Childhood
in Crossroads

Childhood in Crossroads

Cognition and Society in South Africa

PAMELA REYNOLDS

David Philip   Cape Town and Johannesburg
Wm. B. Eerdmans   Grand Rapids

IN MEMORY OF A CHILD, LINDIWE GAYIZA,
WHO SHARED HER LIFE WITH ME, AND
A WOMAN, MONICA WILSON, WHO SHARED HER
KNOWLEDGE.

First published in 1989 in southern Africa by David Philip, Publisher (Pty) Ltd,
208 Werdmuller Centre, Claremont 7700, South Africa

ISBN 0-86486-117-6

Published in 1989 in the United States of America by Wm. B. Eerdmans
Publishing Co., 255 Jefferson Ave., SE, Grand Rapids, Michigan 49503

ISBN 0-8028-0477-2 (USA)

Printed by Clyson Printers, 11th Avenue, Maitland 7405

Contents

MAPS

FIGURES

Acknowledgements

Grateful acknowledgements are due to the Editorial Board of the University of Cape Town for a grant in aid of publication of this book.

The book is based on a dissertation submitted to the University of Cape Town for a Degree of Doctor of Philosophy, 1984. The field work was supported by the H M Chadwick and Smuts Memorial Funds, Cambridge University. A University of Cape Town Postgraduate Research Scholarship and a Human Sciences Research Council Bursary enabled me to analyse the data and write up the thesis.

I wish to express my appreciation to the Department of Social Anthropology of Cambridge University and of the University of Cape Town for offering me both encouragement and the freedom to pursue novel forms of fieldwork. I have been particularly fortunate in having had the guidance of three excellent supervisors. Professor Monica Wilson was unfailingly supportive throughout the period of preparation, research and analysis. Dr Esther Goody tutored me from 1978 to 1980 and Professor Martin West from 1981 to 1983.

My major debt is to the people, particularly the children, of Crossroads. And my thanks are due to my husband Norman and our children, Talitha, Portia, Sabaa and Abigail, for enabling me to do the study.

The photographs were taken for me by Sandra Burman, Peter Templeton and Norman Reynolds, and the manuscript was expertly criticised and shortened by Ginny Tyson. My thanks.

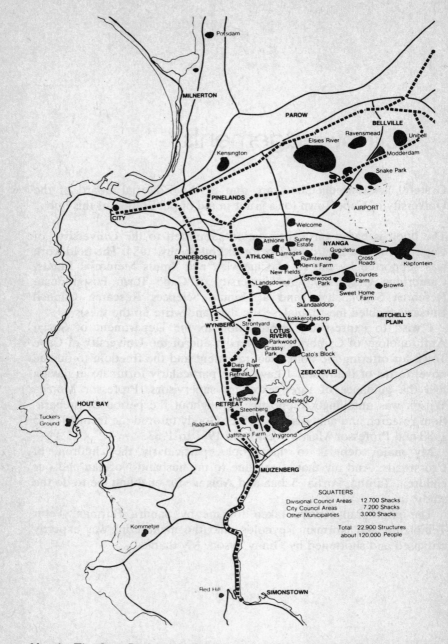

Map 1: The Cape Peninsula. The shaded areas are squatter settlements.

A view of a school, some shacks and the Table Mountain range in the distance

Children playing in my room

My room at the back of a shack (far right)

A shack in Crossroads

A mother and child at the
entrance to their yard

Salvaging zincs after a fire

Three of the children who were not attending school

Children on swings

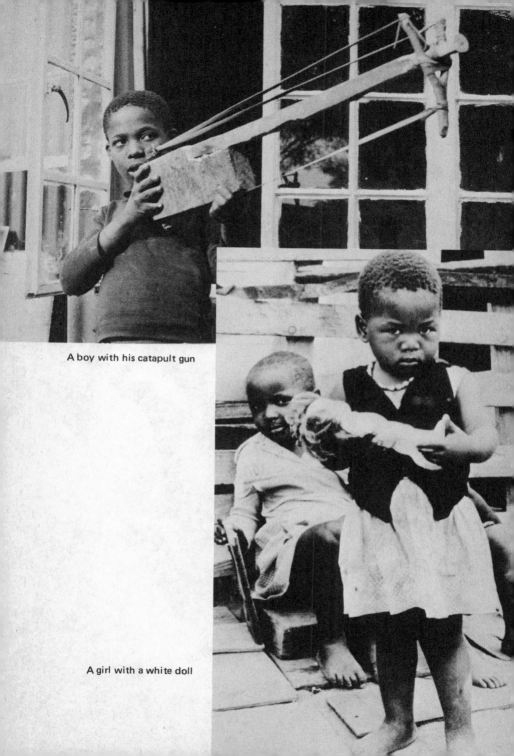

A boy with his catapult gun

A girl with a white doll

A girl with her charge

Boys gambling in the street

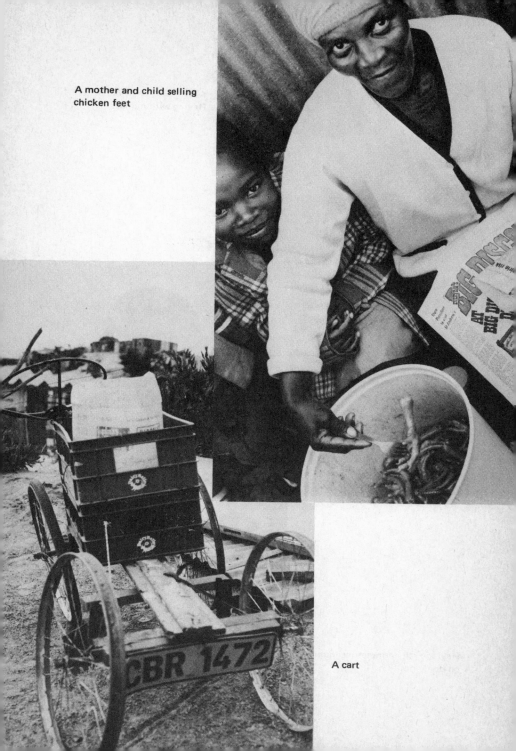

A mother and child selling
chicken feet

A cart

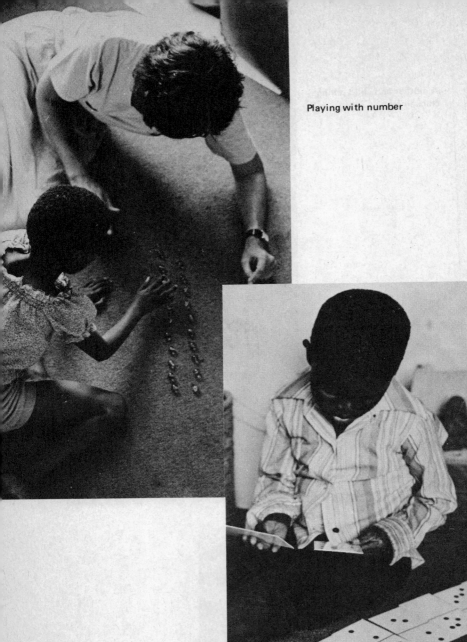

Playing with number

Playing with asymmetrical number
on dominoes

1

Introduction

My own observations show that we have rated the powers of children too low and that there is no knowing what they cannot be given credit for (S Freud, 1918: 584).

The book is the result of an ethnographic study of 7-year-old children in a South African squatter settlement. The aim of the work is primarily anthropological in that it describes and analyses all aspects of life as experienced by children of a particular age. As the subjects were children, the analytic tools of the anthropologist were, of necessity, extended to include some borrowed from the psychologist.

Within the study, I have emphasized children's cognitive development with the hope that by combining systematic observations and psychological testing I may contribute to formulation of an empirical scheme for collection of data on child thinking-processes. Research was conducted for eighteen months, from August 1979 to January 1981, in the Crossroads squatter settlement, situated on the Cape Flats about twenty kilometres from the centre of Cape Town, South Africa (see Map 1).

The study depends upon ethnographic data on the Xhosa culture gathered by other anthropologists, in particular upon the work of Monica Wilson (née Hunter). Aspects of Xhosa existence, including ritual patterns and child-rearing norms, are not elaborated upon except as they relate to the life experiences of the children in the study. The Xhosa make up the greater part of the Crossroads population.

In response to a challenge from psychologists and anthropologists I applied anthropological methods to explain and describe childhood and to clarify assumptions about cognition in relation to cognitive development. In taking up the challenge, I determined to draw on the techniques of psychologists on the assumption that they had developed dependable tools to describe child cognition. Much of anthropological writing on childhood generalises about all children and leaves one curious as to the nature and range of their experience. Malinowski

(1931) described the child as 'the appropriately moulded organism', a statement that brings to mind Lorenz's goslings rather than children. In ethnographic literature about African peoples reference is frequently made to 'the African child' as if such a composite creature exists. There are obvious reasons why this is so. Children, unlike adults, do not have sets of belief patterns, rituals, symbols, artifacts or economic activities that are clearly articulated and representative of common actions, values or thoughts. Children merge with, contribute to and are integrated into the cultural whole, but the culture does not directly represent them. Therefore, one's information about the way in which children experience the world must derive in large measure from the children's own behaviour and expression. Children grow and their testimony alters more rapidly than the adult's.

To describe the life of a 7-year-old Xhosa child in a South African squatter settlement in 1980, it was necessary to focus on the lives of relatively few informants. The question of the extent to which the microcosm represents the macrocosm bedevils anthropologists. Although I have not resolved the quandary, I have addressed myself to an imbalance within it: that is, to the particular in the form of the individual. As Mary Douglas (1978: 5) says, 'The first source of [our] troubles as cultural anthropologists is that we have no adequate conception of the individual.' She believes that the solution is to ensure a better account of social context. A similar theme can be identified within psychology. For example, Greenbaum and Kugelmass (1980: 142) observe that cross-cultural researchers have not 'adequately depicted the mechanisms by which culture may affect individuals'. I studied closely the lives of fourteen children for a year in order to accumulate sufficient data upon which to consider links between society and the individual.

If some account was to be made of the experiences of children in an urban squatter camp clinging to the fringes of a large industrial city, then the problem of how to record aspects of social change had to be faced. Monica Wilson (1977: 28) believes that social change is manifest in 'minute particulars' (a phrase borrowed from William Blake, 1804) and that it can be recorded if attention is paid to social process. I paid attention to the minute particulars of children's maturation and their experience of major socio-economic upheavals.

Creativity at the cultural level emerges from the experience of individuals during childhood, how they negotiate their claims and construct their culture. Children in South Africa have paid dearly, too often with their lives, to do just that. We need to begin to make connections between individual creativity and the renewal of social instructions.

I am interested in people's construction of their culture and in each person's construction of self. So was Joyce (1937: 183), who wrote:

As we, or Mother Dana, weave and unweave our bodies, Stephen said, from day to day so does the artist weave and unweave his image. As the mole on my right breast is where it was when I was born, though all my body has been woven of new stuff time after time, so through the ghost of the unquiet father the unliving son looks forth. In the intense instant of the imagination when the mind, Shelley says, is fading coal, that which I was is that which I am, and that which in possibility I may come to be.

In the children's accounts of their experiences, in their descriptions of their families, their views of Crossroads, their paintings, their stories, their clay-modelling, their puppet-play, their games and songs, I sought signs of their conceptions of self and indications of changes in those conceptions, particularly in relation to socio-political occurrences. In my opinion, this theme of re-creation underlies Piaget's theoretical formulations. For him the main problem of genetic epistemology was 'the explanation of the construction of novelties in the development of knowledge' (Piaget, 1970a: 77). His notion that each child re-creates knowledge has fertilized the search for explanations of the re-creation.

Thus far, I have mentioned two themes that run through the study: the relationship between individual and society, and change as a continuous individual and social occurrence. A third theme describes and analyses situation and context specific to the nature of cognitive processes. Cole (1978: 629) argues that, 'We need, in effect, an ethnography of cognitive activities, where the nature of each activity is probed by a variety of observations, including experimentally contrived ones.'

Many psychologists interested in cross-cultural research have reiterated the call for attention to be paid to the situation and context in which cognitive processes are observed or measured. The call is a little puzzling to anthropologists as they have always attempted to provide 'concrete specificness and circumstantiality' with any field data (Geertz, 1973: 23). M. Wilson (1948: 11) suggests that one of anthropology's major contributions to social studies is 'the insistence of synthesis', and Douglas (1980: 54) believes that 'the work that thought does is social'. These beliefs are not exclusive to the discipline. Marx, for example, thought the very definition of a problem depends on the experience of a particular way of living; and Mao said that, 'It is man's social being that determines his thinking' (Starr, 1979: 46).

What is new in the psychologists' call is their invitation to anthropologists to join them in seeking alternatives to existing theory and assumptions within the arena of cognitive development. Psychologists are aware of the need to combine laboratory testing with detailed knowledge of the culture in which the tests are used. For example, Irvine and Carroll (1980: 218) give a checklist on an experimental rationale for test data collection across cultures and point one concludes thus, 'In short, gain an insider's or participant observer's view of the target cultures.' An anthropologist may be forgiven for wondering if some psychologists do not underestimate the difficulties involved in obtaining such a view. This study demonstrates the complexity entailed in an ethnographic report of just one year of childhood.

I worked with children because there are very few detailed accounts of children's lives in the anthropological literature. Little is known about childhood from children's points of view. There is a sizeable amount of material in psychology on children in third world countries but, given the nature of the discipline, there has been little attempt to relate findings to social context. There is no intrinsic reason why the insights and techniques within anthropology cannot be applied to the world of children. I worked with black children in South Africa because there is a need to document their experiene in an oppressive society.

In working with the children of Crossroads I borrowed liberally from psychology and used the test material that I appropriated in ways that can scarcely please psychologists. My purpose was not to contribute to psychology in terms of validating or expanding tests, but was to borrow, to lean on a century of insight and effort in one discipline to highlight interest in another. In Crossroads, I tried to describe as closely as possible the world through the eyes of a 7-year-old. My aim was to contribute to the development of an empirical scheme for the collection of systematic observations in this area. I was interested in tracing the links between child thought and the states of consciousness represented in adults' formulations about society.

METHOD
In this study my intention was simple: its execution complex. I was suspicious, and not alone in being so, of the results of many psychological tests that demonstrate the inferiority of children in non-Western countries to those in the West. At various times it has been held that children in 'other' cultures are less intelligent or that their development is arrested in early adulthood or that they are culturally 'deprived'. I resolved to look closely at the expressions of thought of

some young children. To do so, I immersed myself in the anthropological enterprise. It seemed to me that if I could establish a relationship of trust with children and could work with them in the context of their lives, only then could I begin to recognise the quality of their development. No full ethnographic studies of childhood in Southern Africa exist. Most monographs contain small sections on children, and in some there are substantial sections on initiation (the most comprehensive of which is Richards's study of a girl's initiation among the Bemba, 1956). Blacking's book, *Black Background. The Childhood of a South African Girl* (1964), is a poor contribution. No serious attempts have been made to write an ethnography using children as informants or to study cognitive development in the full context of living and growing in South Africa.

Children aged 7 were selected because that age is pivotal in status for many Xhosa; age 7 is also an important age in Piaget's scheme of intellectual development. Besides, it is the age at which black children in South Africa begin school. Many Xhosa see it as an age at which a child emerges from the first period of childhood, to a time when, traditionally, a boy was capable of herding cattle and a girl of doing many household tasks and caring responsibly for younger siblings. Van Tromp (1948) observes that from the age of 7 a boy has an enhanced social status. He is considered to have more experience and better judgement. Although responsibilities increase, his legal status remains that of a child. Adult opinion in Crossroads supported this attitude towards both boys and girls aged 7. A similar change in status at that age has been recorded elsewhere in Africa, for example by Read (1968) among the Ngoni of Malawi.

As I was compiling an ethnography of 7-year-old children, any child of that age in the community qualified as an informant. Indeed, I observed, listened to, played with and recorded the songs of, many children of all ages. However, as I intended to record the details of children's individual experiences and cognitive growth, I had to select a sample. I had to know each child well. I had to work with each across time and in many situations. I had to devise exercises to draw out their thoughts. I had to win their trust that they might offer me their fears and their dreams. I had to test them on a range of tasks to assess their ability. I estimated that I would be able to follow closely the lives of ten children. The rights of the people in the community to work and live with their children in Cape Town were not secure and it seemed likely that children would fairly often be sent from town to country and back, or shift among kin. Therefore, I began with fifteen children, hoping that only a third might leave the area during the period of study. As it turned out, only one child left, on an extended visit to the Transkei soon after I had begun to work with him.

I selected ten children who were attending school and five who were not. I hoped to gauge roughly the influence of schooling on the children's patterns of play and work and test behaviour. Formal schooling for blacks in South Africa begins at age 7. The school-going children were chosen from the first grade at two large schools. Each school had two classes in the first grade and at least two children, a boy and a girl, were chosen from each class. Five were selected from each school. The method of selection was as follows: the name and shack number of each child (who either said he or she was 7 or was thought by the teacher to be 7) in the four classes was listed. The house numbers that were located in two of the four wards of Crossroads were selected. If the children in the sample lived in two specific areas it would save me a fair amount of trudging across dunes and it would mean also that the children might know each other and their networks of friendship or enmity might be followed. By taking children from four classes in two schools and from different wards, I hoped to ensure against some bias.

From the resulting list, ten names were chosen at random and a visit was made to each of their homes. It was a time-consuming task: introducing myself, explaining my business, seeking information, all in accordance with the pattern of polite discourse that frowns upon haste and relishes exchange. I confirmed that each child was or would be 7 for some months in 1980. Only one family was openly suspicious of me; nevertheless, they agreed to allow me to work with their son, and I did.

It took much longer to find children who did not attend school. Some parents appeared to be ashamed to admit that their children were not going to school. Some said that their children were registered and were awaiting places in township schools, some that they were waiting for money with which to buy suitable school clothes, some that their children were ill and others that the children were returning to the country. It was only through contacts made with the neighbours and kin of families with whom I was working that I came to know children who were not going to school. As their families became accustomed to me and understood my intentions, I found five children with whom to work. These five children were not randomly selected. Three were girls and two were boys and one of the boys returned to the Transkei. The final sample of fourteen children was composed then of eight girls and six boys. The non-school-going children are called *abangafundiyo* (those who do not attend school) and are sometimes referred to in the text as the 'Abas', for short. No remuneration was offered to either the parents or the children. Only on completion of the study did I give the children gifts and contribute to the cost of their school fees and uniforms.

A control group of twenty-five 7-year-olds was selected at random from the list of schoolchildren. A series of Piagetian tests was administered to the sample and the control group in order to give some idea of the extent to which the sample group could be accepted as representative of the Crossroads 7-year-old population. The results are discussed in Chapter Seven.

The approximate location of the sample children's homes is shown on Map 2. The actual location and the names of the children and family members have been changed.

The selection was made during the first three months of research while I was working with 3 to 6-year-olds. During this time, I observed and played with small children so that I could understand something of the nature of the experiences that shape children living in a squatter settlement. I spent most of the time at one or another of eight crèches attended by 600 children. As the community leaders seemed to expect me to contribute directly to the people's welfare, I provided the crèche children with crayons and paper and then from their drawings I produced Christmas cards for sale.

The proceeds from the card sales provided enough nutritionally fortified soup for each child to have a bowlful every day for six months. A small amount of money was given to the leaders. Friends kindly took over the card production and the proceeds have increased dramatically.

Most of the women who ran the crèches were prominent in local politics and I had to learn to steer my way through the tides of political antagonism. Some months later young committee members who had been assigned to work with the same women came to me and said, 'We have heard that you withstood the power of those women. Can you teach us how to do it?'

During the same period, I explored the community and introduced myself to prominent residents. I sought and received permission from the Crossroads Committee to build a room onto a resident's shack. The Committee selected a resident who was a woman of strong and forceful character; as a community leader she had both admirers and detractors. I became her tenant with some trepidation. A local builder and I built my room; my landlady acted as my guide in sifting sheets of zinc from among the stacks in demolition yards, in begging for off-cuts from factories, in sharing the loot and constructing the building. It was an instructive process: I was amazed by the ingenuity and determination that residents displayed in creating homes out of very little and by the resilience with which they dealt with discrimination.

Mary Mmango was my assistant and she worked with me for all of 1980. Her lovely nature, her gentleness with children, her intelligence contributed greatly to the study. She is a resident of Crossroads and a literacy tutor in the community who was studying at night school for her school matriculation certificate. All of our conversations with the children were conducted in Xhosa. None of the children spoke English. Test sessions and many other occasions were taped and the transcriptions were used to ensure accuracy in reporting on the use of language.*

I used two kinds of methodology in working with the children. One was derived from the systematic observations and participation techniques traditional in anthropology; the other involved a variety of tests devised by psychologists. Apart from playing, talking, walking, eating and working with children both in their homes and outside, I invited each child to my room for formal sessions during the year. Mary and I had formal working sessions with each child for about thirty-eight hours.

The school headmistresses and teachers generously allowed me to call the children out from their classes. The sessions followed a loose pattern. We would begin by talking about matters of interest to the child, then about family occurrences such as visits and moves, and community affairs such as riots, accidents, fights, weddings, school outings and friendship networks. Some of these discussions were recorded on tape. Then we would move on to formal testing, which almost always involved the child in an activity such as playing with cards or dice or moulding clay or going through a series of physical exercises. Finally, we would play a game together or draw or play with a family of puppets. The session ended in our having a glass of juice together. Sometimes the children came in groups to dance or sing or paint. Each day some of them would bring their friends and ask to borrow crayons or footballs or marbles, with which they played in the yard. Thus I came to know many children aged 7 or 8.

The children and I grew to know each other well. If the formality of the test situations seems to dominate the text it is because these are easier to report on than are more casual encounters. Participation in and observation of their activities were vital to the description and

* My grateful thanks are due to Gerry Zondo of the University of Zimbabwe for expert help with the transcriptions.

interpretation of the test results. An overall plan guided my involvement with the children. I wanted to find out about their own passage through time, and about their notions of space, kinship, dreams and order. These topics would inform me about much of their cognitive understanding of their world. Within these areas, I selected tasks or exercises that seemed likely to serve my interest. I behaved rather like Lévi Strauss's *bricoleur* in assembling from amongst the psychologist's tool bag that which seemed to suit my purpose.

I made an effort to probe the children's ideas on a topic from many angles and across time. For example, in studying their use of kinship terms, I used three different interview formats that had been devised by psychologists; throughout the year I also taped discussions with the children during which they used kinship terms while talking about their families; I recorded the way in which they used the terms in their homes and in play; and I used a family of puppets to elicit use of a set of kinship terms that were not ego-centred.

Foucault (1980: 82) makes a plea to scholars to examine what he calls 'subjugated knowledges', blocks of historical knowledge present but disguised within the body of functionalist and systematising theory. He explains that they are

. . . a whole set of knowledges that have been disqualified as inadequate to their task or insufficiently elaborated: naive knowledges, located low down on the hierarchy, beneath the required level of cognition or scientificity. . .it is through the re-emergence of these low-ranking knowledges, these unqualified, even directly disqualified knowledges (such as that of psychiatric patient, of the ill person, of the nurse, of the doctor – parallel and marginal as they are to the knowledge of medicine – that of the delinquent, etc.), and which involve what I would call a popular knowledge *(le savoir des gens)* though it is far from being a general commonsense knowledge, but it is on the contrary a particular, local, regional knowledge, a differential knowledge incapable of unanimity and which owes its force only to the harshness with which it is opposed by everything surrounding it – that is through the re-appearance of this knowledge, of these local popular knowledges, these disqualified knowledges, that criticism performs its work.

In searching for the local knowledge of intelligence of Crossroads residents, I gathered life histories and held unstructured interviews with many of the residents, including the sample children's parents and guardians. I also held meetings with groups of literacy tutors, school teachers, crèche leaders and young executives of the Crossroads Committee. I met with a group of women for four hours once a week over a period of six months. Each of the thirteen women was a student at the literacy training centre. Each agreed to explore with me in a group situation their lives, especially their memories of childhood. The women called our meetings *Inkumbulo Yakwantu,* which means the remembrance of things past. Out of their memories and their accounts of the present, I sought to weave the cloth upon which the pattern of the 7-year-olds' lives might stand in relief.

An obvious corollary to a study of children in an urban area in South Africa is a study of children in the countryside. Had I the time, I should have liked to have done such a comparison. In January 1982 Nozizwe Nyakaza from Crossroads and I spent a month with children in the Transkei. We drove some 3 000 kilometres altogether. I decided to look at children in Pondoland, taking Monica Hunter's study of the area in the 1930s as background on traditional beliefs. From our base near Port St John's we foraged out each day into the countryside, taking with us a good supply of bread and jam and cool drink. Once in the countryside, we would walk into the hills and settle beneath a tree and wait. Some children would gather around and we would talk and play games and explore the countryside together as well as share the bread and drink. In that way, we met many herdboys. We also went into small villages and talked to adults and children. We travelled widely around Eastern Pondoland and interviewed ninety children between the ages of 5 and 12.

Pondoland is beautiful. Swimming in the sea, collecting mussels, eating oysters, fishing, hunting weasels, making clay models, dancing, singing, walking along the beaches and over mountains with children was satisfying and fitted much more the image of the anthropologist at ease beneath the shady tree than did the urban study. The loveliness of the hills and the fun we had did not hide the poverty. A rural ghetto is almost worse than an urban one. The dependency of the rural area on earnings in the towns and cities is clear; so too is the destruction of family life by migratory labour patterns. I confirmed a few hunches and learnt as much as I could in a short time (see Appendix F for a brief report). To have learnt more, an in-depth study would have been necessary.

A word of caution must be sounded. It was not by design that I had two children in the sample whose mothers were *amagqira**. However, I did consciously seek to discover the conceptions of childhood of *amagqira* and, in consequence, there may be a bias in my data towards the representation of traditional attitudes and beliefs. I was surprised by the resilience of these and fascinated by the manner in which they were

---

* *amagqira* – traditional healers. Singular *igqira*.

entwined with modern views.

In the text that follows, I have endeavoured to account, at least in part, for my contributions to the Crossroads encounters. Some readers may dismiss my account of cognitive understanding of the children because, they may say, the children's understanding was shaped and altered by their year-long relationship with me. There is no simple rebuttal. Their skills on a series of Piagetian tests were compared with a control group half-way through the year. If so few hours can alter a child's understanding, then the educational system is under indictment.

URBAN SQUATTING

A UNICEF policy specialist (Donohue, 1982: 24–5) has estimated that as of 1980, 369 million children and youth below 15 years of age lived in the urban areas of less developed regions of the world, including, for these purposes, South Africa. Of this number, 129 million were in the 0-5 age group. Within the next eighteen years the number of children under 15 years of age is projected to grow to 666 million, with 232 million under 5 years of age. Figure 1-1 shows the percentage of urban children in each region in relation to the total world urban child population. It illustrates the phenomenal rate of increase in sub-Saharan Africa as against all other regions of the developing world.

	Northern Africa	Sub-Saharan Africa	Latin America	China	Other East Asia	Eastern South Asia	Middle South Asia	Western South Asia	Cyprus Turkey Israel	Melanesia-Micro-nesia Polynesia
2000	6,3%	15,8%	21,2%	16,5%	2,6%	8,2%	23,0%	4,0%	2,2%	0,2%
1975	5,1%	8,4%	24,1%	23,2%	3,4%	8,4%	22,1%	3,0%	2,2%	0,1%

Source: United Nations Population Division as assessed in 1980 (computer print-out).
Figure 1–1: Percentage of Urban Children in Each Region in Relation to Total World Urban Population, 1975–2000.

In 1975, sub-Saharan Africa was 21 per cent urban; by the year 2000, it is expected to be 38 per cent urban. In that 25-year period the urban population is projected to grow from 66 million to 252 million in absolute terms. This means a fourfold increase of 186 million people. By the year 2000, it is estimated that 59 per cent of all population increase will be taking place in urban areas, and that urban areas will grow two and a half times faster than rural areas (5,36 urban versus 2,09 rural growth – Donohue, 1982: 27).

In South Africa, however, despite a percentage increase in the overall number of blacks who were urban residents (see Table 1–1 in the Appendix), the period 1970–1980 has seen a major population shift of Africans away from the urban areas to the homelands.* While the number of Africans in white areas increased by 13 per cent in the last 10 years, the homelands' population increased by 59 per cent in the same period. The figures represent an opposite to the established trend in all other developing countries. It must be borne in mind, however, that calculations are problematic as there is a hidden illegal population in the cities. The black population of Cape Town is said to be close to double the official figure (F Wilson, 1975: 175). One possible explanation for the high population growth of the homelands is the inclusion within their borders of large African townships. Another explanation is that migrant workers are defined as residents of homelands rather than of urban areas despite the fact that migrants spend an average of eleven out of twelve months at their places of work (Gordon, 1981: 68).

For West (1980: 128), the picture is clear:

. . . the majority of the African population lives outside the so-called homelands, outnumbering whites in all 'white areas' by at least two to one.

The six million or more urban Africans at present outnumber white urban-dwellers by nearly three million, and based on current projections will increase to fifteen million by the year 2000, compared with the estimated white urban population at that time of just over five million.

Basing his calculations on two assumptions, Simkins (1982) antici-pates that for the rest of the century in South Africa either there will be continued demographic pressure on the homelands, which have experienced a great deal of it already over the past quarter-century, or pressure will be put on the metropolitan areas, which are better able to deal with it from an economic point of view. Simkins (1982: 11) comments that, 'Of course, immigration of four million Africans over the remaining years to 2000 implies a great deal else: nothing less than a fundamental realignment of political forces in the South African arena.' Further, Simkins (1982: 6–7) points out that whichever of the two assumptions he uses in his calculations, in the year 2000 the proportion of blacks living in the homelands would still be slightly higher than it

---

* Homelands are areas set aside by the South African Government in which blacks are supposed to live and from which they derive or will derive their only citizenship rights. The use and misuse of words in South African politics is a terminological minefield. For convenience I shall use terms such as 'homelands' but do not mean thereby to endorse their legitimacy.

was in 1950. The masculinity ratio and the proportion of people between 15 and 64 would be much the same in 2000 as it was in 1980, implying a continued imbalance between men and women and between people in the dependent and income-earning age ranges. He predicts that at the end of the century, a substantial part of the metropolitan population would still be living on a non-family basis.

In South Africa the existence of black urban 'squatting' has been an official problem from the days of the earliest white settlement. Jan van Riebeeck wrote in his journal on 10 February 1655,

Only last night it happened that about 50 of these natives wanted to put up their huts close to the banks of the moat of our fortress, and when told in a friendly manner by our men to go a little further away, they declared boldly that this was not our land but theirs and they would place their huts wherever they chose. (As quoted in Davenport and Hunt, 1974: 11)

The artificial dichotomy over land and the lack of freedom to settle and sell one's labour that characterises the South African condition have led to such distortions of wealth, of access to resources and services and of employment that urban squatting has become an economic necessity for many blacks.

Table 1–2 (in the Appendix) illustrates the enormous concentration of black poverty in the countryside, on white farms and, particularly, in the homelands. Eighty-five per cent of the world's poor live in the countryside. Using the Poverty Datum Line of R200,00 per month for South Africa, Reynolds (1981) has shown that 93,7 per cent of South Africa's poor are in the countryside.*

Simkins (1981b) has calculated the divergence between predicted urban growth according to GNP per capita and South Africa's actual growth (Table 1–3 in the Appendix). The divergence has grown from 1,9 per cent in 1960 to a staggering 13,4 per cent in 1980. The figures show the relative stagnation of urban growth, a testimony to the growing panoply of racial legislation which, over the last two decades, has prevented the natural movement of rural blacks to town. In another work, Simkins (1981a) has shown that the proportion of blacks in the homelands has grown dramatically over the same period, from 40 per cent in 1960 to 54 per cent in 1980. Read together, the tables illustrate the pressure to move to town. It can be analysed in terms of economic necessity but it incorporates vital moral elements.

* In March 1983, R1,10 equalled US$1,00.

URBAN BLACK POLICY

The first shacks in a settlement that came to be known as Crossroads were erected in February 1975, on the sands of the Cape Flats. By 1979, when I began to study children there, some 20 000 people were living in about 3 000 shacks.*

Almost every squatter in Crossroads was Xhosa. That they had to build shacks of zinc and scraps in the sand dunes among the wattle trees, and that they should be classified as squatters and be vulnerable to imprisonment, expulsion from the area and loss of their homes arise out of their political powerlessness. A government that does not represent them controls their movements through legislation to do with race classification, migrant labour and Group Areas.

In South Africa most of the 3 780 000 Xhosa people are citizens of the so-called independent states of Transkei and, since 1981, Ciskei: their rights to work and live in other areas are controlled by a battery of legislation strictly enforced. The Bantu Homelands Citizenship Act of 1970 provided,

. . . that every African who was not a citizen of a self-governing territory was to become a citizen of a territorial authority area. Such persons would retain South African citizenship only in terms of international relations, and would still be required to hold South African reference books (passes). The new citizens of the territorial authority area were to be given certificates of citizenship issued either by their authority or by the South African government acting on its behalf. This was the beginning of the implementation of the Nationalist policy for making all urban Africans citizens of homelands. (West, 1980: 135)

West notes that the South African government's definition of a Transkeian is very broad, and includes birth, residence, linguistic, kinship and cultural criteria in determining who may be deemed a Transkei citizen, in terms of the Status of Transkei Act of 1976 (West, 1982a). He observes that,

When the Ciskei gained 'independence' in December 1981, virtually every black person in Cape Town became a technical foreigner. The implications are clear: nearly 100 000 people are subject to instant deportation in the Cape Peninsula, without even the minimal recourse to the law which exists in terms of other influx control legislation.

Since 1968 blacks from the homelands could only come to Cape Town on one year contracts, without their wives, children and any other dependents (see Reynolds, 1984). Most contract labourers are

* The story of the people's struggle to establish their homes and secure the right to live and work in the Cape Peninsula is complicated and can only be told as part of an analysis of the political and economic reality of South Africa. The full story has still to be written.

housed in single Bachelor Quarters and some in other registered accommodation in townships set aside for black occupation. In Cape Town, there are three townships for blacks: Gugulethu, Nyanga and Langa. Selvan (1976) points out that whereas contract workers technically live singly, in actual fact single quarters in the townships have women and children in them. He estimates the ratio of men to women as ten to one. Contract workers often bring some of their young children with them from the countryside, although these children will not qualify for permanent residence in the areas.

At the end of 1974 there were 33 093 black children living legally in Cape Town (see Table 1-4 in the Appendix). The official estimation of the African population residing legally in Cape Town was distributed between the different areas as indicated in Table 1-4 (Graaff and Maree, 1977: 3). Official provision in 1976 allowed for only one in every 4,7 workers to live with their families (Ellis et al, 1977: 19). Seventy-nine per cent of black workers are housed without their families: 37 000 women live in the homelands without their men (Ellis et al, 1977: 53).

In 1981, Dr P Koornhof, the Minister of Co-operation and Development, quoted the *de facto* black population of Cape Town as being 199 600 and the *de jure* black population as 114 164. Thus over 84 000 or approximately 42 per cent of the black population in Cape Town is there without permits (Hansard No. 4, August 1981; Col. 231). (SAIRR, 1981–2: 11)

With the 'independence' of the Ciskei in December 1981, almost all of Cape Town's black population is now made up of 'foreigners' and only those with Section 10 rights under the Urban Areas Act have any security at all. Only a permanent qualified resident may have his wife to live with him and only if there is suitable accommodation. Shortage of housing serves as grounds for the total refusal of entries from rural areas and extremely limited granting of transfers to wives from other prescribed areas.

Two cardinal principles of urban black policy are that municipalities and employers are made responsible for housing blacks and that blacks are not allowed to acquire an interest in land from a non-African owner without the President's consent. The effect is that Africans may not legally reside outside the locations, villages or hostels that are specially set aside for them, unless they are domestic servants living on their employer's premises or are residents in specially licensed accommodation (SAIRR, 1954).

During 1980, when much of the field work was done, 8 113 black women and 7 747 black men were arrested in the Cape Peninsula on charges under influx control legislation. The arrests were carried out by officials of the Administration Board (formerly called BAAB) that falls under the Department of Co-operation and Development. In 1980, the South African Police arrested 467 blacks for the same 'offence' in the same area of the Cape Peninsula (SAIRR, 1979–80: 20). I have kept the figures of arrests separate to highlight the role that the Department of Co-operation and Development fills. Charges are laid in the Commissioner's Court in Langa and those who are arrested are detained in police cells and frequently sentenced to R60,00 or sixty days for being in the area illegally, and R10,00 or ten days for failure to produce a pass. According to West (1982a: 437) the 'normal' fine of R70,00 represents approximately two to three weeks' wages for unskilled workers.

The number of women arrested in the Western Cape has increased dramatically to a state where 30 per cent of all arrests of women in the major centres take place in the Cape Peninsula. It is the only area in the country where more women than men are arrested under the pass laws (West, 1982a: 467–8). Lange has estimated that workers can come to an urban area from a homeland and end up better off even if they spend nine months of every year in prison; less imprisonment than that could result in living standards several hundred per cent better than had they remained in a rural area (*Finanacial Mail,* 12 October 1979, referred to by West, 1982a: 465).

CROSSROADS

Crossroads is situated south of D F Malan Airport in an extension of Nyanga township and is bounded by Klipfontein Road, Lansdowne Road and Mahobe Drive (see Map 1). Initially the land was owned by the Cape Divisional Council and later it came under the charge of the Bantu Affairs Administration Board (hereafter called BAAB). In 1978, it was said to house 25 per cent of the black families in Cape Town (Platzky, 1978: 1).

The area is triangular with a perimeter of some 3,3 kilometres. It undulates across the dunes. Depending upon the time of day or the season, Crossroads alters its mood. It can be harsh and vibrant on a summer's day or eerie and silent in the thick soup of a Cape Flats' fog.

Three thousand shacks jostle for room and yard boundaries fight with public pathways for the right to exist. The dunes have been tamed and the terrain is rather like the surface of a peach pip. Sand permeates everything and on a windy day a pen carves grooves through the grains in order to write. There are few trees apart from the odd brave Port

Jackson Willow and the bluegums that stand sentry on two sides of the triangle. The third side is bordered by an unsettled area that fills with pools of water in the wet season: places where young boys dare each other to venture. The Phillippi Industrial Area, a Boys' Rehabilitation Centre, administrative buildings and the black township of Nyanga East border the rest of the settlement.

In 1978-80 the few remaining open spaces were claimed by children at play, footballers and hawkers. Three hubs of activity focused on two of the schools and on the string of hawkers' stands lining the track between the settlement and Nyanga East. The University of Cape Town's Urban Problems Research Unit estimated that in 1980 10 per cent of households in Crossroads were surviving on money earned from trading and production and more than 100 small businesses competed in the marketplace on the fringes of Crossroads (West, 1982b: 174).* Two of the three schools were used as community centres and came to be identified with different political groups. Shelters were erected for the mobile clinics of the Divisional Council that visited twice weekly. The University of Cape Town's student health service held clinics twice a week in one of the school buildings. The Roman Catholic Church housed the adult literacy centre and other church structures also served the community in a variety of ways. At the end of 1979, eight crèches catered to the needs of nearly 600 children under the age of seven. By mid-1980, the Empilisweni South African Leadership Assembly clinic had been established to meet the primary medical and health needs of the Crossroads Community.

Innumerable small shops attached to people's homes and other businesses – car-repairing, watch-making, tailoring – formed a lively informal sector. Shebeens (places where illegal liquor is sold) varied in size and quality: one, that I visited, was owned by an ex-convict and it boasted a fine view of the Peninsula's mountains, a comfortable lounge suite and a television; another offered no more than a smoke-blackened parlour lined with barrels of beer.

The struggle to secure the right of the people to stay in Crossroads was long and harsh. Despite constant threats of removal, many pass raids, shack demolitions and other forms of harassment the people refused to leave Crossroads.

By the end of 1979, the people of Crossroads had been assured that

* In October 1982 officials of the Western Cape Administration Board demolished more than 200 of the stores that supplied vegetables, meat, clothing and building materials to the squatter community. Business was later resumed and a monthly rental was imposed on stall-owners.

their houses would not be demolished unless they vacated them for some reason or if they fell into arrears with their rent. They were to be housed in a new township, the only drawback of which was that relatively high rents would be charged. The township is called New Crossroads and it borders Nyanga East. Movement to New Crossroads began in November 1980, when the first of 5 000 families moved into brick houses. As each shack was vacated, it was demolished.

In early 1983, both townships are still in existence and, as Government funds for building more houses are not available, it is likely that the original settlement will continue to survive for some years. New squatters, temporarily housed in tents, have grafted themselves onto Crossroads and are battling to secure rights just as the Crossroads residents did.

Population

In December 1977, Maree and Cornell (1978) conducted a sample survey in Crossroads that included 288 houses and 1 785 residents, 8,5 to 10 per cent of the population. They found that there were 6,2 persons per household of which 3,2 were adults and 3,0 children. Seventy-seven per cent of the houses were occupied by one family and 22 per cent by two families; very few by single boarders. One hundred per cent of the sample was black. The average size of families living in the settlement was five. Fifty per cent of the household heads were qualified to live in the Cape Peninsula, of which 44 per cent fell under Section 10(1)(b). This group represented 22,1 per cent of all household heads. As qualifications under Section 10(1)(b) required that a person must have worked for ten years continuously for the same employer or have resided in the area for fifteen years continuously before 1968, it is probable that they had each lived in the Cape Town region for at least nineteen years. The other 50 per cent of household heads were probably in the area illegally.

Of the spouses, 9,3 per cent were qualified and 90,7 percent were not qualified or failed to specify their status. A large proportion, 21,8 per cent, of children above the age of 16 years were born in the area. This partly reflects the fact that many of the spouses, 17,9 per cent, have been in the Cape Town Region for more than sixteen years. Not all of these children necessarily have the status granted to those born in the area.

Origin of the Squatters

The majority of the residents came from the Transkei: 67 per cent of household heads and 70 per cent of the spouses. Twenty per cent and 13,7 per cent respectively came from the Eastern and Western Cape. Not all of them came from a homeland.

Employment and Income

The survey showed that 81 per cent of the household heads in the labour force worked in the formal sector and 11,2 per cent in the informal; 1,8 per cent were in both and 6 per cent were unemployed. The informal sector included the people who sold fruit, vegetables and clothes; tailors; car mechanics and travel agents. Those in the formal sector earned an average of R24,30 per week and those in the informal sector, R28,30 per week. Spouses earned only R9,50 on average per week. The average weekly income of all adults in the sample was R21,30. The total weekly income of a family with 1,2 breadwinners was on average R24,10.

Past Demolition Experiences

Of those in the sample, 34 per cent had experienced the demolition of their homes: 13,9 per cent had had one house demolished; 9,6 per cent two; 8,2 per cent three and the rest had had four or more houses demolished. If their homes in Crossroads were demolished, 72 per cent intended to build again in the Cape Town Region. Only 2,3 per cent of household heads said that they would sent their wives and children to the countryside and 0,6 per cent said that the whole family would go. Those who either gave no answer or did not know what they would do make up 15,6 per cent of the sample.

The authors conclude their analysis with the following statement:

The employment and income situation demonstrates why the Crossroads residents are in the Cape Town Region in the first place, namely to earn money and make a living. No less than 94 per cent of the heads of household are employed with the informal sector making an important contribution to both employment and the income of families. This needs to be contrasted to Transkei where most of the families come from and where the opportunities for formal and informal sector activities are virtually nil. It is thus sheer economic necessity that drives Africans from the Transkei and other rural areas to the Cape Town Region where opportunities do exist for making a living. It is in the light of this that the intention of the overwhelming majority of families to remain in Cape Town in the event of their houses being demolished has to be seen. For the same reason the demolition of African squatter housing will not solve any problems. It will merely displace most of the residents from the demolished squatter area to other residential areas and put an added strain on already overcrowded accommodation (Maree and Cornell, 1978: 7).

Most of the dwellings are made of sheets of zinc (corrugated iron) on a timber frame, lined with plastic, cardboard and paper, and with a wood or cardboard floor. Some are well furnished and decorated inside. Walls are often neatly papered with rejects from shops or factories and one is frequently startled by the incongruity that they present – magazine covers of the British Royal Family, posters calling for the protection of 'Our Beautiful Cape' – in relation to the immediate environment. Space is often very cramped and there is not always adequate protection against the wet and cold in winter, and the heat, wind and sand in summer. Apart from the supply of water, the major preoccupations of day-to-day living are transport to work; access to schools, hospitals and shops; crèches, because they enable the mother to work; and the problems of heating, cooking and lighting. Fires are a serious hazard because paraffin stoves are often used for cooking and paraffin lamps or candles for lighting. As one resident said, 'We sleep on our graves.'

Research in Crossroads

I chose to study in Crossroads for several reasons. On principle, I did not want to ask the South African Government for permission to work among Xhosa children. In 1979, I would have had to have sought permission to enter those urban areas that were set aside for black people. Crossroads was, and still is, a squatter settlement and in 1979 it had not yet been branded a particular colour and therefore did not fall under legislation that controlled entry on the basis of people's race classification. Although Crossroads was declared a black township in April 1980, and whites had, theoretically, to obtain permission to enter the area, the law was not enforced.

Another advantage of working within the Crossroads community was that a significant amount of data collection and analysis had been done by researchers in a variety of disciplinary areas. Given the nature of the intimate and intensive study that I had planned to do among a small sample of children, I needed access to data of a different order, the sort that anthropologists have frequently collected themselves.

As I was interested in documenting the lives of some Xhosa children in 1980, I was concerned to study those whose families were struggling against the political and economic forces that tear so many black families apart. Those blacks who have the right to live with their families in Cape Town form a minority. The people who created the squatter settlement at Crossroads represent the majority who do not have that right. The legislation that controls the rights of blacks to live, work, purchase property, be with their families or travel at will is complex and throttling. It would take a Solzhenetsin to trace the laws' effect upon them. As Joan Robinson (1960) said, 'With most problems nowadays the economic answers are only political questions,' and, likewise, there can be no analysis of childhood and cognitive development in South Africa that does not raise political questions.

MAP 2 Approximate location of the homes of the sample children
       in Crossroads

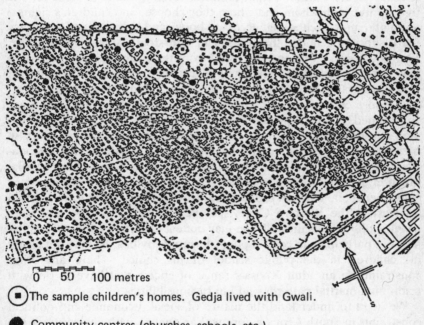

```
0    50   100 metres
```

(■) The sample children's homes. Gedja lived with Gwali.

(●) Community centres (churches, schools, etc.)

Source: Base map compiled by UPRU from information provided by the
Municipality of Cape Town, 1978.

2
The Children in Time

In considering the lives of children in a South African squatter settlement, it is necessary to bear in mind the reasons behind the existence of given conditions. The South African economic and political realities create turmoil within families, forcing adults to fight for the right to live with whom and where they choose, and children's rights – to uninterrupted schooling, access to books and lights, need for privacy – are subsumed under these. Men in Crossroads spend, on average, 12,5 hours every working day away from their families; their children may not live with them near their places of work unless Government sees fit to grant them temporary rights hedged with conditions.

A Xhosa child is born of a man and a woman whose movements are constrained by official prohibitions. They may not live together near the man's work-place; each must seek and receive permission to work in prescribed areas; the man must live in officially registered accommodation; he may not bring his children to live with him without official sanction; he may not live in an area that suits his notion of economy or convenience; he may not move at will from job to job nor town to town (at least in the Western Cape, see West, 1982b: 171); he may seek training only in certain skills; he may not eat in certain public places; he may not participate in certain public leisure activities; he may not enroll his children in the public school of his choice. There are other constraints to an adult Xhosa's range of choice that have to do with traditional marital patterns and kin responsibilities.

We need to understand the nature of social, economic and political constraints in South Africa before we can analyse with any accuracy the nature of relationships between adult and child. These relationships shape and nurture cognitive development and analysis of intellectual growth must take into account the character of the adult–child relationships. Appendix CI and Table 2–1 in Appendix G give basic data on the children's parents and guardians. Appendix CII gives sketches of the children's lives.

From interviews with each child, and with her* parents and guardians, I compiled profiles of the life histories of the children from birth to the present. As an aid to discussion with the children, I cut out cardboard figures to represent the child at yearly intervals. The figures were first used in a Piagetian seriation task wherein the child had to place the figures in order of size. Once the child had accomplished the task, we talked about birth and growth. We took each figure in turn and discussed where the child had been at that age, with whom she had lived, what she remembered and how she felt about that time in her life. I knew a fair amount about each and could remind her of episodes or stages in her life.

This chapter is a report on the child's life history and self-image. I shall tell you about the children as they told me about themselves. I was trying to do two things: to describe what it is like to grow up a Xhosa child in the decade of the 1970s in South Africa, and to record children's consciousness of their growing and becoming.

Let me introduce the children. Among the girls there is Tozama who is lively, confident and articulate; Peliswe who is fragile and exquisitely polite; Zuziwe who is gay and quick; Yameka who is quiet and observant; Saliswa who is considerate and sensitive; Nomvula who is solid; Lungiswa who is worldly-wise; and Gedja who is gregarious and fun-loving.

Among the boys is Mlawu who is conscientious, gentle and sure; Cebo who is a charming, naughty clown; Togu who is shy and warm; Gwali who is a bumbling, laughing, big-hearted fellow; Hintsa who is vulnerable and retiring; and Nukwa who is a sea-anemone – he opens and retreats.

BIRTH

Birthdays are neither noted nor celebrated year by year. The Xhosa culture provides ceremonies that perform similar functions in focusing on the individual and cementing her into the community (see Hunter, 1936: 159f). For the child, time is divided differently from the unilinear progression that marks the Western concept. Only Tozama immediately used the cut-out figures as steps signifying a growth process.

Ten of the fourteen children were born in the cities, that is, in areas that have been proclaimed as the preserve of the whites. Nine of these were born in Cape Town and one in Port Elizabeth. The other four

* The Xhosa language is not hampered by sex differences in pronouns, distinctions being made on other grounds, and the feminine pronouns used here and elsewhere imply female and male.

were born in the Transkei. Six children said that they had been born in the Transkei, whereas they had been born in Cape Town. It seems odd that their families had not stressed their rights in the city as 'Cape Borners'.

Half of the children were born in a hospital and the other half at home with a trained sister in attendance. Of the births in the Transkei, only one occurred at home. In the context of discussing birth, I asked the children, 'From where did you come?' Nomvula said, 'I was born in a stable in Bethlehem', and Zuziwe replied, 'I came from heaven'. With further questioning both girls said that babies came from the hospital. Eight of the fourteen children believed that babies are either given or sold to their mothers by the hospital or are bought in a shop. Some examples of their reasoning on the puzzle of birth follow:

Tozama said, 'I was born in the Transkei in the house. Mother said that I was fed on a bottle not the breast. Babies are made in hospital. I don't know who makes them.'

(Do babies grow in a woman's stomach?)

'Yes.'

(Why do you say they come from the hospital?)

'Mother says babies are bought there. She is telling the truth because she said so.'

Tozama later questioned her mother closely about birth and I was justly chastised for interfering in culturally sanctioned ways of transmitting knowledge.

Hintsa told me, 'I was born in the EmXhoseni in a hospital. I know where babies come from: the hospital.' Two months later the following exchange was recorded between Hintsa and his father.

Hintsa: 'Mama told me that I was not born. She got me from the baboons on the mountains. Is that true?'

Father: 'Yes, it is true. I, too, was with her and we bought you from the baboons in the mountain.'

Hintsa's younger sister: 'I know where mama got you. She bought you from the hospital, from that doctor who gives the heart of a pig to a human being.'

Hintsa's friend: 'A person can't be right with a pig heart, because he will do all things done by the pig.'

Hintsa (annoyed at having had his conversation hi-jacked): 'Do not talk about an older person, you children.'

Both Nukwa and Togu declared that at birth they were too young to know whether or not they had been bought. Lungiswa was certain of her origins:

'I was bought from a shop. My younger sister was bought at the hospital. Mother was very thin before she was born. My mother told me that I was bought at the shop. I don't believe her. I believe that I came from the hospital. I don't know where the hospital got me. My baby brother was a gift from the hospital.'

Mary, my assistant, was at the time of these discussions fairly large with child. Lungiswa, Mary and I talked about the baby. Lungiswa looked amazed but stuck to her theory. Later in the discussion, I asked when her father had left their home and she said:

'I was one and my sister was still counting the months.'

(I was told that he only left a year ago?)

'Anna [her mother] is telling lies. The next baby has his own father.'

This observation coupled with one of her dreams, which she told me a month earlier, suggests that her understanding of the birth process is more complex than she was willing to admit either consciously or unconsciously.

Lungiswa's dream: I went outside to the house next door to see a little baby. I found that the baby was not there as the girl had not finished giving birth to the child. She was still in the hospital.

She used the verb *ukuzala,* to give birth. In the discussion, I reminded Lungiswa of the dream content. She remembered it and commented: 'The other child is coming from her mother's tummy. I did not.'

The other children claimed not to know from where babies came but three of them, after some discussion about Mary's pregnancy, said that babies came from the mother's tummy. They were Cebo, Peliswe and Yameka. Despite the same discussion, none of the others budged from their views.

Saliswa was the only child who said immediately upon being asked that babies are born from the mother. She told me:

'I was born in the Transkei. In my mother's house: it was in the home of my father's parents. Babies come from the stomach. They stay inside until the stomach is big. My mother fed me on the breast. I remember when my brother was born [he was four years her junior]. He came from the stomach. I saw him come. I was shut outside. I was afraid. I was glad when he came.'

Saliswa's mother is an *igqira* and has given birth to fourteen children. Whether or not a child had younger siblings did not seem to affect their ideas of birth.

It is a belief widely subscribed to by the women of Crossroads and one recorded in anthropological literature on the Xhosa that a baby is made from the menstrual blood of a woman and the semen of a man (Hunter, 1936: 145, and Hammond–Tooke, 1962: 71). An *igqira* told me:

'The child's mother in nature is created out of water [semen] and is created with blood, both of these things. Whereas she is created through water and blood, the mother makes the baby with blood only. The blood that she builds the child from is the same blood we call menstruation; and her husband pours water in his wife's womb. Now the foetus grows in the womb and then emerges from it.'

A child's deficiencies may be traced to weakness in either the semen of the father or the blood of the mother and appropriate steps can be taken to propitiate the ancestors to balance the forces of power within the child. Many women in Crossroads, particularly those who had not been to school, had as children been led to believe that babies were either bought at the shop or born from the knee. One woman re-enacted the birth of her first child and had the other women rocking with mirth as she squirmed on the floor trying to catch a glimpse of her knee from which the baby ought to emerge. Traditionally, there were sanctions to keep young married women separate from unmarried girls, thus blocking a natural channel of information.

Older women used to say, 'See, the children of today are wise. They know about the origins of babies. They are too wise and afraid of nothing. Thus they get into trouble.'

Mrs Bhurhu, Peliswe's mother, also expressed common fears when she said: 'As Peliswe grows up, I will worry that she will marry and leave me. I am afraid that she will have a child before marriage. I have not told my children about conception. It is not the Xhosa custom.'

JEALOUSY

The children and I discussed the birth of younger brothers and sisters. I was interested in seeing whether they would admit to feelings of jealousy, and whether there were legitimate channels for its expression. In most households, great play was made of the baby. For example, Mrs Hleke upbraided her 14-year-old daughter, saying:

'Oh, why do you eat my baby's apple? As you were the first child to be born, you were grown by your father and me. Now you eat everything: you do not want my child to grow big like you.'

Later, the little boy said, 'Mama, I want cheese with my bread,' and she responded, 'Yes, my baby, you must get it for you are my last born. Anything you like, you must get.'

The first-born took retribution on the following day. The little boy was crying for a toy camera and his sister said, 'Call the police, Zuziwe; 'phone for them – there's the child crying.' The child stopped in fear just as his mother returned from work. She asked, 'Why is my child crying?' and her first-born answered, 'He is hungry. He said that he wants more bread.' No one in the room exposed her. On another day, Zuziwe, who was the next oldest child, demanded of a friend, 'Why did you hit me? Why did you hit Sonwaba [her small brother]? Sonwaba is my mother's child, don't worry him.'

Zuziwe told me about his birth, saying, 'I was not glad when he was born. When I returned from play, I heard that there was a son in the house. I was not happy.' Her position as the baby had been usurped.

Monica Hunter (1936: 119) recorded that in Pondoland the exclusive right to cultivate a certain area was inherited by the youngest son of the woman cultivating that area (before Crown rules were applied). In addition, a woman's pots, baskets, hoe, axe and stock belonging to her in her own right were inherited by her youngest son (120). Perhaps the regard paid by mothers to youngest sons in Crossroads reflects the special nature of the bond as did the Mpondo inheritance rules.

Of the sample children only Yameka was an only child. Nevertheless she lived with her mother's brother and his wife in Crossroads in order to help with the care of their 2-year-old daughter. Peliswe, Nukwa and Gwali were the youngest in their families. Gwali had had a younger sister who had died. Ten of the children had younger siblings and six of them had two younger than themselves. All but three denied having felt jealousy at a baby's birth and many expressed gladness in recalling the occasion and in having younger brothers and sisters.

Those who admitted feelings of jealousy were Zuziwe, whose remarks are recorded above, Togu and Lungiswa. According to his mother, Togu was his father's favourite child but his younger brother stole the place. Togu said of this child's birth, 'I was glad when he came but I was jealous. I am not jealous now.' Lungiswa has two younger siblings of whom she says, 'I was not pleased about the birth of the child who is straight after me. I did not like her because she had big eyes and they made it worse by burning her just under the eyes. It was an accident. I was also jealous when the other baby was born. He was ugly, but I was pretty as a baby.'

FAMILY ATTITUDES TO RITUAL AND CHILDHOOD

Among the families of the sample children, a number of variables determined whether or not traditional customs concerned with birth and growth were performed. The variables included the place of birth and domicile of the child; the family's commitment to Christian beliefs; scepticism of the value of traditional ways; the detection of signs in a child's behaviour; and, for sacrifices, the availablity of capital.

Four of the mothers who gave birth at home in Cape Town disposed of the placenta in a customary way. Three of them preserved the cord, and, upon their return to the Transkei, treated it according to the tradition of their husband's family; the fourth mother buried the cord in Guguletu, a black township. A fifth woman gave birth to her child in a hospital in the Transkei and was therefore unable to handle the placenta according to custom. She disposed of the cord in a traditional manner. Five other mothers said that they did not perform the traditional acts at birth because they were in Cape Town, which is not 'the place of the shades', or because the birth occurred in hospital. Three mothers did nothing because, for one of them, to have done so would have been against the family's Christian beliefs; and the other two were sceptical of the ritual's value. I do not know what rituals Yameka's mother performed after her birth. Her mother's brother intended to offer a sacrifice to the ancestors of his family in order to place the child under their care, because, being illegitimate, she did not fall under the protection of her father's ancestors.

Only two children, Togu and Tozama, had had an animal killed on their behalf. Both occasions were ten days after the baby's birth. Hunter (1936: 155) described it among the Mpondo thus:

A day or two after the mother comes out of confinement the father kills a goat to make an *imbeleko (ukubeleka,* to carry a child on the back) in which to carry the child. There is no calling on the ancestors, neither gall nor bladder is used, and the goat is not necessarily killed in the kraal, but if the killing is omitted the child may get sick for it.

Four other families planned, so they said, to kill an animal for their child within the next year.

Mlawu, Yameka and Tozama were to have the final joint of a finger cut off (*ingqithi*), the last only if 'she asks for it' or if a sign is given. It was a practice observed by only some groups and its purpose was preventative. Some said that if it was not done, the child would fall ill and perhaps die. Boys had the last joint of the small finger on the left hand removed, and girls the last joint of the fourth finger (see Hunter, 1936: 264–266, for an account of the custom as found among the Mpondo). Two cases follow giving mothers' accounts of the rituals that have been or will be performed for their daughters. Both mothers are *amagqira*.

Case 1

Mrs Qasana bore Siliswa in a shack in the K.T.C. squatter camp. She said that no ritual was performed as her marriage custom ordains that everything must happen in the Transkei. However, the Xhosa midwife who officiated told Mr Qasana to bury the placenta secretly, which he did. When the cord fell off, Mrs Qasana kept it until she returned to the Transkei five months later and there she mixed it with mud and covered it in the wall when smearing the hut at her husband's home.

The sacrifice of a cow is planned and will be held in Crossroads. The cow must be red and the child's body will be smeared with red, the colour being a sign that they are propitiating the shades. The child will wear white beads around her neck and must stay in a room during the entire three-day proceedings. On the first day, the cow will be slaughtered, on the second there will be feasting and on the third the bones will be buried or burnt. The ritual is to introduce the child to the shades. If it is not held, the child will do something very strange as an adult: she will be incontinent, even as a woman her sphincters will be uncontrolled. Or she may be a thief. The sacrifice should be offered now, Mrs Qasana said, as the child sometimes wets her bed.

At the age of 20, Saliswa will be initiated *(ukuthombisa)* in the Transkei. Although Mrs Qasana has had the final joint of her fourth finger cut off as a child it will not be done to Saliswa as it is not the custom of her father's family.

Case 2

Mrs Ketshe bore Tozama in Cape Town, in their lodgings in Guguletu. A male relative dug a hole outside at night in which Mrs Ketshe buried the placenta, which was covered by a white cloth. The place had to be where no one walked and away from grass. Should grass later cover the place, the placenta must be dug up and buried elsewhere. If there is grass, the child will fall ill and grow thinner like the grass. She kept the cord and buried it in soft soil in the Transkei. If that had not been done, the child would have died. Ten days after Tozoma's birth, the house was cleaned and a sheep slaughtered. As Mrs Ketshe is an *igqira*, her teacher came to officiate. The teacher predicted that the baby would be rich as an adult and would live by the work of her hands. The animal skin was used to make a blanket for the child. Pieces were cut from the sheep's pelt and placed on the child's wrists as a sign of the blanket.

In 1979, a second sacrifice was made on the child's behalf to introduce her to the ancestors. The ceremony is performed when the child's behaviour signifies the need for it, which is often detected in toilet habits, Mrs Ketshe said. Tozama dreamed of a goat and said that she could hear a goat's cry. The animal for this sacrifice must be a goat. Her finger will be cut if a dream about it occurs. Tozama's little sister had asked for the ceremony: that is a sign and it will be done for her.

Tozama will be initiated and there will be ritual linked to her calling to be an *igqira* and to her marriage should circumstances demand them.

Tozama described a ceremony that she had witnessed at a neighbour's house in Crossroads. It is noteworthy for the attention to detail and clarity with which she focused on important incidents. Her account follows:

'I have seen many Xhosa rituals. Many here. I enjoy them. (Once) there were many people at the back of a house. A goat was slaughtered for a little girl. My mother said that the girl had been dreaming that she had a goat. The dream is a message from the shades. She stopped dreaming after the sacrifice.

'There was a white goat with a black neck. One man made it fall down. They brought a knife; they cut the neck off and took the skin. They cut the goat into pieces. They brought a dish and put it down. They put the head next to the dish so that the blood must flow into the dish, all of it. When they were busy cutting it into pieces they found a kid *(itakane)* inside the goat. It was dead already. The kid was thrown away. When the goat was well cooked, nobody wanted to eat the meat. They said we cannot eat this kind of meat and others said that it must be taken to their side (of the yard). It was brought in a big dish to them. Then there was also a dog with long hair just like yours. It spilt all the meat and the men cried for the meat and another man took the rest from the pot. When they were about to eat it, they said that they must look first to the East then to the West and they took it back to the pot as it was not cut into pieces. There was also a drum of Xhosa beer where the others were busy drinking. Everybody said, "We are not satisfied with the meat, we must drink beer." They saw a man fall down and so did another and the rest of the meat was taken from the pot and placed next to the men and they woke up. My story is finished now.'

I enquired from her mother about the sacrifice. She said that it had happened as her daughter had said. The offering was not accepted by the shades: the custom had not been fulfilled. Tozama had headaches afterwards.

Of the fourteen families five had performed some traditional ritual on behalf of their children and five more said that they planned to hold some. Of the remaining four, one family would not because of Christian beliefs and three others thought the rituals unimportant. Two of the latter were women without husbands.

Scepticism was expressed with some ambivalence. For example, Cebo's father did not believe in the efficacy of rituals but was planning to sacrifice a goat because of his son's continual bedwetting. He intended to 'watch and see the effect'. Hintsa's family had not fulfilled any customary requirements and his mother feared that the shades would be annoyed. To avoid their retribution, she was wondering whether she ought to make beer and tell them to wait as she intends to fulfil the customs. Many adults expressed unease over their isolation from their ancestral past.

ILLNESS

Ritual on behalf of a child is often conducted only when a child's behaviour indicates a need for it; such behaviour might be bedwetting or dreams, or when a child asks repeatedly that a particular ceremony be performed. The ritual focuses family attention on the child and reaffirms care and support. It may also be performed in response to a child's illness or anxiety. The cause may be identified as originating in the shades' displeasure at the neglect of ritual that forges and maintains links between the child and the past.

When a child falls ill, the parents may first try home remedies before consulting a Western-trained doctor, or an *igqira,* or an *ixwhele* (a herbalist). Sometimes the parents refer to two experts, usually if there is something inexplicable about the illness or if it continues for a long time. The usual childhood ailments and many other illnesses are seen as natural and not in need of explanation. There seemed to be no set pattern to decide by whom an illness should be treated. Saliswa, for example, suffered quite severely from asthma *(isifuba)* for the first few years of her life. Her mother (an *igqira)* often rushed her to hospital. She thought that her being too fat was a cause of the illness, but she did not seek further causes. On the other hand when the child was three months old she would scream and scream when the weather was bad and her mother attributed her behaviour to worms in her cord. She cut small incisions around the navel with a razor blade and sprinkled powdered medicine on them. The baby was given some of the medicine to drink. The treatment worked: the screaming stopped. Togu had similar incisisions made in his forehead and cheeks to cure sore eyes.

Six of the children were said by their mothers not to have suffered any illness apart from the usual childhood ailments. Of the other eight Saliswa, Lungiswa and Togu had been ill with asthma. Each remembered the attacks as frightening and Lungiswa told me a dream in which she was hospitalized during an attack and her mother was crying. Many people in Crossroads suffered with asthma. Mlawu's father did and so did Hintsa's mother's sister. I met the latter just after she had been released from a major Cape Town hospital. She gave me a form given to her upon discharge and asked me to read it to her. We sat on a wooden bench in the shack at dusk as a south-easter whipped up the sand: the form read like a poor joke. It exhorted the asthmatic patient not to have too much furnishing:

Do not have: upholstered furniture, rugs, furry toys, bookcases or other dustcatchers.
Do not use: feather quilts or comforters.
Dust control: The bedroom should be vacuum-cleaned thrice weekly and mopped down with a damp cloth once a week.
Do not lie or sit on the grass.

Three of the children had been hospitalized for loss of weight, usually as a result of diarrhoea. Peliswe had had paralysis of one side of her face which her mother linked to distress that followed an accident in which Peliswe's brother had been injured and her mother's brother killed. Tozama had had an illness which had been diagnosed as *ukuthwasa,* by a white doctor at Worcester, a small town in the Cape. *Utkuthwasa* means 'to appear' and is seen as an illness that is a call to be initiated as an *igqira.* The illness is often feared and the call may be resisted. As an *igqira,* one is never entirely free of illness.

The child's illness began with a dream in which a man threatened to kill her. The doctor whom the family consulted told her parents to handle her carefully, to let her do as she wished and not to punish her. Tozama was pleased with the doctor's prescription. She described the experience thus:

'I have had serious illnesses. I was sick and I went to the hospital. The doctor said I am a doctor myself and so my mother must not punish me. Mother does not punish me. She did before. I was glad of that news. I am happy that I will be an *igqira.* I have everything now to be one: beads and clothes. I do not know when I will become one. I am not afraid. I am not afraid of the sickness. I can dance.'

The case reveals the implicit psychological attitudes of those involved. The parents were concerned about the child's nightmare and her nervous, listless behaviour. They sought advice on handling her.

The specialist proclaimed that she was in need of special attention and understanding for which he gave an acceptable, traditional explanation. The warmth and concern expressed by her family and an impressive stranger reassured the child and her 'calling' singled her out for attention and interest.

Togu, who had suffered from asthma until he was aged 5 or 6, had spent the first five months of his life in hospital because he had double pneumonia soon after birth. His mother visited him once a week and his father every day. Both Togu and Cebo had been badly burnt by hot porridge and boiling water, respectively. Most of the children had had minor burns. They were burnt when playing around the tins of coals which were used to warm the shacks in winter.

Three of the children had a brother or sister who was seriously ill. Hintsa's sister had tuberculosis; Zuziwe's had tuberculosis and retina plastoma: and Gwali's brother suffered with convulsions and was 'not right in the head'. Zuziwe's sister, aged 10, had lost an eye in 1975 as a result of cancer and she needed weekly monitoring to assess her reactions to heavy medication. Zuziwe on a number of occasions expressed both jealousy at the family's concern for her sister and pity for her, especially when her affliction drew the curiosity of strangers. Her parents had consulted both Western-trained and traditional doctors and swung between trusting the one lot and the other. Of necessity, the family had lived near a city hospital for five years.

Gwali's elder brother, also 10, had convulsions and was slightly retarded. Gwali said of him, 'Loyiso is sick. Not in his head. He has convulsions *(ukuxhuzula)*. He is sensible but he swears.' Loyiso was an uncontrolled boy, and Gwali used to watch his antics with amusement and concern. When he was ill, Gwali would stay beside him and not leave the house until he was better. He caused many incidents during which I was able to observe the reactions of adults and children to his undisciplined behaviour. Once he climbed into my car, quite naked, and demanded to leave with me. Fortunately his mother was at home and she firmly extricated him, laughing all the while. On another occasion, he came to my room and asked if he could play inside with the children. I said no because we were working. He picked up a brick and made as if to throw it at me as I stood in the window. The other children, including his brother, just watched. I stood my ground and he threw the brick at my house instead.

On the third occasion, I was helping to erect a nutrition centre when Loyiso joined me. As was his wont, he began to swear at some adults nearby who were trying to get a motor car started. After a time, one of the women picked up a thick stick and chased Loyiso, who hid in my skirt. I grabbed the woman's arms, saying that he was not right in his head. There was a tussle before she yielded. Loyiso, however, resumed his abuse and a man cuffed him hard on the head. The boy had been playing to a delighted audience of small boys who laughed at his misfortune. This time he just leant on me for comfort. It is unusual to see children behave in a manner that draws attention and not much quarter was allowed for Loyiso's obvious lack of control. His family always handled him gently and with humour. They would not admit to his being slow-witted, although they were glad when the possibility of special schooling was offered to him. Both parents worked and the two boys were left at home largely unsupervised.

SEPARATIONS

Despite the laws and economic controls that force black families to live apart, five of the children had lived all their 7 to 8 years with both parents in Cape Town. Three others had been separated from them for only about a year each while living with a grandparent in the Transkei. Another three had always lived with their mothers: Yameka in the Transkei until 1979, when she was sent to care for her mother's brother's child in Crossroads; Gedja in Cape Town in either her maternal parents'. home or her mother's sister's; and Nukwa in the Transkei and then in Crossroads. None of the three had spent much time with their fathers because, respectively, Yameka's father had failed to pay *lobola* and her mother had been recalled by her natal family before the child's birth; Gedja's father had not married her mother nor assumed full responsibility for Gedja; and Nukwa's father, until he was killed in an accident, would return from the mines in Johannesburg for only three weeks a year.

The remaining three children in the sample had spent considerable periods of time away from one or both parents. Nomvula lived with her mother in the Transkei until 1976, when, because of serious illness, her mother left her and joined her father in Cape Town where she had been referred to a city hospital. Cebo had lived apart from his parents for about three years at different times. He spent those years with one or the other of his grandmothers in the Transkei. Lungiswa had been separated from her parents for three to five years. The exact time period was difficult to establish because the topic roused heated controversy within the family, especially between the mother, who said that Lungiswa had spent five years in the countryside with her maternal grandmother, and the child, who claimed to have been apart from her mother for only a year. Besides, mother said that her husband had only left the family in 1978; Lungiswa said that she was but a year old when he went. The squabble is interesting in that family mythology was in the making. Teenage family members were the best informants on such issues, not being concerned with either status or moral rectitude. Lungiswa's mother had to include her husband in the family history until the last-born child had been conceived: the children saw no need for such finessing.

In all, the children had spent more than half of each of their lives in Cape Town. Of their accumulated years, they had spent one-tenth away from their mothers and one-third away from their fathers. Most of the time spent separate from fathers had been lived with a grandparent in the Transkei.

Eight of the children had one or more siblings of school-going age living elsewhere. I do not know of figures that show how many years Xhosa children spent apart from their mothers and fathers. In talking about her family, Tozama expressed her feeling of loss when her father left her:

'Father left us once in the Transkei. I don't know for how long. It worried me because I wanted to go with him and he disappeared. He was away a short time. He returned to us. I have been away only from my mother for short times. It is not all right, I get hungry when she is not there: there is not enough to eat. Nomvuyo [her 14-year-old sister] cooks too little. I know my grandparents. I only know my grandmother on my mother's side. Grandfather is not alive. I do not know about those on my father's side [they died when her father was a young man]. I have spent a long time with my grandmother. I like to be with her. She cooks porridge for my father. She tells us stories (iintsomi) but it is long since she stayed with us. She is like my mother but she is not an igqira. I would like it if my whole family lived together.'

Of the twenty-five children in the control group, 56 per cent were said to have always lived with both parents. At the time of the interview, 20 per cent were living without one parent: one had no mother, three had no fathers because their mothers were unmarried, and another had no father as he had deserted the family. Forty per cent of the children had lived apart from their fathers for 48 per cent of their lives, and 16 per cent had lived apart from their mothers for 36 per cent of their lives. The figures overlap as some children lived apart from both parents for some of the time. While the existence of a squatter camp at Crossroads enabled many of the families to live together, it is still remarkable that 56 per cent had contrived to be together for all of each child's seven years. The data are probably conservative in detailing the length of separations between parent and child because it was in the interests of Crossroads residents to affirm marriage over any other liaison and to establish settlement in the camp for as many years as possible. Besides, in a single interview, I was unable to trace the details of family moves to and from the countryside. Such moves often meant that a child would be left in the care of a relative for extended periods of time.

MOVES

Having considered the amount of time that the children in the sample had spent with their parents or grandparents, let me now detail the number of moves they had experienced in their short lives. No child had lived in less than three different homes, whether shack, rented room, mud hut or a corner of the bachelor quarters. Five of them had lived in three homes; five in four homes; two in five homes; and one each in seven and ten homes. Sometimes the number of places belies the number of moves. Cebo, for instance, had lived in Langa with his parents, in the homes of his paternal and maternal grandmothers in the Transkei, and in Crossroads with his parents, but he had moved six times between the city and the country apart from short visits.

Five of the children had lived in one or more shacks in squatter settlements around Cape Town prior to their move to Crossroads. Three children had watched their homes being demolished. Everything was broken in all their homes. Their families built again and later moved to Crossroads.

Peliswe and her family had four shacks demolished before their eyes. Peliswe had been three months, twelve months, eighteen months and 3 years old on these occasions. Their house in Crossroads was threatened but not demolished. During the last demolition, Peliswa's mother clambered out of the shack through a small window and ran into the bushes across the road in order to escape being sent back to the Transkei. She was caught and brought back. She was told that she must be gone by the weekend (it was a Tuesday). The officials said that they did not care where she went; it was not their business. Peliswe was in the house crying as her mother escaped.

TRAUMA AND FEARS

The women told me how they thought their children had been affected by having been involved in or having witnessed demolitions, riots, police raids or family distress caused by imprisonment*. The children, too, told me how they had felt. The impressions given by mother and child sometimes differed but more often dovetailed. I interviewed mother and child separately and on different occasions.

The children in the sample talked about various experiences during the troubles between 1975 and 1980. I refer you to the chapters on dreams and play scenes for indirect accounts of the impact. Three children were described by their mothers as being very fearful and the member in the family most disturbed by such events. Each of them had lived in Crossroads since its inception: each had been tied to mother's back as she ran into the dunes chased by the inspectors who came to catch those without passes. Zuziwe was with her mother when she was arrested and taken away in a police van. Hintsa and Saliswa had been at home when their shacks had been demolished. Here is a verbatim report of Mrs Hleke's description of her daughter – she spoke in English:

'Zuziwe is very scared of riots and runs to hide. In December 1976, when the people fought, I carried her and she kept her eyes closed, being afraid of the things [curved knives] that can cut off your head. The residents of Nyanga were fighting those in bachelor quarters when the children were closing the shebeens.* Houses were burnt. The people of Nyanga ran to Crossroads and they were kept out. It was bad: I think the people of Crossroads did wrong to keep others out as they were killing each other. Zuziwe is not naughty but very sensitive and screams if her rights are abused. She cried much as a baby. People said it was because I loved to listen to the radio while I washed when I was

* Between 1975 and 1980, three major upheavals occurred in the community and they became, like the eclipse, part of the people's calendar reckoning.

* During the 1976 student riots that originated in Soweto and spread to Cape Town and elsewhere, beerhalls were a main target of student anger. Some 67 were burned as early as the end of June (Geber and Newman, 1980: 145). A member of the Soweto Students Representative Council, formed in July 1976, is quoted by Geber and Newman (145–146) as saying:

'There are more beerhalls than schools and you find these beerhalls are situated right at the terminus of the buses, station and offices where you pay rents. So when your father comes home from work he either goes to the beerhalls or pays rent. . . .

'These beerhalls [are] what is breaking down and lowering dignity of the Black people. It is taking money from their parents and their fathers are coming home drunk. Beerhalls messes up all the Black people in Soweto. The beerhalls are made by the government of the White people.'

Students held the same attitude towards shebeens where liquor was illegally sold. Students' anger and frustration precipitated fights within black areas. Mrs Hleke is referring to one in the above passage.

pregnant with her.

'If I die, I am concerned about her fastidiousness. She is a sensitive somebody. She hates quarrels. Runs from them. She goes to another house and hides her head on the bed. She has improved a little. She resents accusations and abuses and harps on her injuries.'

Mrs Qasana described her child as follows:

'Saliswa has seen riots in Crossroads. They upset her: she was disturbed by the tear gas [she suffers from asthma]. I told her what was happening. When she was 4 years old, her father was imprisoned and the child was crying and asking for him. She understood that it was because of the pass. Once I too went to prison: she was 1 year old and was with me. She was my bail as I was told to leave because of my baby. It was a bad experience.'

The only fears that Hintsa admitted to having were these: 'Elephants make me afraid and dogs. Not you. I was afraid of you a long time ago.' His mother, Mrs Lusizine, described his response to troubles thus:

'Hintsa saw the riots at the school in 1978. He told me that a policeman had helped him and had told him to return home or he would be hurt. He went out of the school but was afraid of the [police] dogs. He had bad dreams and was restless but the little girl [his sister] was worse. Still she does not want to go to school as she says she nearly died. I say nothing to them. I comfort them. Hintsa does not tell me his dreams. I think he dreams a lot. Our house was demolished at Brown's Camp when Hintsa was 4 years old. He was afraid. Later I was arrested on my way from work to Crossroads for having no pass. I went to jail for a night. Bail of R50,00 was paid by a Roman Catholic Sister. It happened in 1978. It was my only arrest. Hintsa cried and could not sleep that night. He was the most upset. My sister bought Complan to calm him. He is always the one to get the most upset. I don't know why.'

These are the three who would not, could not talk directly about such experiences. They were the only ones who were described by their mothers as sensitive and particularly troubled by such matters, apart from Tozama whose own views and mother's opinion will be discussed shortly. Three mothers said that their children were untroubled by similar events. Lungiswa's mother said, 'She is not disturbed by riots. She is rather interested'; and Gwali's mother, 'He is not bothered by riots or other demonstrations'; and Yameka's mother's brother's wife, 'She is unaffected by riots or demolitions of other people's houses.' Yet the children did express fears. Lungiswa said, 'Mother has been to prison. She and others were going for training to Hanover Park and she was caught for the pass. I was very upset. I was well once she was out. I am now afraid of the police.' Gwali told me, 'I have seen houses knocked down and houses burnt down. I am afraid for my house. I do not dream about it. My mother's house never burnt.' Finally, Yameka said, 'I have seen houses knocked down in Crossroads. I think nothing but I am afraid.'

Gedja and her mother both asserted that she had seen riots but that they do not worry her. Mother and child were born and their births were registered in Cape Town and they have the right to live in the Peninsula. They left the Nyanga East township in 1978 to live in Crossroads and have not directly experienced pass raids or demolition threats. They have, however, been witness to many upheavals including the bus, school and meat boycotts of 1980. Nukwa expressed similar bravado saying, 'I am afraid of nothing'; but his mother said that he is afraid and that whenever there is trouble he asks to return to the Transkei.

The other six children openly expressed a variety of fears and they were confirmed in their mother's understanding. Togu expressed fear of demolitions and of trouble in Crossroads. He added, 'I do not go into the forest as I am afraid of snakes. I am only afraid of snakes and policemen. I am also afraid of my teacher. I am not afraid of you.'

Cebo, for all his brash front, admitted fear of police and trouble in Crossroads. His mother was too anxious about his behaviour to worry about his reactions. She said, 'Cebo is naughty with his neighbours but not at home. I worry about his naughtiness and his nervousness. I am afraid that he will grow up bad.'

As on many topics, Tozama was articulate. In response to the query: 'Of what are you afraid, what worries you?' she said,

'Sometimes father has no work. Nothing happens then. There is little to eat. People worry. I don't. I have seen both riots [1976 and 1978]. They worry me. I am afraid for myself.

'I am afraid of the teacher and of not doing well. I am afraid to play outside at night. If there is a thunderstorm, I just stand. I cannot run. I am afraid in the night of people going around and of the spirits. Even if I am with someone, I run leaving the person behind as they cannot help me against the spirits. No one told me about the spirits. I have not seen a spirit. Another child at school, Mandisa, said that a giant *(ingqongqo)* will eat you at night. I think it is true. I have not asked my parents. If someone is beaten at night, people will be afraid to come out and help.

One day we were sent by mother to buy paraffin. As we rounded the corner, a man in a black coat gestured to us with his finger to come. I ran. Nomvuyo was left. There were two men; one was hiding behind a pole. We did not buy the paraffin.'

She related two other incidents of the same nature and, a few months later, the following occurrence was recorded in which Tozama's fears landed her in trouble.

At 6.10 one evening, Mrs Ketshe sent Tozama and her 11-year-old sister to the shop to buy salt and pepper. Ten minutes later they returned:

Tozama: 'Here are the things you sent me to buy, Mama.'

Mother: 'Why were you so long? Are there a lot of people in that shop from which you bought these?'

Sister: 'Yes, Mama, there were lots of people in that shop, and the people who are selling are children.'

Tozama: 'You are telling a lie, we were watching people fighting on the side of the road. They were fighting with knives; one stabbed the other next to his nose nearly in the eye.'

An hour later, the same two girls were dispatched with jug in hand to buy milk for supper. They returned shortly but without the money and having spilt the milk. They told their mother that a *skollie* (ruffian) was coming towards them and they ran in fear:

Mother: 'What have you done, you two stupid children? What kind of person was that?'

Tozama: 'He looked like a *skollie*.'

Mother: 'How does a *skollie* look?'

Tozama: 'He was going from side to side in the road, and then we got a fright and then we ran.'

Mother: 'This brightness of yours, Tozama, is not good, for that person was just drunk: he was not going to do anything about you. There are still many more people in the street. You can't simply run for nothing. What are you going to have for your supper now? Here is money. Nomvuyo [her 14-year-old daughter], go and buy milk, for your father has nothing to eat with his porridge, I do not worry about you two. Take water and make tea for yourselves.'

CROSSROADS DEATH ACCOUNTS

In attempting to place the child in time – his or her past, present and future hopes or ambitions – I talked to each of them about a dramatic incident that occurred within the community. I sought some idea of their understanding of a major upheaval; how they observed and recalled the occasion; how they differed in their reactions; how their reactions fitted into their own and their mother's descriptions of the impact of trauma in the past.

Each child and I talked about a week of trouble in Crossroads in the days immediately following it. The accounts are fascinating: they range from Zuziwe's refusal to say anything (she was the only one who did) to Tozama's extraordinary detailed observations. Before discussing them, I shall give a brief account of the trouble. At about 9.00 a.m. on the morning of 11 August 1980, as I sat in the Hlekes' home, the loudspeaker that is used to convey messages from the Crossroads Committee to the community passed close by. The message was, 'If a member of your family left for work this morning via the Nyanga Bus Terminus, you should check if he/she is lying dead.' The people said that the police were forcing workers to violate the bus boycott by boarding the buses against their will. Students reacted and a battle ensued. There was an atmosphere of unease in Crossroads that morning. Soon after 12.00, Mary and I were stopped by residents near the road to Nyanga East. They told me that as I was white I was in danger and that I should leave Crossroads, taking the Lansdowne Road not the Klipfontein Road, as trouble was about to break out. I left, and five minutes later the students came over the dunes singing. In the afternoon they gathered near the Klipfontein Road and stoned two cars. The driver of one, Mr Beeton, was stabbed and hit and he died at the scene of the incident. Another car driven by Mr Jansen was hit by the stones. His car stopped and the students overturned it and set fire to it. He managed to escape from the burning car and threw himself into a puddle of water. The police arrived and took him away – he died shortly afterwards. In the daily paper next day, there was a picture of the man sitting in the puddle: a terrible picture. During the week, another man was killed by the students and a young boy was shot by the police. It was a week before Crossroads was quiet once again.

In the children's accounts of the violence, it is clear that none of them understood the causes. Most of them realised that white people were in danger, although they were puzzled as to why the students were so angry with them. Eight of them identified the crowd as children of the townships or of Crossroads. Seven others labelled the crowd as the children of Black Power, or of the Comrades, or of Mandela. Four children got some of the facts wrong: Saliswa said that soldiers' cars were stoned and that Mr Jansen was a policeman; Gwali and Togu said that the police burnt the cars; and Nukwa was sure that the white men would have killed me had I come to Crossroads that week. Two of the children dreamed of the trouble.

Hintsa's dream: 'I dreamt about those children of the riot, burning the car. I was near them. I was not afraid. I did not want to be one of the children.'

And Lugiswa's: 'I had a dream that I was burnt. The children of Black Power burnt me while I was on the road. I cried. No one came to help. I woke up in the morning. I did not tell anyone the dream. It was on Monday night after the burning.'

Peliswa recounted her 13-year-old sister's dream: 'The soldiers surrounded Crossroads and Mr X* was there and they said, "Yes, Kaffirs, we are going to shoot you."'

Tozama's account of the trouble follows. It is clear, vivid and moving. She told it all – the gore, the action, the response, the emotion, the humour – with a slight smile and intense concentration: 'The children of Black Power came from the Klipfontein Road across to near my house holding a red flag. There arrived a car with a white man. These children just ran to it and threw stones at the windows. The man was hiding himself with his hands. They turned the car upside down and lit it with fire while he was still in it. He tried to come out. He came out and was on fire and threw himself in the water. The soldiers arrived and the children ran to hide in Crossroads. The soldiers were trying to throw sand and water on the car and the ambulance arrived and took him. He was still alive. After a while we heard that he had died. My mother said that we must stay at the back of the house because she did not want us to see what was happening.

'I cried. I wanted my father. There were women who came to our house and they all cried. The blacks were not killed. Only whites. I don't know why. My parents did not tell me anything. My father was in the hospital during the trouble. He was getting tablets. I was afraid that my father would be hurt. It was right outside my house, near the tap at X4 [a church]. I was afraid at night after that. If we are sent outside at night, we are afraid to go past X4.

'I have not seen the children throw stones before. One child was shot by the policemen. The children removed the bullet from her knee. They removed it with a bottle top. I saw the child shot by the police. She ran away and the children gathered around her. This was near X4. The policeman saw them only after the bullet had been taken out. It was a girl from Crossroads, from house number –. She is not at school. She is an old child, over 15 years. She is fine now: no longer limping. A girl was the first to throw stones. I saw her. I also saw – throw stones. She is

* An official who had been in charge of the settlement until recently.

from Crossroads. The rest are from the townships.

'The newspaper said it was not the children from Crossroads but the township children who killed the man. I felt sorry for that man. My mother said, "It seems as if that man is just like my child." The other girls from the township, while the policemen were throwing tear gas, took off their panties and peed on them then wiped their faces. The Crossroads children were here when the township children came along the Klipfontein Road. They joined them. They were mostly township children and some from Crossroads.

'You would have been killed if you had come. The man was finally unconscious.

'The child of number – was shot to death. The children went to that house. He was found at the hospital and was brought back in a coffin. I did not see him being shot. The people from Crossroads and the teachers came to my house because they thought my brother was the one who had died.'

A little later during the same session, she told me how her uncle *(malume)* had tried to warn her family that trouble was coming:

'My uncle wanted to tell us what was going to happen that week. My mother took it easy and did not listen to him. He was afraid that you would be hurt. Now my mother wants to stay at his house in Guguletu because they hear things before they happen. Another lady from Crossroads saw a white lady coming towards the children after they had killed that man. She waved her hand to tell her to go. The children were angry and wanted to burn her house. She ran away.

'The students were asking for petrol from a Crossroads man. They were not given it. My mother would have given it to them as she was afraid they would kill her.

'My uncle came to my house and asked what is happening. He wanted to know the names of the children because he knows them. My brother would only give a name of a youth group. I do not know if he wanted to take them into prison. Only one boy from Nyanga, called –, mentioned all the names of those in his group. That was wrong because they were all taken to prison.

'The township children came to school and made the older children join them. A teacher's sister was taken. She went. While they were going she said she wanted to pee. She was lying. They waited. She returned and then said she was thirsty. They said, "We will wait." She ran out of the back [of the shack]. The children came and told her sister that she had gone and that they would punish her. They returned later and found her and forced her to join them again. They saw the police and the girl said, "We must hide or we will be shot." They hid and she escaped to another house. They did not get her again. My mother told us this story saying that we must not go to school. We stayed home.'

In the above account, Tozama expresses fear for her father's safety and pity for the white man; she observes with interest survival techniques (how to remove a bullet from the knee and how to avoid being overcome by tear gas); she analyses the composition of the crowd; she expresses disapproval of informers and wonders about her uncle's knowledge and interest in the affair; and she recalls the details of an incident involving intimidation.

Her mother's account of the death of Mr Jansen represented the torn emotions of many adults in Crossroads. On the one hand, she was sympathetic towards the students and their cause, but on the other hand, she wept for those who suffered as a consequence. Mrs Ketshe was ill after the week of trouble and went on a visit to the Transkei to 'release' her body. She told of a woman who saw Mr Jansen being killed and had laughed and laughed and laughed. When she returned home and was cooking, her primus exploded and she was badly burnt on her face and hair and body. It was, said Mrs Ketshe, God's revenge.

I neither wish to understate the impact that trauma may have upon a child's life nor do I wish to exaggerate the impact. The children were remarkable for their quiet dignity, their poise, their curiosity and their openness once trust had been established. Relationships within families seemed to be characterised by the calm expression of warmth and acceptance. There lies the miracle: the strength of the family despite the system. Should you consider that these children were unfortunate in their experience of family separations, moves, contact with demolition, riot, the imprisonment of family members and similar upheavals and, therefore, not representative as a sample, then I refer you to the substantial literature within South Africa that documents the impact of the system on black lives and suggests in outline the experience that huge numbers of black children encounter.* Few studies are available that tell about the reality of day-to-day life of black children, except perhaps for the autobiographies of writers. To borrow a phrase from Habermas (1968), much of children's experience of repression in South Africa is 'unequivocally identifiable suffering'.

* Some of the literature is referred to in the Introduction. Other writings include: Desmond, 1978; Nash, 1978 and 1980; Thomas, 1974; Wilson, 1973; Reynolds, 1984; Burman and Reynolds, 1986.

SELF-IMAGE

As an index of the children's self-image, I gave each a circular mirror to inspect. After a while, the child was asked to describe what he or she saw when looking into it. Once the description had been given, I asked, 'If you were to meet a person who looked like that, what would you think of that person?'

In their descriptions, they used the words black (-mnyama) and white (mhlophe). Five described their faces, which was all that could be seen in the mirror, as black and five as white. Two others used both words to describe facial items and another two used no colour term. I presume that black and white referred to relative hues. I never heard the children use the words for pale or for light or dark complexion. Lighter skin shades were admired by some in the community and it was this preference that advertisements for skin lighteners exploited. Mr Ketshe was away from home when his daughter, Tozama, was born. Upon his return, he teased his wife saying that the baby was too black to be his.

All but two of the children said that they would admire or like a person such as the one reflected in the mirror; Gwali, however, refused to acknowledge kinship with his reflection rather as he had refused to identify himself with the cardboard figures that were purported to represent him at different ages. Nukwa was vexed by his image but denied that it was his. He said,

'The face is white. The eyes are white. If I were to meet this person, I would say that I would be irritated (ukucaphukisa). As for me, I am beautiful but this person I see here is ugly.'

Lungiswa called her reflection ugly and said that she would not like someone who looked like her reflection. Her description was:

'The shape is like David [her younger brother]. The face is black; the nose is white; the chin is white; the cheeks are white; the teeth are white; the tongue is white; the ears are black; the head is black; the feet are black; the knees are black; the arms are white; the neck is black; the eyes are mixed (ukuxubana) black and white. Lungi [her nickname] is not beautiful: she looks ugly. I would not like that person.'

Some months later, the following conversation between Lungiswa and her friend was recorded:

Boy: 'Did you hear what Zolani said, Lungiswa?'
Lungiswa: 'No, I didn't hear him.'
Boy: 'He says that you are ugly as a vomiting medicine.'
Lungiswa: 'I am all right, I didn't ask to be beautiful.'
She was, I thought, an attractive child.

TASKS

Consensus among the adults of Crossroads was fairly general as to the age at which children could be expected to perform certain tasks. At age 3 or 4, a child can be sent on small errands to nearby houses. At 5 or 6, he or she can fetch a small bucket of water from the tap and shop for one or two items. Just before the age of 7 a child is expected to be able to complete any straightforward household task efficiently and quickly. Between ages 8 and 10, a child should be able to buy or sell items with fixed prices. By age 10, a girl should be capable of handling any household job and by 14 she should be able to run the house, including food-preparation and cooking.

There seemed to be little division in labour between the sexes up to the age of 8. The children in the sample, had, on a regular basis, to complete two or three of the following tasks: to collect water, sweep and wash the floors, clean the yard and toilet seat, wash and dry dishes, wash their own underclothes and sometimes care for small children. One boy prepared the family tea each morning and another washed his blanket that he frequently wet at night. One girl resisted doing housework and was given the tasks of cleaning the yard and toilet seat.

Cebo's mother said that his duties were to sweep the kitchen and toilet, wash his blanket and collect water every day but that he only did them well if she was at home. However, if she returned home late on a Friday evening, she would find that he had lit a candle in her bedroom and had brought in the washing all of his own accord. Two other mothers praised children for conscientiousness and thoughtfulness. Mrs Ketshe said that Tozama is not told what to do but she takes on tasks such as sweeping and washing the floor on her own. On her father's return from work, after he has walked across the sand dunes from the bus stop in Nyanga East, she washes his feet and his socks. When he sleeps, she tucks in his blanket and says, 'Father, if you die, I will be upset and die.'

Mrs Qasana said that Saliswa washed dishes, swept and washed the floor, and collected water regularly and, although there were many children to share the work, she took upon herself more than her share. Here is the skeleton of an observation made in the Qasana home in June. It was mid-winter. Saliswa did not go to school.

9.30 a.m. Somtshakazi* (the young bride who is the wife of a man from Mr Qasana's clan) asks Saliswa to dress. The children are still under their blankets. The child rushes to the tap for water and asks an older girl to warm it. All the children wash.

* *Umtshakazi* – bride.

9.45 Saliswa helps her sister to feed the baby. The bride prepares the fire tin and they gather round it. They talk and sing like members of the Church of Zion. They run around the fire while singing. The bride asks them to stop and stand away as Saliswa was burnt last time they played like Zion members.

10.00 The bride asks Saliswa to wash her pants and vest. She pours soap and water into a bowl and Saliswa washes them. She washes her socks too and the bride rinses them and hangs them on the line.

10.20 The bride tells the child to take the fire tins to the side of the house. She does, then takes up a broom and sweeps the floor. She washes the dishes and her sister rinses them.

10.45 Saliswa plays sticks with her brother. They fight. She pulls off her cousin's [the 14-year-old child of her father's half-sister] hat and she is chased and ordered never to do it again or she will be beaten.

11.00 Saliswa hides herself in her mother's bedroom. She emerges. Cleans the pot and warms stamped mealies for their meal.

CONTROL

In an attempt to estimate the degree of control that the parents exert over the children, and the manner in which each child perceives that control, I asked, on different occasions, the mother and child who selects the clothes for the child to wear each day, what choice he or she has in attending school, accomplishing tasks, selecting friends, playing away from home and ranging through and beyond Crossroads. Predictably, the amount of control exercised by parents varied. For instance, it ranged from the restriction of Peliswe's movements to three houses, the occupants of whom were relatives or people well known to the family, to the freedom allowed Gwali to move anywhere in Crossroads and even as far as his grandparents' home in Nyanga East.

Of the six boys, five could range anywhere in the settlement. Cebo's mother forbade him to go to the sand dunes beyond the shacks or across a major road into the forest, but she was aware that he did go. Only Mlawu had to play near his home and let his mother know where he was. Half the boys were given no choice on school attendance, what to wear or eat or whether or not to do their tasks. The other three, Nukwa, Hintsa and Gwali, did more or less as they pleased. Nukwa's mobility was hampered only by the injunction that he should be home by sunset. His mother told me that he decides for himself when he wants to go to school. In fact, he stopped at the end of July. I asked:

(Is he not too small to make such a choice?)

'No, he can think for himself.'

(How does he know what he will need when he is an adult?)

'If he grows well, he will know.'

Nukwa said, 'I no longer go to school. Mother says I must not go as she has no school fees.' The truth lay somewhere between their explanations. Mother, indeed, had no money, but as there was a school boycott in progress, few parents were paying fees. Nukwa disliked school, especially the classroom chaos and boredom under the boycott conditions. His mother could not enforce his attendance as she did not monitor his movements. Besides, she held to a traditional attitude of child development in which it is believed that adults must not stifle the emergence of a child's talents and that the child will find the growth path best suited to him.

The mothers of both Cebo and Hintsa told them to go to school, but both knew that often their child did not. The following exchange between Cebo and his father was noted on 14 November 1980, at 8.00 p.m.:

Father: 'Cebo, did you go to school, my little boy?' (Cebo tries to hide himself for he had not been to school.)

Mother: 'Bring water for me to drink my tablets please, Cebo.'

Father: 'But he has not yet answered my question. Did you go to school, Cebo?'

Cebo: 'Yes, I went to school: at the time there were no children. They had gone home.'

Father: 'Why did you go when the others had gone home, Cebo?'

Cebo: 'At that time, at that time, Daddy . . .'

Father: 'Do not be tricky, young man. Can you not tell me the truth? Why do you cheat me?'

(Cebo does not answer but hangs his head.) Then he says, 'We have not yet gone to buy paraffin. Your washing water will be cold tomorrow morning.'

Father: 'O.K., my boy, let's go together and buy paraffin.'

Relative to the boys, the degree to which the girls were free to range in Crossroads was curtailed, but it varied amongst them. Peliswe's movements were carefully monitored, and four other girls had to play near home; another had to inform an adult in the house as to where she would be; the seventh girl was given a large triangle from home to mother's sister's house to mother's friend's house within which to explore; and the last child, Gedja, could go anywhere in Crossroads. The above are the mothers' views of their children's freedom of movement. Interestingly, five children gave different accounts of their mobility: two suggested more restrictions than had their mothers,

Hintsa and Gedja, and three declared that there were no controls on their movements within Crossroads, Yameka, Tozama and Nomvula, whereas their mothers had said that they could only play near home and not explore the area alone.

The mothers of the three girls who were given more freedom worked. I observed that all the children (except Mlawu and Peliswe, whose mothers carefully watched their movements) ranged far through Crossroads, although their usual beats were well defined.

Only Gedja, among the girls, was given much choice in selecting clothes, deciding what to eat or in accomplishing tasks. Tozama could select her own clothes, but she had to go to school and eat what she was given. She said that she could stay away from school for one or two days when she chose to. Again, the conditions under the boycott affected the situation.

POSSESSIONS
The children had very few personal possessions. Among them they owned one broken bicycle, two broken wind-up cars, one ball, one length of skipping-twine and some hoopla wire. At different times during the year the boys owned cars but they usually broke or were stolen after a while. The children had six exercise books and three textbooks among them; some exercise books were kept at school. They had, too, eighteen utensils – mugs, plates, bowls – that were designated as the child's own and an average of sixteen items of clothing each; the clothing ranged from Saliswa's seven (four dresses, one skirt and a pair of shoes) to Lungiswa's thirty-six items. Lungiswa's mother used to hawk clothes and so she had a large wardrobe. Their clothes were usually kept in a box or a suitcase beneath a bed. Yameka owned a black plastic bangle and Tozama a traditional outfit, consisting of: an *inkciyo,* a bead apron in black, white, green and blue; an *isiyeye,* a necklace in white, green and blue beads; a shawl and a skirt in *ibhayi,* a blanket cloth of orange. She was very proud of it. Her mother, a seamstress and an *igqira,* had made it for her.

It is impossible to say what impact their lack of possessions had on their learning. No doubt the lack of opportunity to manipulate, order and construct things that were made out of materials uniform in shape, colour or texture towards particular ends rendered the children less confident when faced with formal tasks in a test situation. Similarly, their lack of exposure to pictures and written stories made the introduction of reading and writing a more complicated process. However, their use of rhythm, their repertoire of songs, their own song compositions and their ingenuity in play warn against placing too great an emphasis on their lack of possessions. The children's own activities and the objects and plants available in the environment offered a rich base upon which education skills such as classification and numeracy could have been founded.

SCHOOLS

In 1955, the Government passed the Bantu Education Act. It has been the source of much anger and frustration among blacks because it is thought to offer an inferior education, and because of its initial insistence on the use of mother-tongue instruction up to Standard Six and the use of Afrikaans and English in the teaching of many high-school subjects. The Report of the Commission of Inquiry into the Riots at Soweto and Elsewhere from 16 June 1976 to 28 February 1977 (Cillie Commission), found that the riots were caused by dissatisfaction with the medium of instruction and with Bantu education (SAIRR, 1981: 501).

According to the Minister of Statistics the amount and the percentage of the gross national product in the calendar year 1978 allocated to education was as follows (including the Transkei and Bophuthaswana):

	Amount R-million	% of GNP
White	1 009,8	2,62
Coloured	196,7	0,51
Asian	95,2	0,25
African	253,6	0,66
Total	1 555,3	4,04

Source: Hansard 4Q cols 185–6 quoted in SAIRR, 1981: 459

The estimated per capita expenditure during 1978–79 on school pupils of the various racial groups was given by the responsible Ministers in the assembly:

	Including Capital Expenditure R	Excluding Capital Expenditure R
White	724,00	640,00
Indian	357,15	297,31
Coloured	225,54	197,20
African in 'white area'	71,28	68,15

Source: Respectively Hansard 3Q col 103; Hansard 2Q col 42; Hansard 4Q col 187; Hansard 2Q col 96 quoted in SAIRR, 1981: 460.

The SAIRR (1981: 460) calculated the pupil/teacher ratios for 1980 from statistics supplied by the Department of Statistics:

White	1 : 18,6
Coloured	1 : 28,8
Asian	1 : 25,6
African	1 : 45,9

(The number of pupils and teachers in the 'independent' homelands are not included.)

The above figures indicate the disparity between the Bantu and other education systems in South Africa.

A full account cannot be given here of the nature of Bantu education, its efficiency in terms of the overall development of South Africa, or of the distress that it has caused among blacks (see Auerbach, 1979; Gerber and Newman, 1980; Malherbe, 1977; SAIRR, 1979, 1981; Steyn, 1969 and UNESCO, 1972).

I shall report little about the children's school experiences. Ten of those in the sample attended two schools in Crossroads that had been founded by the community with aid and assistance from church and other organizations.

Their very existence was testimony to many people's strength and optimism. One of the buildings was bulldozed down by official decree and rebuilt with community and Urban Foundation funds. The schools were symbols in the locality and focus points of a political rivalry that culminated in a murder in October 1979; after which one side gained and held dominance throughout 1980. One school was the headquarters of the Crossroads Committee during the year. The teachers of that school, all of whom except one were women, were leaders in the community and they represented both the power of the women and their fury as the men divested the women of that power.

The two schools differed in a number of respects, the most significant of which was their identification with factional allegiance. The teachers of one all lived in Crossroads whereas those of the other came from the townships, which was a source of jealousy and suspicion and handicap in the establishment of good teacher/community relations. Both schools fell under Government control at the end of 1980, which was seen to be a victory by the teachers as Government would then be responsible for paying teachers' salaries and benefits.

I shall report little about classroom activities and atmosphere because the creation of the schools and the position of the teachers was part of a complex picture that I observed keenly but did not study in sufficient depth to report with confidence. Besides, the schools were in a transitional state and cannot be seen to represent the school experiences of a wide group of children. Another reason for setting schooling aside in this work is that I was anything but an objective observer. I found the conditions appalling – the crowding (sometimes 150 children in a small room); the lack of furniture, paper, pencils, books; and the control wielded through the stick. While I admired those who established the schools, I did not approve of the way they ran them. I did not feel that basic conditions need be so bad; that is, the adult/child ratio, the lack of use of materials from the environment and the misuse of the stick.

A school boycott in the Western Cape effectively stopped teaching from June 1980 to the end of the year (see SAIRR, 1981: 501–20). In one school, little work was accomplished for the rest of the year. The situation in this school was extraordinary: children sat in the classrooms all morning doing nothing. Older children were placed in charge of order and abuse resulted. A teacher from the other school, however, was proud of having taken all her children successfully through the syllabus despite the boycott. She used to smuggle in the day's lessons on a scrap of paper tucked into her brassiere despite threats from students that they would burn down her house if she continued to teach. Whether or not one thinks that she was right to disregard the command of boycott leaders is a political judgement.

For most children little formal learning was acquired during the year. In the situation, it was not possible to estimate the value of classroom activity without making political statements of either community or national implication.

TIME
The children's response to questions about time were not very informative. Using a watch and a cardboard clock with movable hands, we talked about day and night, the seasons and the years. The children synchronized their days according to the behaviour of parents, teachers and other children. Daylight and sunset were their most important markers. Here is what Tozama said:

'I get up at eight or nine. My brother tells me the time. I go to school with the others. When the sun sets, I return for supper. Teachers tell us not to come to school at weekends. I know when the month has ended. You can see it up there [the moon]. I see the year has ended through the calender *(icalendi).* Also it tells me when I am a year older.'

Most of the children said that they did not know when a month or a year had ended, nor were they told when they were a year older. This confirms the children's lack of involvement in a sense of growth or age progression measured in even steps. In Chapter 7, we shall see that the seemingly simple task of placing cardboard figures in order to represent the child at each year was problematic. None of the children could tell the time, but all knew what watches were.

AMBITIONS
Four girls wanted to be nurses and one a teacher. None of them saw any obstacle in reality to prevent them from achieving their goals. Another girl wanted to be a Western-trained doctor or a driver, but she granted that in reality she would probably be a char or a baker. A seventh girl wanted to be a factory worker and the last girl a clerk who could type *(ukuxhaxhaza* – a fine clicking word); both supposed that they would really be chars. Of the boys two wanted to work in a factory, two wanted to be clerks, and two said that they would be drivers.

3
The Play and Songs of Children

Chapter 3 records the play and songs of children aged 10 or less who live in Crossroads. I needed to know what games the fourteen children played, when, where and with whom. It was, obviously, not possible to observe their play in isolation and I therefore recorded all instances of play in the society of children that I observed during the eighteen months, whether or not they involved a child from the sample.

Young children in Crossroads spend time either at a crèche or at school, at home with kin or neighbours or at play in the sand. They travel very little and there is no organized entertainment for them. No library is within easy access and there are only a few privately owned television sets in the settlement. Some children listen to radios but none that I knew could determine when to listen in peace to particular programmes. Family outings to church, visits to adjacent black townships and occasional shopping expeditions to peri-urban centres provide children with their major form of entertainment outside the settlement.

I did not record children's play with the intention of establishing any theoretical point of view. There is a rich literature on the subject* and there is a need for an analysis of play in the South African context. It is an aspect of poverty that people, including children, may live within fairly close proximity to a variety of facilities yet not take advantage of them. In South Africa access to beaches and public amenities is, often enough, determined by the colour of one's skin, but even when no restrictions exist opportunities are not always taken. One reason, in Cape Town at least, is that blacks are forced to live far from the areas of play monopolized by whites and the cost of transport to and from is high. Of the fourteen children none had been to the zoo, none had walked on either of the ranges of mountains (Table Mountain and Hottentot's Holland) that are visible from the dune tops in Crossroads,

* For further reading on children's play see: Bower *et al*, 1982; Bruner *et al*, 1976; Finley and Layne, 1971; Garvey, 1977; Mead, 1928 and 1930; Millar, 1968; Piaget, 1951 and Singer, 1973.

only a few had visited the city centre and only two had swum in the sea.

In analysing the children's ideas about space (see Chapter 4), I was surprised to find that they paid little attention to features of the landscape outside the settlement and that, for them, the origin and end-point of routes was not of great interest. I should not have been surprised. When children are denied access to and, therefore, a feeling of community with the terrain through either poverty or discriminatory legislation, they may be denied a sense of control over or connection with that terrain. A comparative study around that point could be fruitful. Few matters that relate to the development of cognition can be studied in isolation. A child's use of space, particularly in play, reflects the child's liberty and wealth, which reflects the nature of the economic and political realities of that child's society. An obvious point but one grossly neglected by those who write about cognitive development. I do not mean to imply that privileged children in the South African context use play or develop notions of space that are necessarily superior but only that the criteria against which they are measured should not be biased.

The chapter has two sections: one on the play and the other on the songs of young children in Crossroads.

PLAY
The following collection of observations of child-play celebrates the innovation, ingenuity and imagination of children. Some useful pointers that contribute to the general thesis emerge and some methodological issues suggest themselves. The bulk of the incidents of play that have been recorded occurred outside and were noted during the course of other investigations. At the scene of play the number of children involved, an estimate of their ages, their sex, the materials used, the space occupied, the rules in effect, and, when possible, conversation, roles and interaction were noted.

The most striking feature of all play was the ingenuity with which materials found in the environment were put to use. Materials used in play fell into three categories: those manufactured for play; those found in the environment and adapted for play; and those borrowed from the adult world. In the first category, I noted in use only five varieties of items that had been specifically manufactured for the purpose: balls, spinning-tops, dolls, playing-cards and cars. There were few of each in Crossroads. Substitutes were more commonly found. In the second category, there were twenty-eight varieties of items that formed the material base from which playthings were made. They were salvaged from the environment, particularly from rubbish dumps. There was a large city dump near Crossroads and when tip-trucks arrived, women and children could be seen walking behind them, foraging for useful scraps. Factory off-cuts were a good source of supply for certain materials such as small rounds of wood that were used as draughts, or wire for making vehicles. The materials most often used besides the ubiquitous sand were bricks, stones, rope, string, wire, plastic bottles, sticks, wooden off-cuts, bottle tops, elastic, tins, milk bottles, boards, zinc, springs, wheels, nails, rubber, plastic sheets, pieces of coal, cloth, hide and nylon thread. The third category included items borrowed from home such as spades, combs, slippers, bias binding, *sjamboks* (whips), shoes, drums and bicycles. Coins, begged, borrowed or earned, were another popular item if we stretch play to include simple gambling games played by young teenagers.

The uses of sand were myriad. It could be moulded into homes; constructed into roads; thrown for dogs to catch; carried in tins as water; bounded as rivers for swimming; dug in for treasure; shaped for cakes; carved into holes for 'jacks'; drawn in, and even used to stuff down an enemy's nose and mouth. A child simply had to squat and begin to re-create the medium and, in a wink, other children would join the game. Maree and Cornell (1978) estimated that in Crossroads there were 6,2 persons per houshold of which 3,2 were adults and 3,0 children. As there were some 3 000 shacks, the child population was estimated at about 9 000. In the homes of the families with whom I worked, there was an average of 6,8 children per house. It is possible that there were many more than 9 000 children. Playmates were readily available.

Among the crazes that swept through the child population were hula hoops (made of iron), spinning-tops and swings. Suddenly, so it seemed, every child was swaying his or her hips to keep an iron in motion. The hula hoop craze had blown in. Even tiny children undulated with nonchalance. Just as suddenly, something else suited the children's mood: spinning-tops, perhaps. One elaborate game involved a top that was spun on the ground and then lifted while moving. The tops would vanish and soon swings would magically hang from every lean-to as if spiders had spun them in the night. Occasionally an outside event such as the Gerry Coetzee and John Tate boxing match would spark off a craze. Cloth would be carefully wound onto children's hands to form most realistic gloves; fights would be staged, sometimes amidst the full paraphernalia of rings, towels, trainers and heckling audience.

Apart from such crazes, the most popular forms of play were making houses and roads in the sand and cars out of wire. I only noted a fraction of the instances of such play. Nevertheless, out of the play situations recorded, one-tenth pivoted around houses and roads and another tenth around wire cars. The third most frequently noted scene was play with drums, usually accompanied by *amagqira* songs and dances. Fourth position was shared by doll- and ball-play, then hopscotch; other sand play, *uchiki* – a form of 'jacks' or '*chuckies*'; card games; gambling and boxing. Together these ten forms of play made up half the scenes.

Houses in the Sand

The houses varied in the complexity of their design, the variety of materials used and in the numbers of the children involved. For example, one small girl playing alone etched the plan of a house in the sand using two plastic spoons; in contrast, thirteen children built a village in the dunes using a wide selection of scraps, leaves and household items. In the latter example, two girls began to build on a high soft dune and within an hour thirteen children (seven girls and six boys) were 'extending', so they said. The first house was made of sand with 16 cm high walls that had been firmly stamped and patted. Some walls were made of brick. Angles were clear and walls, beds and tables were shaped with a small piece of linoleum. The assignment of space was organised and the furnishing elaborate.

26 March 1980

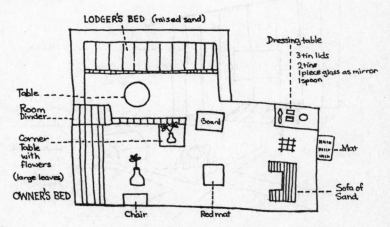

The 'owner' was a girl of 10 and her 'lodger' a girl of 7.
Figure 3–1: House in the Sand – Number One.

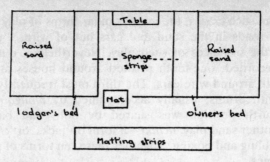

Figure 3–2: House in the Sand – Number Two.

In this house, too, the 'owner' was a girl of 10 and the 'lodger' a girl of 7.

An hour later, thirteen children all 10 years old or less had collected broad leaves and had stuck them like hedges into the sand walls. There were five new rooms, in one of which two boys were asleep on brown paper beds.

Four girls aged 10, 8, 7 and 6 made the following complex near their school.

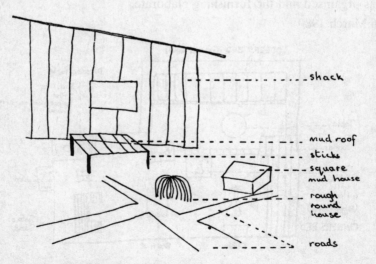

Figure 3–3: House in the Sand – Number Three

59

Six children aged between 4 and 7, of whom one was a boy, made large mounds in the yard. They used bricks, plastic bottles and glass jars in the construction and the same for carrying 'water' to the site, that is, sand.

30 April 1980

Figure 3–4: House in the Sand – Number Four

A storekeeper's child aged 8, and five friends between 5 and 11 years made a house outside her parent's shop.

19 June 1980

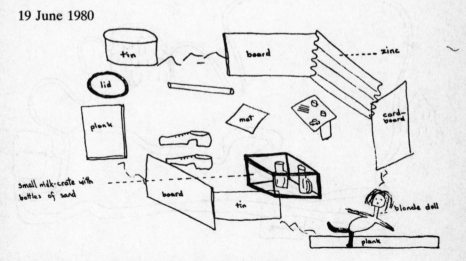

Figure 3–5: House in the Sand – Number Five

Seven boys and one girl aged from 4 to 10 made a scene in a narrow space between a wall and the road. They used empty packets of Omo soap, Joko tea and Lexington cigarettes, pieces of zinc and some iron pipe.

Figure 3–6: House in the Sand – Number Six

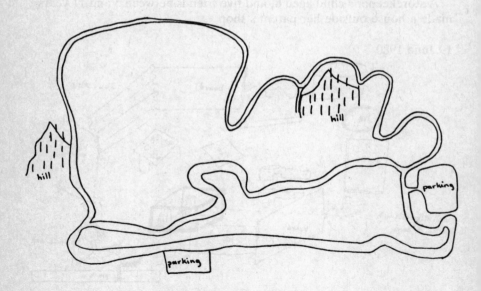

Figure 3–7: A Road Network in the Sand

Roads

Road networks were often complex and carefully elaborated. A group of boys aged 7 to 9 landscaped the following on a side-road within the settlement, covering an area about 6 x 4 metres. Roads connected parking areas, hills and forests (bunches of sticks) rather like Figure 3.

In another road network, two boys of 5 and 8 years used round wooden off-cuts painted brown and green as the traffic lights. Occasionally a child would have a metal car or plastic vehicle, but often bricks would be used as cars. Six boys aged 3 to 5 used bricks on 12 August 1980, and three children, aged 5, 7, 9, including a girl, used two pieces of wood nailed together on 6 May 1980. They made a wide road, scraped 2,5 cm into the sand with the banks built up, and they used bricks and planks to make a tunnel. One child had a small plastic car and the others had blocks of wood. The girl seemed to be directing the play.

Wire Cars

Iimoto, cars made of wire, could be seen at any time although production increased dramatically when 'imports' of wire hit the 'market'. The designs ranged from the elegantly simple to the mechanically intricate. The principal elements of the car consisted of a long steering-rod, which the child could hold as he ran, attached to a base that rolled. The simplest was a wire fixed to a plastic bottle:

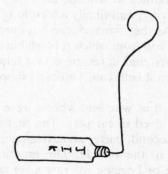

Figure 3–8: Car Design – Number One

The basic materials were wire and wheels made from the bottom of plastic bottles, tin lids, buttons, cotton-reels or wood, or taken off old prams or toys. Most cars were made by boys between the ages of 7 and 14, although some fathers made them for their small sons.

Out of the innumerable instances of play with or the construction of cars that I saw, I recorded twenty-two involving eighty-seven children and almost as many cars. One design was fairly widely used (Design 2), but the rest varied.

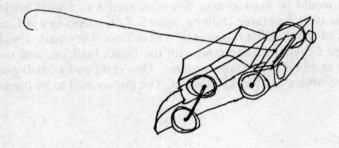

Figure 3–9: Car Design – Number Two

Road rollers, trucks, buses, motor cycles and particular car models were made. Vehicles were among the few possessions that boys prized and they featured in their dreams and quarrels. In one Saturday morning scene, three boys aged 9, 7 and 5 had collected wire, string and plastic bottles and were each making a car. They began by cutting off the bottoms of the bottles as wheels, then they attached wire frames held together with string, and finally added long wires topped by rings as steering-wheels. As they worked, the boys argued as to who owned which bit of material and from which rubbish bin it had been taken. The 9-year-old finished first and in response to a request for help from the youngest, said, 'I cannot help you. I must go shopping. Take your car to the garage.'

Essential items such as wire and wheels were used in barter. There were four stages involved in car play. The first was the acquisition of some materials; the second, barter and exchange; the third, production; and the fourth, use of the vehicle. The production process involved boys finding, buying or begging for raw materials, often taking them quite far afield. The younger ones were slowly led out into the wider world of scrap yards and factories by the older boys. Having acquired materials, a process of barter or exchange often occurred. Once I saw twenty boys, who had made a good haul, set up a factory beside a road within Crossroads (14 November 1980). Actual production was a learning situation and involved much discussion. Saliswa's 9-year-old brother made a car in a neighbour's yard and had in attendance eleven children between the ages of 3 and 8, some of whom offered help while others watched. He had obtained the wire from a nearby factory and was busy making a Toyota. He used two half-bricks and a stone the size of his fist to hammer the wire into shape. First he made the steering-rod fixed to an axle and two front wheels:

Then he made two frames and

began to combine the whole.

Figure 3–10: Car on the Assembly Line

Once made, cars were used in single play, or in small and large groups. Race tracks were meticulously planned and passionately lapped. Cars seemed to fulfil the same functions as dogs on leads, for they allowed the driver/master to explore the environment while visibly occupied in some necessary activity. Boys ranged far and wide in finding materials and in driving. Rallies were sometimes held over the dunes and through sizeable puddles.

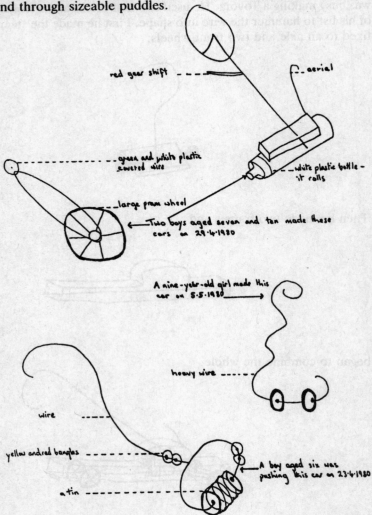

red gear shift

aerial

green and white plastic covered wire

white plastic bottle – it rolls

large pram wheel

Two boys aged seven and ten made these cars on 29·4·1980

A nine-year-old girl made this car on 5·5·1980

heavy wire

wire

yellow and red bangles

a tin

A boy aged six was pushing this car on 23·4·1980

Figure 3–11: Some Car Designs

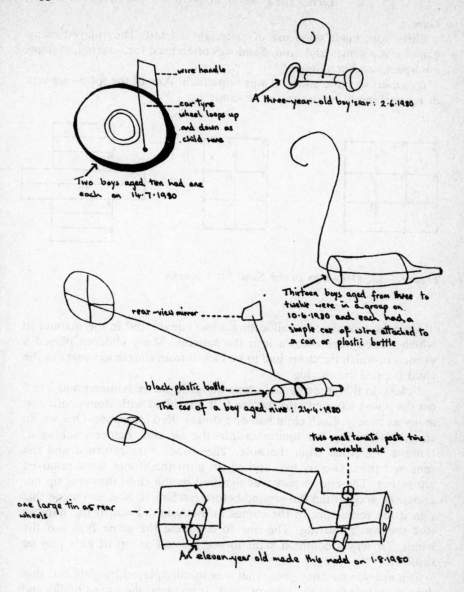

Figure 3–12: More Car Designs

Games

Girls, too, made good use of materials at hand. They played many games using stones and sand. Sand was often used for washing, making mud-packs and cooking.

Ugqaphu was one game. It was hopscotch. Any of the following sets of squares might be drawn in the sand:

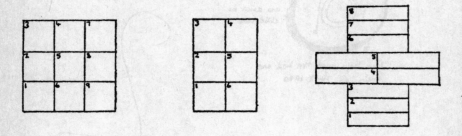

Figure 3–13: Drawings in the Sand for Ugqaphu

Variations occurred in allocating a rest square and in the manner in which stones were thrown into the squares. Many children played a version in which the stone had to be kicked from square to square as the child hopped on one leg.

Uchiki: in this stone game, a hole about 12 cm in diameter and 3 to 5 cm deep was scooped into the sand. It was filled with stones, often as many as twenty. Each child had one stone called *iqununda*. One would start by throwing her *iqununda* into the air and, before catching it, remove one stone from the hole. The stones were returned and she removed them two by two and so on until the stones were removed altogether. The end of play was signified by the child throwing up her *iqununda* and patting the ground before catching it. She also made that sign if the remainder of the stones in the hole did not fit the number that she was removing. The one to complete the game first was the winner. It was a common sight to see a small group of girls playing skilfully.

Stenana was another game that was usually played by girls and that drew materials from the environment. It involved the use of bricks and a ball. Six bricks were piled in the middle of an open space and, in the game I recorded in detail on 8 March 1980, two children stood close to the pile while two others stood further out and on either side of them.

Figure 3–14: Sketch of Children Playing Stenana

The object of the game was to hit with the ball the two children in the middle: when one was hit, she would wait to one side until the other was hit whereupon it would be their turn to throw. If neither of the two was hit and the ball went far afield, the two in the middle quickly knocked over the pile of bricks and had to rebuild it before the ball was retrieved. When the ball was fetched, they could be hit but could resume building if the ball went astray again, and so gain one 'game'. On this occasion four girls between the ages of 9 and 16 were playing in a fenced-in yard.

Upopi/dolls: in doll play, I recorded nine scenes involving eighteen girls and a boy of four. Frequently, sticks, plastic bottles and other items were used as dolls. I watched an *igqira's* grandchild of 2 persuade a girl of 5 to tie a slipper to her back with a diaphanous red scarf and then sing and dance her 'baby' to sleep (24 October 1980). There were a few fair-haired dolls around but I saw no black dolls, probably because there are few for sale in the shops. The game was not played by children over the age of 8 and the doll play of those between ages 6 and 8 involved scrummaging through dustbins for pieces of cloth with which to make doll's clothes.

Violence

There was a notable lack of violence, actual or pretended, in the children's games. I saw only two children with guns – one child's gun was made of a heavy spring that he had bent over:

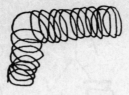

Figure 3–15: A Gun Made from a Spring

and the other's was a cow's jaw. I noticed only two fights, one between Cebo and a boy his age (5 August 1980) and another in which one boy of 6 or 7 years sat upon a boy about his size while be poured sand down the unfortunate's nose and mouth (24 November 1980). The only bullying that I saw was officially sanctioned by teachers in the classrooms. The society was violent enough: for example, one young teenager was seriously beaten on the head with a brick by two adult men for attempting to pick their pockets, and a child under 10 was locked in the boot of a car for stealing from a hawker. There must have been more fights and more cases of bullying than were visible, but in a crowded space filled with children it is surprising that more were not in evidence. Sometimes I saw little children practising throwing stones and burning car tyres in the dunes just as older children were doing in their fights for political rights.

Girls tended to throw verbal missiles at one another. Perhaps following the example of some adults, children sometimes used offensive language and sexual innuendoes to tease each other. For instance, after a set-to Zuziwe's friend said to her, 'I will suck your breast, Zuziwe,' and in her mouth was a balloon (23 October 1980). Once Gwali teased a girl his age by dancing close behind her with his pelvis stuck forward. Annoyed, she turned quickly and pushed him hard. He laughed delightedly and ran off, leaving her to continue on her way (14 September 1980). A girl of 8 years, having run out of verbal abuse, showed her bottom to a boy of the same age as a gesture of disdain (24 October 1980).

There were many other incidents of play that could be described: the making of aeroplanes, beer, fire-tins, guitars, drums, catapults, draughts and the playing of games like soccer, 'cats and mice', skipping and 'fox'. There were games of pretence in which children were fleas or *skollies* (rascals) or herdboys or trains. There were children who drew in the sand, organized drill and piggy-back races.

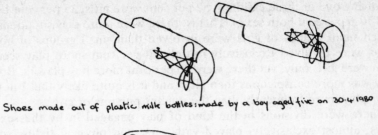

Shoes made out of plastic milk bottles: made by a boy aged five on 30.4.1980

A catapult-gun made by Cebo's cousin aged fourteen: 14.8.1980

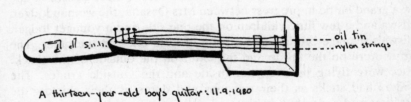

oil tin
nylon strings

A thirteen-year-old boy's quitar: 11.9.1980

Figure 3–16: Examples of Items Created by Children for Play

Sexes

Out of the play situations that were recorded, 42 per cent involved boys only, 33 per cent girls only and 25 per cent girls and boys. One-third of the situations involved girls only, although girls were involved in only 40 per cent of the 200 play scenes recorded. One reason for this was that boys gathered in much larger groups than did girls. Out of seventeen scenes in which ten or more children were at play, eight were all boys and none was all girls. Out of the seventy-one play scenes involving two or three children, 52 per cent were girls, 35 per cent boys and 12,6 per cent both sexes. That is, there were more play situations in which small groups of girls were involved than small groups of boys. Boys were involved exclusively in only 10 per cent more play scenes than were girls only, yet there were 20 per cent more boy players. Boys' play was more conspicuous than girls' and it is quite likely that I noted their play more frequently than the quieter pursuits of girls.

There were divisions in the kind of play engaged in by the sexes. Boys, almost exclusively, played with cars, had physical fights, spun tops, gambled, played draughts, marched, played with dogs, and made catapults. More boys than girls played with balls, boxed, fought with sticks and ran races.

Girls played with dolls and ropes and the stone game. More girls than boys played hopscotch and card games. There seemed to be similar numbers of both sexes in *amagqira* play and games involving drums, sand, swings, hula hoops and trains.

Age

In the varieties of play that were recorded, only three adults were seen as participants. One included a young man playing cards with a girl of 10 (27 March 1980) and the other two instances included Mrs Qasana and her lodger who were active combatants in a mock war in the Qasana home. One morning (28 October 1980), I passed the shack and saw a grand battle in progress between Mrs Qasana, the woman lodger, Saliswa and a few little children on the one side and a younger lodger, Saliswa's teenage brother and a gang of little ones on the other. The former were on the inside and the latter on the outside of the shack. Shoes were flying between the Inside and the Outside armies. The Insiders had sticks as their weapons and doors as their shields: the Outsiders had a *sjambok* (whip) and a variety of missiles (shoes, etc.). As I watched, the Insiders retreated to the front bedroom shrieking and laughing as boots were hurled through the door and the *sjambok* cracked through the window. It was all tremendous fun.

My assistant, Mary, would not stop to watch. She walked on and waited for me. Other adults looked disapproving. They explained that it was a show of 'less dignity'. Even Hendrik, a teenager who had recently arrived from the Transkei, looked askance. 'How,' asked Mary, 'can children learn respect if they beat the mother and play the fool?'

At the scene of play I would ask the children their ages and estimate them. About 70 per cent of the incidents involved only children between ages 5 and 10; in 15 per cent there was one child or more of 4 years or less and in another 15 per cent there was one child or more over the age 10. In Crossroads, the years between 5 and 10 formed a span of time that was quite free and carried few responsibilities. Apart from running a few errands, performing a few household duties and fetching water, little was expected of children between these ages. The duties of a herdboy and a child caretaker in the countryside make greater demands on children during these years.

I saw little child-care by children under 12 years. The ages of those involved in play given above support the observation. There was, I suppose, little child-minding because of the dangers that surround living in an urban situation. Most houses had roads fairly close by and few yards were fenced. Houses were small and crowded with little space where dangerous items such as paraffin, matches and rat poison could be safely stored. Cooking and heating facilities were dangerous and there was no *umzi* (household grouping) with attached space over which all adults wielded some authority and responsibility. If the prime care-taker, usually a mother or grandmother, had duties elsewhere, it meant a long journey and many hours away from home during which children could not be expected to assume full responsibility for toddlers. There was, of course, some care of youngsters by older siblings as the figures suggest: in 15 per cent of the play situations children under 4 were included and only 3 per cent involved only children of 4 years and under.

Children over 10 years played some soccer and hopscotch and they boxed and gambled, but they were less often seen on the streets. There was no high school in Crossroads and many of them were at school either in the Transkei or the townships. A major reason why they were not seen at play, given the lack of adequate study facilities and organized activities including sport, was that they, especially girls, were given heavy responsibilities in the home that left them little free time. Besides, a certain sense of decorum was demanded from girls over 10 years.

In Crossroads, girls over 10 years often ran the house while their mother worked or became involved in political or church issues. The burden of work for many of them was quite heavy. They were responsible for younger siblings yet they could not wield much authority. Both Zuziwe's and Tozama's elder sisters, aged 14, found it difficult to handle their quick and headstrong younger sisters. On one occasion, Mr Ketshe called the 14-year-old to him and reprimanded her for being angry with the younger ones. A conflict in authority between parental expectations and town ways often occurs at this age. It is complicated by the dangers of the girl falling pregnant.

I noted children at work in other occupations. Some examples follow. One 12-year-old boy gathered grass after school each day to feed his father's eight cows for which he earned R1,00 a week. A 9-year-old boy helped his mother chop wood to sell. A girl of 7 helped her mother with laundry for which the mother earned R2,00 a load. It was not unusual to see children hawking produce prepared by their mothers; on one occasion (28 November 1980), seven children, the oldest of whom was 7, were selling potatoes for 20c a bag and had been told to sell them all before returning home despite the fact that it was raining. Boys would build go-carts out of pram or tricycle wheels and heavy plastic milk boxes with which they collected water and wood for housewives. For a large plastic barrel of water they would charge 35c and 10c for a small one. They gathered wood from the trees across the main road and charged 40c for a cart-load. Children over 10 years attended customers in the small shops or at the hawkers' stands. Others helped with businesses such as tailoring and the making of tin trunks that were conducted in the homes.

A closer study of children at work would need to be made to estimate their contributions, direct or indirect, to the maintenance of the family. Many play situations were interrupted by demands made by adults to take a message, shop or perform some duty. One adult expressed her annoyance at seeing a child doing 'nothing' and said that such a state of affairs should not be tolerated.

SONGS

Song and dance can be seen as part of play. While few songs were expressly composed for children, songs were taken from the repertoire of the churches, political commentators and *amagqira;* the songs selected suited the children's needs in terms of voice exercise, body co-ordination, symbolic re-enactment and communal sharing.

When children in Crossroads sing, they always move with the rhythm. Movement and song are inseparable. During the first three months of fieldwork, I spent much of my time with children aged 6 and under in the crèches. Often as many as one hundred children would be gathered in a small room and they would spend a good part of each day singing and dancing. Sometimes a single session would last for two hours. A woman would lead the singing, but a child would introduce the group into the next song. Many songs had dance steps and gestures that accompanied them. One song was particularly moving. It had a chorus of 'turu rurururu turu . . . ' that sounded like doves in the bluegums. The children would bend low from the waist as they sang the chorus and shuffle their feet in a quick, fancy rhythm. The meaning of the song contrasted sharply with its gentle sounds and steps:

Asina mthuthulezi watsha ngumlilo.
Thumela uLazaro anthi unothixo phina
Turu rurururu turu ruru turu
tururu turu ruru.
[We have no nanny (comforter), our nanny is burnt.
Send Lazarus and where is God?]

And so it was with many songs. Behind the harmony, hidden in the beat of the little fat thighs of girls and the quiet foot shuffle of small boys would be words of anger and loneliness and despair. Here are three songs that were sung by children aged 5 or under:

Jo ndenze njani kulomhlaba?
Oh, ndenze ntoni. Kumnyama
pambi kwam?
[How can I live in this world?
Oh, what can I do? It is so dark
ahead of me.]

Sisi, Nomatamsanqa, uhlola.
uMama noTata abasifuni,
be sitengela oTsotsi
Basihlaba ngemela.
Sis, Nomtamsanqa, uhlola.
[Sister, Mother-of-good-fortune, you are
singled out.
Mother and father do not want us,
They sell us to thugs,
They stab us with knives.
Sister, Mother-of-good-fortune, you are
singled out.]

Walila umzi akatyiwa sashiywa
nguLipano. Xwalile pantsi
kumhlaba amatombo enja aka ko.
[The cry of the nation*
People could not eat when we mourned
The death of Lipano.
He is buried in the ground
like a dog's intestines.]

---

* Or 'the village mourned'.

The women said that they taught the songs to the children. Many of the songs were brought from the Transkei and some were composed in Crossroads. I have, in most cases, used the translations given to me by women in Crossroads, although they are not always very literal.

I collected over one hundred songs from children most of whom were 10 years old or less. Some of the songs were recorded in the crèches and many were overheard as children played and sang and danced in the dust of the dunes or around the *imbawula* (tins filled with burning coals) in winter. The songs fall in three major categories, each roughly equal in size: those derived from churches, political commentary and tradition. There were two minor categories: the songs composed by children and the songs that made social comments. I shall give examples of each in turn, after a discussion of music and learning.

In terms of their content, there were few songs that seemed to have been composed for children. Most songs, however, use repetition and sounds as if they are the instruments of the voice; the effect for a child must be something like an English nursery rhyme such as 'The Grand Old Duke of York,' which originally was a political comment. Children often took simple refrains and made them into songs like the following:

Loli, loli, loli, loli
Mthumele, mthumeleni,
Iyho, yo-yo, iyo-ho.
[Loli, loli, loli, loli
Send him, send him
Iyho yo-yo, iyo-ho.]

Siya' emthatha, emthatha
Thima, siya emthatha.
[We are going to Umtata . . .]

Children almost always sang in groups. One might begin and others would soon come to join in. They had sizeable repertoires. On 21 November 1980, seventy children aged 5 or less were gathered at a crèche in a room that measured 12 by 15 m. They were singing *Nkosi Sikeleli iAfrica,* the country's national anthem.* I watched two 3-year-olds listen and copy and slowly gather confidence until they too were singing and dancing with accomplishment. The children next to the little ones appointed themselves tutors and they would slow down to

* A leaflet written by Professor D.D.T. Jabavu of Fort Hare Native College, South Africa, published by Lovedale Press (South Africa) gives the history of this hymn. It was composed by a lay preacher Enoch Sontonga during the First World War. The Xhosa hymn to freedom, 'Nkosi Sikelel' iAfrica' (God Bless Africa) was translated into other languages. It expresses a national yearning for political liberation.

demonstrate a step or emphasize a phrase. I recorded many instances in which a woman would sing to an infant and dance him in her hands, or drum for a toddler to dance.

On an evening in August, I watched an old man teach fifteen children to sing and dance. His drum was a large tin covered with hide. It had a hose pipe for a handle. He would drum and the children would dance. He would stop and talk and they would repeat what he said. He taught three 5-year-olds to sing:

'I am praying that I can pass my exam.
I call on my ancestors.'

A child of 6 took over the drumming. Then another. The old man used to teach them when he returned from foraging for scraps to sell. The children loved him and used to crowd around him on his return.

In November, I came across ten children aged 7 or less who had formed an orchestra in a space tucked between a house and a fence. Their instruments consisted of a plastic bucket turned upside down, sticks and tins half-filled with stones. What was noticeable about the children's play with music was that it was ordered, purposeful and sustained.

Older children would not dance quite so freely in the open, but they would sing as they walked. For example, three 12-year-old girls sang the following as they walked through the shacks one July morning:

Ilizwe lethu, iSouth Africa,
Lisithembisa ngenkululeko.
Kuthiwa masiziphathe ngokwethu
Thina bantsundu.
Imithandazo yethu bantsundu
ngaba wankele na enkosini?
[Our country, South Africa,
Promises us freedom.
It is said we black people
should rule ourselves.
Are our prayers, we black
people, heard by God?]

The first time that I saw Yameka, she was dancing with ten other children all under 9 years of age. They were playing in a yard beneath washing-lines and were using a large green plastic bottle as a drum. A child of 4 was drumming as the children sang:

Ye, mfazi ophekileyo
khauphake kulanjiwe
Siyamphothula O! Hai.

[Hey, woman who has cooked
please dish out, we are hungry.
We are grinding him (like mealies).]

The song probably comes from an *intsomi* (folk tale).

There seemed to be conscious efforts made to teach songs and rhythm and dance steps. There was more involved than simple repetition. A mother would beat to the rhythm of her child's feet; and older children would patiently repeat a step for a little one to follow; another may take over from an incompetent drummer and play a little and then hand back the sticks for him to try again; the old man gathered the children together to teach them: 'They must learn,' he said.

While in the Transkei in early 1981, I discussed learning and music with Father Dave Dargie and his marimba players at Lumko. Father Dargie's excitement about the complexity and intricacy of Xhosa vocal music was infectious. He rejects the theory that natural talent explains Africans' musical, ability and says that it is carefully taught. He remembers seeing a woman teach her 2-year-old a simple song and then harmonize with the child's efforts.

There were six children playing in Father Dargie's group that day. They ranged in age from 6 to 15. One was an 8-year-old girl. They played well and the youngest, whose father was a song composer, was particularly talented. Afterwards, they explained to me how they learned. One said, 'Men sing more than women in the Church and at home. Yet it is the mothers who sing to the small children. It is from them that they hear the sounds. We used to listen to the women's songs. We do not know who created them.' They insisted that on learning to play the marimba, one must first know the song and then the notes can be found. A 15-year-old said, 'I hear the note that will suit in the instrument. If the note sounds wrong, I change it and seek another note.' A 10-year-old added, 'Father Dargie shows us the notes, but it is reminding not teaching. You first know the song and then you know the notes. You touch, touch all the notes and you get the one that suits the songs. You need not be clever to play. You must be interested and do it with your heart. Someone might be teaching you, but you will take your own way of making music.'

The other children repeated the themes of creating music through love of it and of finding the notes rather than being taught them. They thought that a child who had been starved of music would not be able to learn to produce it. They confirmed my observations at Crossroads that in learning musicality there is a core of instruction, yet room for innovation. A woman uses her voice, her rhythm, her words in relation to the age of the child with whom she makes music. She and the child create together: she does not sing to the child but tunes her contribution into his attempts. Similarly, the older child creates with the younger. It is a learning process, not based on imitation and observation but on an intricate mesh of tones and syllables of rhythm and rhyme. A study of the process would inform us about learning and teaching techniques.

Church Songs

Church songs were taken from every denomination and many of them had political overtones. One that was often sung was 'The Rivers of Babylon'. Three of the church songs follow:

Ulizwi wadal' amazulu homhlaba
Ulizwi wadal' amazulu homhlaba
Wadala wadal' amazulu waphumla
Wadala wadal' amazulu waphumla
[Word created the heaven and the earth
Word created the heaven and the earth
He created, created the heaven and He rested.]

Ze nihlale ngokonwaba
Ze nihlale ngokonwaba
Ze nixel' uAdam no Efa
Bethel' emyezweni we Eden.
[You should stay in happiness . . .
Like Adam and Eve
In the garden of Eden.]

Uzugcin' imithwelishumi
Ebhalwe kwincwadi engcwele.
Ukuba waphule wamnye
Uyaphule yonk' imithetho.
[You should keep the ten commandments
Written in the Holy Book.
Should you break one of them
You have broken all the commandments.]

Often the songs from the Zion churches were sung as part of a re-enactment of a church gathering with an all-child congregation. The leaders might be the children of church members, but many other children joined in. The occasions were remarkable for the intensity with which the children acted and their faithfulness to detail and expression. On 20 November 1980, I recorded this scene:

About twenty small children, most of whom are under 6 years of age, are singing Zion songs near Mary's home. One drums on a plastic bottle as the others run fast in a tight circle singing –

> *Bavumeleni abantwana beze kum,*
> *Jerusalem halala–ho–o–ha.*
> [Let the children come to Me,
> Jerusalem halala–ho–o–ha.]

One girl falls in the dust and another falls upon her holding her down as if she was in a frenzy; one hand is in her hair as she prays for her recovery. The manic actions are imitated to perfection. They run and run, making a dark track in the sand. Sometimes they twirl and hum. Three children have sticks: one has tied green cord to his and some in his hair. One child kneels to pray and another punctuates the prayer with the drum:
'I am praying for our Bishop'
Drum rolls.
'And our priest'
Drum rolls.
'And especially for our people'
Drum rolls.
They sing and clap and run again. So fast. A girl kneels and drums. One falls and predicts the future. I cannot catch her words.

There was a similar scene in September 1980, on the outskirts of Crossroads near the hawkers' stands. This time a crowd of twenty-two children all under 8 years of age were being led by a woman who was a member of the Zion church. She had been called by the shades to become an *igqira* but her family refused to finance her training so she turned to Zion. Not very successfully, the people said, as she acted crazy. Sometimes she would kneel on the road in front of my car to bless me, becoming, like the sanitation truck, something of an occupational hazard. On this occasion, she was dressed in an assortment of clothes with beads and a cow-hair fringe around her waist. A towel was pinned by one corner to her bodice and a child held it behind her as they danced around and around and around. One child drummed on an upturned orange bath-tub and the unlikely congregation ran and sang songs of Zion. One boy carried a palm frond with a white cloth tied to it and another a stick bearing a cow's tail. People stopped to watch and smile.

Political Songs

Songs with political content formed the largest group. Many of them were freedom songs that I gathered while the children were boycotting their schools. These were sung most often by small groups of children between 9 and 14 years old. Some examples follow:

Ayabaleka, ayasab amaBhulu
Ayabaleka, ayasab amaBhulu
Ayangena, ayaphuma ayadidizela
ayasaba amaBhulu.
[They are running away,
The Afrikaners are afraid . . .
They are coming in,
they are going out,
The Afrikaners are afraid.]

AmaBhulu akwelizwe ayosbel' emanzini.
AmaBhulu akwelizwe ayosbel' emanzini.
Siyohlala sisodwa emhlabeni wethu.
[The Afrikaners who are in this country
are going to escape to the water . . .
We are going to live alone in
our country . . .]

Unzima lo mthwalo
Woyis' amadoda.
Unzima lo mthwalo
Woyis' amadoda.
Thin' aikhathali noba siyakhonkxwa
Sizimisele inkululeko.
[This load is heavy
Even for the men . . .
We don't care whether we are chained
We are standing up for freedom.]

Vula Botha siyankqonkqoza,
Vula Botha siyankqonkqoza,
Khulul' uMandela asikhokele,
Khulul' uMandela asikhokele.
[Open, Botha, we are knocking . . .
Release Mandela to lead us . . .]

Sikhalela izwe lethu
Elathalthwa ngamBhulu
Mawayek' umhlaba wethu
Mawayek' umhlaba wethu.
[We are crying for our country
which was taken by the Afrikaners.
They should leave our country.]

Sixakekile kwilizwe
lakhokho bethu.
[We are concerned about
the country of our forefathers.]

Singabantwana benkululeko,
Siyayifuna inkululeko.
[We are the children of freedom,
We want freedom.]

Other songs carried more general political messages. The crèche children often sang:

Anqonqoza amajoni afikile
Ye, ye, ye mama, ye majoni afikile.
[The soldiers knocked
they have arrived
Ye, ye, ye, mama, the soldiers have arrived.]

The police were often called soldiers *(amajoni)* by the children. The next song comes from the repertoire of one of the school choirs:

The nation is dead. Orphans are all alone.
The world is dead. Nations are killing one another.
Villages have lost their sons and daughters.

Among the blacks, it is all problems.
Among the whites, fear reigns.
It is sorrow and anguish all around the world.
All happiness is gone.

Father who is in Heaven
Listens to all prayers
He washes away sorrow
And anguish from the earth.

Some songs reflected people's dislike of legislation that controls where they live. The following was sung by Nomvula and her friends as they stood around an *imbawula* on a cold July evening:

Xelelam amapolisa
kuba umzi ngowam
nabantwana ngabam
aandithethi naba' andinapasi
kuba umzi ngowam
nabatwana ngabane.
Yiza mthanam.

[Tell the police
Because this is my house
and the children are mine
I'm not talking even if
I have no pass
because the house is mine
and the children are mine.
Come, my progeny.]

Others reflect despair at being unable to find a home:

Nombuyiselo ndiboleke iaddress
ndihlalele e Ciskei
Ndaliwa, ndaliwa e Transkei.
[Nombuyiselo, give me an address
I live in the Ciskei.
I've been rejected, been rejected
in the Transkei.]

Or the refusal to accept the free train ticket to the homelands that is given by the authorities to those whom they refuse permission to live in the cities.

Wakha wambonana umntu okhwele
i-aeroplane?
Suda naye loliwe.
Andisoze ndiye ekoloni.
Hamba naye loliwe,
Andisoze ndiye ekoloni.
[Have you ever seen a person
flying in a plane?
Take off with him, train.
I won't go to the colony.
Go with him, train.
I won't go to the colony.]

The homelands were sometimes referred to as colonies as in the above song. A final song in this section reflects politics within the community. It, too, was sung by the school choir:

What has happened, my father's son?
It looks as if things have gone wrong.
Crossroads has been demolished.
It is a painful situation, a painful situation.

What are we going to do now?
Where will we go, my father's children?

Let us go to Crossroads
and build it up although it is fallen.

We shall go, we shall leave
We shall go right down home.
Our home is at Crossroads
We shall live in happiness
We shall live there in happiness in Crossroads.

Traditional songs

Traditional songs, most of which come from the *amagqira,* formed
another group of songs that were often to be heard sung by children
aged 10 or under. As may be expected the words of these songs are
stranger and the meanings less clear. However, they were not relics of
tradition long since forsaken but reflected beliefs still held by many
people in the community. For example, there was a young man whom
we shall call Absalom who worked as a driver of a hotel delivery van
until he was bewitched by evil spirits in 1974. He and his family believed
that ants had been placed inside him and had driven him crazy. Both his
parents lived in Crossroads although they were separated. His mother
had passed Standard 7. She had consulted a number of *amagqira* at high
cost as well as trained doctors. The young man had twice been
hospitalized. In 1980, he used to berate whites in Crossroads and, as he
had slashes across his face that had healed but that still held the
stitching thread, he made a fearful impression. One of the songs that
Saliswa and her friends sang referred to such witchcraft:

Khauve zenyuk imbovana
Hawu yehe, yemtaka nomama.
[Just here the ants are going up
Hawu, yehe, my mother's child.]

Here are some examples of songs in this group:
Zuziwe sang this as she played alone in her home in October 1980 –

The children of being sick
I am sleeping with a goat blanket.

Hintsa sang this in December 1980 –

They are coming tomorrow,
They are coming,
The children of the spirits.

One of the signs that the shades are calling someone to be initiated as
an *igqira* is that animals appear before one or in one's dreams. They act

as totems or guides in the initiation process. Some children playing in the road were heard to sing –

Namhla kudibene ingwe ne ngonyama
Namhla kudibene ingwe ne ngonyama.
Wen' uyabizwa, uyabizwa, uyabizwa.
Wen' uyabizwa, uyabizwa, uyabizwa.
[Today the leopard and the lion are meeting . . .
You are being called, called called . . .]

I had often tried to discuss certain details of Saliswa's life profile with Mrs Qasana and I had usually failed because she was busy attending to her patients. Therefore, I resolved to sit in her home one day and wait until she was free. She had, at least in part, been avoiding me because she found it tiring to answer my endless questions. On an October morning, I settled down with Mrs Qasana's cheerful permission, in a corner of her front room to wait.

She went off to see a patient and her family took it upon themselves to entertain me. We began at 9.00 a.m. with thirteen children, including Saliswa, Zuziwe and Gwali, two teenage girls and two women in the room. By 11.00 a.m. there were twenty-seven children, three teenagers and six adults. The young children danced and sang the songs of the *amagqira* for three hours. The boys took male roles, using different steps from those of the girls, and often humming like trains in a tunnel. Each song was accompanied by definite steps. Saliswa danced with amazing grace. People arrived with bigger and better drums and many children took turns in beating the rhythm, including Saliswa's 4-year-old brother, who was most proficient. Those who were not very able were lightly teased but not denied a turn. Here are some of the songs. They seem simple without the harmony, the parts, the repetition, the actions:

Kwawuleza sangoma
Liyakhala ixesha
[Quickly, diviner,
The clock strikes.]
Camagwini salahleka
Sebabibi, camagu!
[Blessing on you, we have lost our way
Both of us, Blessings!*]

Molweni zangoma;
liyabulisa igqira.

* *Camagu* is a greeting to the shades, pl. *camagwini.*

[Good morning, great diviners;
The diviner greets.]

It was 12.00 before Mrs Qasana returned and we retired to her room to talk.

Children's Compositions

A fourth, smaller category was of the songs composed by children. Three examples will suffice. Cebo sang the following as he leafed through a magazine one evening at home:

> There is a baboon
> under the cave.
> It says something surprising –
> that it wants to smoke.

He sang another two evenings later:

> *Mama, ndiyeke, ndiyeke*
> *ndiye eskolweni*
> *Heyi – hey – hey ndiyeke*
> *ndiye eskolweni.*
> [Mother, leave me alone, leave me alone
> let me go to school . . .]

The third example is noteworthy because of its reverberations across time. On 28 March 1980, three girls aged 4, 7 and 9 and a boy aged 5 were playing outside the house of the grandmother of three of the children. The 7-year-old girl was a neighbour. The mother of the 4-year-old was unmarried and lived with and supported her mother. The father of the other two was blind and lived with his wife in an institution in the Transkei. Grandmother was heard castigating her grandson for telling the neighbour that the house was not her home. She added that it was not his either as his home was in the Transkei. It was an odd remark for a grandmother to make. The child was angry and played quietly on his own in the sand while the three girls merrily chanted a song, dancing round him and poking him:

> *Awungowalapha nawe asilokhaya*
> *lakho eli.*
> [You do not belong in this house
> This is not your home.]

The boy did not react. He and his sister had come to live with their grandmother two months before the incident. A few months later, she ran away. Despite the efforts of many of us, including radio and

newspaper appeals, she was not found for three weeks. She had asked
for shelter from a woman in a township house and fabricated a name
and a story about her arrival by bus from the Transkei. She was brought
back to her grandmother's home in Crossroads but ran away again a
day after and was eventually found in a home for abandoned children.
She and the woman in charge had formed a strong, loving relationship
and the woman wanted to adopt her. Grandmother was prepared to let
her be fostered out for a year or two but would not countenance the
shame of having her adopted. She was a small, attractive woman with a
dimpled smile that hid an iron control of her family. Her remark to her
grandson in March echoed down the year in his sister's unhappiness at
grandmother's home.

Social Comment
This is a loose category containing songs that comment on the times.
Some were to do with school attendance:

> *Mama no tata zeningangxoli*
> *Kuba andiyang' eskolweni*
> *Mana no tata zeningangxoli*
> *Kuba andiyang' eskolweni*
> *Utishala undibethile.*
> [Mother and father,
> Don't be cross with me
> Because I did not go to school . . .
> Teacher has beaten me.]

Others with place of origin:

> *Mna ndiyintombi, ndiyintombi*
> *yakwa-Ndebele*
> *Nihlala phaya phesheya kwala ntaba.*
> [I am a daughter, a daughter of Ndebele
> I stay there across that mountain.]

or the need for a place to live:

> *Wi, wi bendilapha nalapha nawe,*
> *He mm he mm he m UThomase*
> *uhlala apha?*
> [Wi, wi I have been here and
> there with you,
> He mm . . . do you stay here, Thomas?]

or they were to do with marriage transactions:

Ndiyamthand' uThuthula,
Watshi uNdabanduna,
Ndizomlobola ngani?
Wenqe wenqe

Wakhalaz' umama,
Wath' imal' ayikho.
Uzomlobola ngani
Wenqe wenqe.
[I love Thuthula,
Said Ndabanduna,
With what am I
going to pay for her?
Wenqe . . .

Mother was not satisfied,
She said there is no money.
With what are you going
to pay for her?
Wenqe . . .]

One needs, in considering the content of the songs recorded above, to remind oneself that they were largely sung by children aged 10 or less. There is an extraordinary admixture of subject matter. Much of it is political and social comment but Christian morality and traditional lore is well represented. Even economic issues arise, as in the last song. One can only wonder at what the accumulated effect is of such training in general knowledge.

SUMMARY

The songs and play of children aged 10 and under in Crossroads showed great ingenuity and imagination and a rich use of available resources. In terms of the demands that a modern education system makes on children, their play did not offer much exercise in fine motor co-ordination that incorporated perceptual differences in colour, shapes, size, etc., in a systematic manner. However, the games that are played could be used as bases for learning, especially the cards, draughts, gambling, stone game, drawing in the sand, hopscotch, the manufacture of cars and song composition. The Cape Flats has about 2 000 species of natural vegetation ready to be collected, sorted, ordered and classified. The children have been denied the opportunity to learn traditional ways of classifying and ordering their environment; their loss has not been replaced by modern methods because education is abysmal and the wider society offers neither library facilities nor other avenues that provide experience in such methods. Given their poverty and given the negligence of South African society to their needs, it is extraordinary that children create such wealth in their songs and play.

The record of instances of play suggests a number of points that are worth reiterating in that they reflect adult attitudes towards play. Few adults involve themselves in the play of children. Play is not seen as sacrosanct and sometimes it is regarded with suspicion as a waste of time. Adults do not seek to direct play and only some attempt to determine with whom a young child may associate. Time is not set aside specifically and materials are seldom acquired by adults for play. Yet adults express pleasure when watching children's games and many admire the construction of wire-cars and offer advice on their design and maintenance. Adults contribute richly in terms of time and instruction to children' education in song, music and movement.

There is a remark that is often found in anthropologists' monographs to the effect that children in non-Western societies learn by 'observation and imitation'. A definition as to what exactly is meant by this is seldom proffered. Children are purported to imitate adults in their play in preparation for adult roles. The remark implies a view of knowledge as a copy of reality. Piaget (1970a: 15) strongly refutes this view, claiming that knowing reality means constructing systems of transformations that correspond, more or less adequately, to reality. He holds that human knowledge is essentially active and that to know is to transform reality in order to understand how a certain state is brought about. In his opinion (1966: 58), play and imitation perform different functions:

It is indispensable to (the child's) affective and intellectual equilibrium . . . that he have available to him an area of activity whose motivation is not adaptation to reality but, on the contrary, assimilation of reality to the self, without coercions or sanctions. Such an area is play, which transforms reality by assimilation to the needs of the self, whereas imitation (when it constitutes an end in itself) is accommodation to external models.

He sees play as a means of self-expression, that is, as a system of signifiers constructed by the child and capable of being bent to the child's wishes. Such is the system of symbols characteristic of symbolic play. These symbols are borrowed from imitation as instruments, but not used to picture external reality accurately. Rather, imitation serves as a means of evocation to achieve playful assimilation. He believes that the function of play is manifested in a great variety of forms, most of them primarily affective but sometimes serving cognitive interests.

In watching children play, in listening to them sing, it seemed clear that they were not imitating a given reality but were using it for a variety of ends including wry comment on society.

4

The Children and Space

SPACE AND THE BODY

The exercises in this section were devised as aids to discovering how the children would handle scale or relative size. The tasks were homespun, and were not meant to be formal tests. I wanted to see with what facility children would use their hands and bodies to describe the relative size and shape of things and how expressively they could describe space with their bodies. And I wanted to see how successfully they could depict relative size with actual objects made out of clay. One series represented the family and the other, vehicles.

I was told that black students in South Africa have problems recording objects to scale and sometimes seem to use modes of perception other than the one expected in formal training: modes of perception more akin to those used by Picasso and Klee than departments of architecture and engineering. Such concerns were in my mind while devising the following six exercises:

1. *Using hands to describe the size of things.* Each child was asked to show me with her hands the size of the following: a bead, a cotton-reel, a teaspoon, a loaf of bread, a car wheel, mother and a house. The order varied.

The exercises are to be viewed in the light of play with children; I was interested in their ability to do the task *and* in the degree to which they would willingly follow instructions in using their bodies, in simulating actions and in paying attention to detail. There are obvious ambiguities in the tasks, such as the fact that beads and cotton-reels vary in size; but their different sizes did not interfere with the purpose. To each of the children's demonstrations, a score was assigned: 0 for a very poor, 1 for poor, 2 for fair and 3 for a good attempt. The scores follow: 24, Tozama and Mlawu; 23, Lungiswa and Saliswa; 22 Zuziwe and Togu; 21, Gwali; 20 Hintsa, Nukwa and Cebo; 19, Yameka and Nomvula; 13, Peliswe; 9, Gedja.

The total possible score was 24.

Most of the children performed with ease and speed and accuracy, changing from a demonstration of the size of a bead, using thumb and finger, to the size of a house, using the whole body to stretch up and out. The bead and the wheel were the items most often misrepresented.

This exercise confirmed the observation reported later in this chapter that some children confused size and age when asked to represent the size of family members in clay. (It is worth reminding the reader that the children spoke only in Xhosa.) Cebo, Saliswa, Mlawu and Gwali each said, 'She is old' as they stood on tiptoes with arms stretched up to demonstrate mother's height. The society's emphasis on the importance of seniority was linked in those children's thinking with relative size.

2. *Drawing hands to scale.* In the second exercise, I drew the outline of my hand and the child's hand on separate pieces of paper that were then hidden behind my back. In turn, the pieces of paper were brought forth and shown to the child who was asked whose hand the drawing represented. No child had difficulty in identifying the owner of the hand. Once this had been established, I drew my hand to scale in a small book and asked the child to indicate how large her hand should be beside mine in the book. Care was taken with the explanation. All the school-children understood the task although Hintsa only did so on his second attempt. Of the children not attending school Yameka made a good estimate on her second try as did Saliswa, although she took some while to understand what was required. Gwali and Gedja, however, failed to understand. Gwali instructed me to make his hand as big as mine in the small book. I did so. We discussed their actual sizes and he agreed that they differed but said that now, in the drawing, they were the same and that it was correct like that.

When Gedja was asked to indicate how big I should draw her hand in the small book relative to the size of mine, she said:

'There is no space to put my hand.'

(Should your hand be the same size as mine or smaller if we pretended to fit it in the book?)

'Smaller.'

(How much smaller? Show me.)

She showed me the size of her hand saying, 'Mine is smaller.'

Five children gave good estimates (Tozama, Hintsa, Zuziwe, Lungiswa and Nomvula) and the others were either one centimetre too long or too short in their estimates.

3. *Outlines of feet and the estimation of size.* A simpler exercise involved the outline of our feet. An outline of my foot was drawn in front of the child who was then asked to estimate on the outline how large her foot would be beside it. All the children understood the task and only Gedja needed a second try.

4. *Body Space.* Architectural students at the University of Cape Town are sometimes asked to use their bodies to describe certain spaces in order to encourage them to perceive space with their bodies. I did the same with the children at Crossroads to see how willingly they would perform the necessary actions and how ably they would act them through. Each was asked to describe with her body the following:
  (i) the space in which you sleep.
  (ii) the space in which you sit upon a chair.
  (iii) the space that you occupy when standing in line.
  (iv) the space that you use when carrying a full bucket of water.
  (v) . . . and an empty bucket.
  (vi) the space that you take up when crying by yourself.
  (vii) the space that you use when playing *ichita* (the stone game).
  (viii) the space that you use when throwing stones.
Apart from looking slightly bemused, the children did as asked. The most interesting facet of the exercise was that culturally shaped ways of using the body were demonstrated. For instance it is culturally accepted that little children may sit cross-legged but that by the age of 6 or 7 girls should sit on the ground with both legs folded to one side or with legs stretched out before them. When asked to show how he sat to play the game with stones, Cebo said that he did not play it as it was a girls' game. We asked him how he sat when playing with cars in the sand and he sat with legs stretched out before him. Mary teased him saying that it was the way girls sit. He responded angrily saying, 'No. It is only because I am playing with the car.'

Most children lay down as if to sleep on their sides with their legs straight (each shares sleeping-space with at least one other person). Over half of them covered their eyes with an arm when showing how they cried. Their demonstrations of carrying buckets were realistic. They insisted that they could not carry a bucket full of water but staggered convincingly with a pretend bucket half-full of water.

5. *The family in clay*. Puzzled by the children's difficulties with Piaget's seriation task and the series of cut-out figures and animals (see Chapter 7), I decided to test them on their ability to represent relative size using material familiar to them. I made a clay figure to represent the child and placed it at the bottom of a piece of paper that was 30 cm in length. The child was told that we were going to make members of her family in clay so that each one was the correct size relative to the model of herself. The child gave me the names of the members of her family whom she wished to be represented. She then indicated how tall each should be on the paper upon which the model of herself was resting. Each child was depicted as a 7 cm high clay figure. I estimated that fathers, on average, should have been made in clay between 10 and 11 cm high and mothers between 8 and 9 cm. Tozama's estimate was closest: she made both her father and mother 11,5 cm tall. Lungiswa, Mlawu, Zuziwe and Gwali made their parents between 13 and 15 cm tall. The rest of the children made them at least twice as tall as the model of themselves. Siblings that were fairly close in age to the child were generally made to a relative size that approximated reality more closely than did older siblings or adults. This may be seen to support the suggestion made in the chapter on Kinship that children may be more child-centred in their understanding of the world than simply egocentric.

Yameka and Gedja made children younger than themselves taller than the model of themselves. The former adjusted her estimate of the height of her mother's brother's child, aged 2, four times before her height was relatively correct. She also made her mother's brother and his wife three times as big as herself. Gedja made her younger brother almost twice as tall as herself on her first estimate. It is difficult to tell whether inability to judge size correctly or self-image affected their estimates.

Cebo made his mother 28 cm tall which was four times the height of the figure that represented him. I asked:

(If you stand beside your mother, do you come up to her knees?)

'No. I would come to her waist.'

(Why then have you made her so big?)

'Just because she is old.'

Peliswe and Nomvula made their fathers extend beyond the top of the paper: they were made 40 cm and 32 cm tall, respectively. Peliswe is the youngest in her family and everyone was made at least twice as big as she. Hintsa indicated that his father, who is tall and thin and who looks rather like a Praying Mantis in the green overalls and floppy child's hat that he wears to work, should be 25,5 cm and his mother 19,5 cm. Then he made his 'granny' (father's father's sister), his uncle (father's brother), Mary and me all taller and close to the top of the paper, as if to say all other adults are quite simply, big.

Many of the children seemed to allow the size of the paper (upon which the first figure had been laid and upon which the child indicated to me how big the next figure should be made) to dictate the size of the adults. It is an important point in considering cognitive development. Why is it that five of them were not deflected in their decision-making by appearances, in this case the given size of a piece of paper, whereas the others were? Age was not a determining factor in this group. Surely one of the early lessons in the rule book that guides children successfully through school goes something like this: 'Observe the parameters of a test situation and make an informed guess as to whether or not they should influence your behaviour.' The rule has its counterpart: 'In certain circumstances it is imperative to set reality aside to give room for other techniques to control your mind such as those of free association or fantasy.' There are no easy guidelines as to when the rules should be applied; experience helps.

Certain conclusions can be drawn from the children's estimates and behaviour. Sixty-four per cent of them seemed to allow the size of the paper that was used as a background for the clay figure to dictate how tall figures relative to the original should be made. While every child could describe verbally or in gesture the correct relative size of family members, few could translate their knowledge into a given medium – in this case clay. Age confounded some of their judgments about relative size. Some were seen to be reluctant to alter their estimates and two children suggested that the original data were incorrect, not their estimates. Performance was obscured by a number of factors.

6. *Vehicles in clay.* Suspecting that the previous task might involve considerations other than those of actual size, that is the child's perception of her position in the family, I asked each child to make the following series of vehicles so that they were the correct size in relation to each other: a cart (the sort commonly used by boys in Crossroads to transport water or wood), a bicycle, a car, a truck and a bus.

In the previous exercise, I had made the clay models and in this one, the child had to make them. There was no time limit. The task was difficult because the shapes of the three large vehicles are easier to represent in clay than those of the bicycle or cart. Only Peliswe performed very well in making the vehicles correct in relative size one to another.

Most of those who made the vehicles became involved in their own creation, causing them to forget what it was that they were supposed to be achieving, namely the construction of models according to relative size. Each child could describe or demonstrate through gesture the correct scale but did not pay attention to the instructions. In task 5 relative seniority seemed to dominate over actual size and in task 6 the difficulty in modelling some items and perhaps the interest in the task obscured the need to attend to relative size.

Conclusion

Out of this series of exercises, we can conclude that among these children competence is easily obscured by other factors in any given situation. The children could describe in words and gesture the correct relative sizes of family members and of a series of vehicles. However, in an exercise involving the transformation of their understanding into materials and a reduction to scale, they seemed to lose track of the essential question involved. The point is supported by the increasing difficulty that the children not attending school experienced as the tasks became more complex. Yameka, who proved to be able on many other exercises, was unable to handle the last two (5 and 6). Only Mlawu and Zuziwe performed well on both tasks 5 and 6.

Play using scale and estimation would be a useful adjunct to formal school teaching.

SPACE AND CROSSROADS

Besides the children's sense of personal scale, I wanted to elicit their cognitive maps of the community within which they lived. I needed to know how they bound their world; what use they made of the territory within that world; their reference to landmarks such as schools, churches, shops, taps; where they played or visited; and whom they knew. Then I wanted to see how ably each child would represent that world in symbolic form. It was necessary to find appropriate techniques that would allow the children and me to share their knowledge and experience in this domain. I sought a format that would both interest and order the children's expression. They were neither familiar nor competent enough with pen and paper to draw maps and with photographs there was the possibility that perceptual error would obscure the true results. To children denied easy access to a variety of symbolic representations such as drawings, photographs, slides and maps, problems of perception could be confounding. The constraints of a non-existent budget and of time precluded the use of model towns such as those created by Bluestein and Acredolo (1979: 691–697).

In his book *The Image of the City,* Lynch (1960: 2) asserts that structuring and identifying the environment is a vital ability among all mobile animals and he believes that in way-finding there is a consistent use and organization of definite sensory cues from the external environment. This organization is fundamental to the efficiency and survival of free-moving life. He is of the opinion that an ordered conception of the environment may serve as a broad frame of reference, an organizer of activity or belief or knowledge. It enables one to order a substantial quantity of facts and fancies about the nature of the world. Such a structure gives the individual a possibility of choice and a starting-point for the acquisition of further information. A clear image of the surroundings is thus a useful basis for individual growth.

Lynch says that it is typical to have a constant tendency to impose regularity on surroundings. In Crossroads the authorities had attempted to impose such regularity on the shacks by numbering each one. However, demolitions, moves and house fires all contributed to disrupt the order and I recall watching with amusement as a group of policemen, despairing at the difficulty in locating house numbers, sought aid from young school-children. The children enjoyed being in a position of choice as to whether or not they would help them.

Lynch identifies five types of element in the physical form of the city on which he sought information that would describe people's image of the city. They are: paths, edges, districts, nodes and landmarks. Nodes are junctions or concentrations that may shift according to the viewer. The elements overlap and pierce one another.

With the above in mind, I set out to discover what images of Crossroads the children had.

I walked with each child in turn from his or her home out into and around Crossroads. First the child guided me around the house and yard, which I sketched, then she was asked to show me where she went, what she did, whom she knew. We talked as we walked about external features like the airport, factories and where the major roads went. We discussed routes to school and church and shops, and where relatives lived. It was an unstructured interview focusing on the child's reality. As the child led, I sketched our route and the features mentioned.

On a later day, I invited each child in turn to my room where a large piece of orange felt (193 × 180 cm) was spread on the carpet and felt cut-outs in various colours symbolizing the features derived from the walks were laid out on the couch. I tried to design the cut-outs according to the way that children represented features such as cars, houses and trees in their drawings. The colours were used to distinguish one symbol more clearly from another and, in a few instances, they represented the actual colour of a building; for example, at the time, the new clinic was yellow. Many houses of Crossroads were painted in bright colours with trim done carefully in another colour.

As the child was shown the cut-outs and identified each one, we repeated the identifications until I was confident that she had mastered them. She was reminded of our walk and then asked to pretend that the orange felt was Crossroads. Together we placed certain boundary features on the map. These included: the mountain ranges; the aeroplanes at the airport; the crossroads and roundabout; trees along the main roads; two buses; sand dunes; and the school nearest to the child's home. We discussed the features in relation to our current position and the child was asked to select a cut-out to represent her home and we placed it in relation to the school on the map.

She was then asked to put everything that she knew about Crossroads on the map. I suggested that she begin by placing things she knew near her home. The aim was to elicit as much as I could of things or places identifiable by name, description or direction, such as friends' houses, routes, tap sites.

The major impression the children gave was of a world closely bound. The children paid little or no regard to external features of the landscape, either on the walk or the map. None used the track of the sun as a reference point in locating places. They had little notion of what was 'out there' and how whatever was 'out there' existed in relation to Crossroads – the world of skyscrapers, ships, road networks, leisure and work. Only two had swum in the sea, one had been to the docks and none had visited the zoo or been to either range of mountains.

For most of the sample children, the world consisted of two patches: one in the Transkei and one in Crossroads and they were linked by the bus. The latter area incorporated parts of the black townships – the post office, the Administration block, the police station, the bus terminus or a church. The children were curious about the world out there but their access to information about it was limited. They pored over magazines, listened to the radio and watched television when they could, although none could read or speak English or Afrikaans, the languages in which television was transmitted.* I often heard children question adults upon their return from work about their experiences; sometimes they were

* A channel using the languages spoken by blacks in South Africa has since been introduced.

rebuked for showing curiosity.

Within Crossroads, nodes were as important to the children as Lynch suggests they are to adults in a city. They were places where people congregated: the water taps (of which there were sixteen placed on the periphery of the settlement); shops; schools; crèches; clinics and hawkers' stands. As Lynch observes, activity makes places memorable. About the same number of nodes that were indicated on the walk were placed on the map. Certain nodes would become a focal point within a particular area. For example, the children of Ward Three knew the house of a man whom they called *Tatakanova* meaning the Father of Nova, Nova being the dog's name. He was a fascinating man and he spoke beautiful English and Xhosa. He had recently completed a fifteen-year prison sentence for selling *dagga*. He was largely self-educated and his talk was peppered with quotes from Marx and Freud. He sold hard liquor from his house, and had the reputation of being a good and generous man and his help and advice were much sought after by his neighbours, including children. Periodically, he would administer de-worming medicine to the children and sweeten it with a lollipop or apple. Parents began to fear witchcraft and he had to stop.

Within Crossroads, only one street had a name: Mpuku Street (the street of mice). The children knew its name and Lungiswa identified it on her map. In another section the owner of a corner house nailed up a street sign that had clearly originated in a smart suburb. The well-ordered roads of New Crossroads were given the names of prominent men in the community to the chagrin of the women, one of whom said, 'It was the women who created Crossroads. When the pot was cooked, the men came to dish up. They do not know from where the fire came and therefore cannot rekindle it.'

Colson, who has studied the Tonga in Zambia for twenty-five years including people's response to settlement, observed (in personal communication with this writer) the extent to which people felt disoriented and troubled in a new environment where paths were not known, names not given to places and where directions and destinations could not be described. People need to create landmarks and to discipline the environment. She feels that this need is almost as important as the need for food. One wonders what dislocation the forced settlement of millions of blacks in South Africa has caused.

No areas were designated for children's play. One boy was shot and killed by the police as he played near the road during one spate of trouble. And one of the girls in my sample was killed by an ambulance as she played near the school in September 1981. The houses bordered two main roads and accidents involving children were frequent. I witnessed two. Children congregated around the school and in a few other areas, one of which was in a cleared space around the new clinic where football was played. Another was at a crossroads within the settlement where boys' wire-car factories and gambling schools were informally established. A third spot was on a high dune on the southern edge of the houses from which the Table range, stretching from Devil's Peak to Muizenberg, could be seen. Here children played *izitye* (dishes) – that is 'house'.

In Chapter 2, we saw that some children's movements were carefully monitored by their mothers. The degree of control over their movements did not seem to be reflected in the world that the children showed me on the walk or the map.

Each of those who did not go to school led me in small circle and, on the map, placed the fewest items with the least degree of accuracy. This was contrary to what I had anticipated. None of them were restricted in their movement by school or parents and I had expected that they would show me a Crossroads well peopled and routed and marked. I presume that the public nature of the walk worried them. It occurred fairly early in our relationship and, undoubtedly, I failed to elicit much from them. However, it was odd that their sense of distance and direction and scale and place were markedly poorer than most of the other children. The skills may be linked to familiarity with other skills such as the spacing of words and pictures on a page to which the school-going children had been exposed in however rudimentary a fashion. Figures 4–1 and 4–2 give an idea of the contrast between one of the best maps plotted by Lungiswa and one plotted by a child who did not attend school, Saliswa.

The children evidenced little difficulty in mastering the symbols used on the felt map. In his study of peoples' images of a city, Lynch (1960) found that paths held a visual dominance among the city elements and were a key influence as networks from which people experienced their surroundings. He observed that people tended to think of path destinations and origin points: they liked to know where paths came from and where they led. Surprisingly, the children did not seem to be curious about this. Few of them attempted to determine where a road began or ended on the map. Its position in passing certain places was what seemed to be important.

I shall summarize the main impressions gleaned from the two exercises:

1. *A positive relationship exists between the number of features that I*

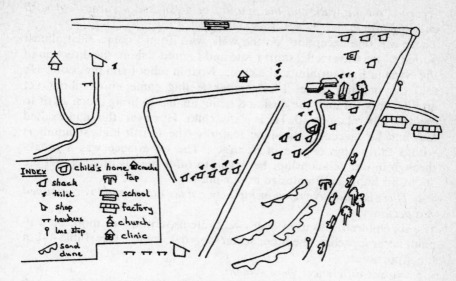

Figure 4–1: Lungiswa's Felt Map of Crossroads

INDEX
⌂ child's home   ❀ creche
◁ shack   ⊓ tap
ﬨ toilet   ⊑ school
▷ shop   ⊑ factory
⊤⊤ hawkers   ⌂ church
⌽ bus stop   ⌂ clinic
〰 sand dune

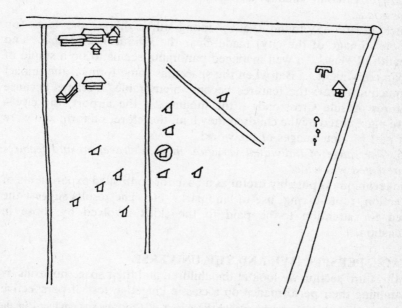

Figure 4–2: Saliswa's Felt Map of Crossroads

recorded on the walk and the amount of detail and accuracy* of each child's felt map.

There was one exception: on the walk with Togu I could elicit almost nothing – we traversed a short route and I noted a shop, the direction of the Nyanga East terminus, the clinic, Noxolo school and my room. He told me nothing more. I remember feeling some ennui about yet another trek through the dust and being unable to bring much spirit to bear on our relationship. He is a shy child. However, the map excited him and he placed twenty-nine features (the fourth highest number) with a fairly high degree of accuracy. The experience was a breakthrough in our relationship: he began to offer me his dreams, tell me about his home and fantasize in our play.

2. *There is a positive relationship between the number of items mapped and accuracy.*

The six children who used over twenty items scored 5 or more on a 10 point accuracy score: the other seven scored 0, 1 and 2 (see Table 4–1 in the Appendix).

3. *No sex differences were evident.*

4. *On neither the walk nor the map did children seem to pay much regard to external landmarks, that is, boundaries or features outside Crossroads.*

Lynch (1960: 45) found that, 'Among other things, the tests (on people's image of the city) made clear the significance of space and breadth of view. . .a well-managed panorama seems to be a staple of urban enjoyment. . .But when the space has some form. . .the impact is much stronger: the features become memorable.' Perhaps because features outside Crossroads – the mountains, the airport, the city – were unexplored by the children they had, therefore, no form and were not part of their images of the world.

5. *The range of individual variation in areas traversed and features represented was wide.*

The technique is possibly useful as a base for controlled experiments of direction, route-taking, use of landmarks, etc. The results suggest the need for attention to be paid to the skills involved by those in education.

SPACE, PERSPECTIVE AND THE UNIVERSE

In this third section we look at the children and their space horizons by examining their performance on a classic Piagetian test of perspective

* Accuracy was measured in relation to a map of Crossroads reproduced in the Introduction.

and by having them describe some of their ideas about the universe. I shall begin the report of the Piagetian test with a quotation from a piece of research done in South Africa that represents the deficit culture view so often expressed in cross-cultural studies. Page (1973: 9–16) wrote:

> Only [Zulu] youths who grow up in town, and attend school from an early age and who consequently associate the invariances of formal measurement with their 'carpentered' world environment are able to progress from the essentially egocentric, topological concept of space to the objective abstractions of the Euclidian one.

Since that was written, such conclusions are viewed with increasing scepticism, although the theory behind them is alive and well. It derives from Piaget's notion of egocentricity and from his test of the co-ordination of perspectives devised in 1948.

Piaget (1972b) admits to having chosen badly in selecting the term egocentricity to fit a particular set of meanings. The terms *egocentrism* and *decentration* are defined as, respectively, the ignorance of or lack of insight into a point of view of another person, and the ability to take the other person's point of view. Generally, a shift from a stage of thought characterized by egocentrism to a stage of thought characterized by decentration is held to take place around the sixth and seventh year of the child. Piaget has constructed a far-reaching and closely woven net of argument, binding together many different features of the development of behaviour around the concept. After massive re-examination of five of Piaget's experiments on children's conceptions of space, Laurendeau and Pinard (1970: 435) concluded that '. . . it is hardly possible to doubt the importance of the concept of egocentrism in the description and explanation of the child's primitive spatial concepts' and '. . . it is regular enough to suggest that it reflects a genuine and consistent form of mental organization' (1970: 439).

Given the importance that the concept holds in Piagetian and Neo–Piagetian theory, and given that age 7 is purportedly a turning-point in the acquisition of others' points of view, it seemed important to ascertain some idea of 'egocentricity' among 7-year-olds in Crossroads. I resolved to stay within the limits of Piaget's definition and to replicate the crucial test.

According to Piaget and Inhelder (1948: 209), a child is able to solve problems involving perspectives only when 'he begins to form coordinate systems or a system of reference. Hence perspective would appear to depend upon operational concepts rather than upon familiarity born of intuition and experience.' To the question why children should be slow in mastering simple perspective relationships, the authors answer that 'a perspective system entails his [the child's] relating the object to his own viewpoint as one of which he is fully conscious.' This, however, implies that the child should be able to distinguish his own viewpoint from those of others and also to co-ordinate it with them.

The experiment which Piaget (1948) devised to investigate the different perspectives on a group of objects viewed by an observer from different orientations had two aims: (a) to study the construction of a global system linking together a number of perspectives, and (b) to examine the relationships which the child establishes between his own viewpoint and those of other observers. The relationships involved in the test are before–behind, left–right.

It is called the Three Mountains experiment. Piaget used a model of three mountains with several clearly distinguishable cues to position. His subjects were 100 children ranging in age from 4 to 12 years. Their task was to imagine and to reconstruct by inference the ways the mountains would appear to a doll which took up various positions around the model. In the version that I used, children were asked to select a photograph corresponding to the doll's position.

The results of the study were classified into four stages, corresponding approximately to chronological age. Thus children of 4 to 6 years (Piaget's stage IIA) identified their own position with that of the doll, and from their inability to free themselves from their 'egocentrism' they assigned their own viewpoint to the doll. Children of 6 to 7 years (stage IIb) showed what Piaget called 'transitional reactions'. They tried unsuccessfully to free themselves from their own viewpoint, although their constructions occasionally came close to the doll's point of view. Children of 7 to 9 years (Stage IIIA) could, however, recognize that the relationships between the mountains varied with the doll's position but were unable to co-ordinate those relationships. Finally, children of 9 and 10 years or older (at Stage IIIB) were able to co-ordinate successfully all the relationships involved for any given perspective. Subsequent research has been done within the same conceptual framework. The findings have not consistently shown egocentric responses.

The Experiment

Materials: 1. A three-dimensional model of three mountains:

(a) Table Mountain in yellow plasticene with a cable station on the top.

(b) Devil's Peak in green plasticene with a plastic deer on one side.

(c) Lion's Head in pink with a white cloud on the top and a plastic car travelling up one side.

The mountain complex is visible from the sand dunes within Crossroads. I had pointed to it and discussed it with each child in an earlier session. Table Mountain was modelled rather high in order to obscure the other mountains from certain angles (see Figure 4–3).

2. Ten colour photographs of the model: eight were taken in a clockwise progression, one was an aerial view and the other was taken from within the complex.

3. A toy camera that was one of the children's favourite toys in my room. We had had a photographic session and had looked at photographs together. Crossroads boasts a number of resident photographers.

4. Five hand puppets with which we had all played during the year. They represented a black family living in Crossroads.

Setting the Scene: Each child was invited in turn to my room; in the middle was the model set upon a table. I took out the puppets and told the child that there had been a family quarrel. The family had gone on a trip to the mountains to take photographs. The quarrel concerns the developed photographs: each family member took a picture from a different place around the mountains. Can the child help settle the quarrel by identifying who took which photograph. In the process, we discussed the camera and the mountain range.

We turned to the model, discussed the view visible from Crossroads (that is position II on the diagram) and walked around, inspecting it. The child was asked to sit at I and given the display of photographs. One puppet was positioned and the first selection was asked for. (Some researchers have argued that requesting the child to select his/her view first imposes an egocentric mould on the task. I, therefore, avoided that.) Each puppet was placed at a different position. The child was then invited to check the selection from those positions, and to make his or her own selection.

Care was taken to relate the scheme to the child's environment and to use materials that were familiar to each child at least since working with me. This was done with Donaldson's (1979: 24) criticisms of the test in mind. She claimed that children fail because it does not make 'human sense'.

The Purpose in giving the test was twofold. One was to test a crucial Piagetian concept. The other purpose was to play with each child across sets of symbolic representations and estimate her facility in transcribing the sets given a context familiar in situation but challenging in content. I also wanted to elicit play with space beyond the child's immediate known field but not beyond her horizon.

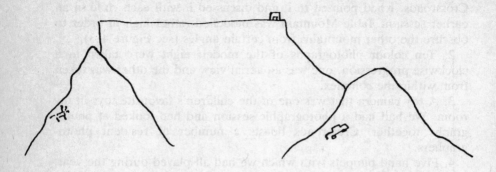

Figure 4–3: Sketch of the Three Mountains Model

Results: Each child selected a view on behalf of a puppet from five positions. After discussion there was sometimes a second choice and, in three cases, a third.

The number of correct selections out of the sixty-five made for all positions was nine. If a second selection is included, then fourteen were correct. No third selection was correct. The view from the position in which the child sat was chosen once on the first selection and once on the second.

Table 4–2 in the Appendix shows the number of times each photograph was selected as a first choice by a child to represent a puppet's point of view.

The mistakes are important in Piaget's interpretation of the results. A child with an egocentric point of view should select either from her own vantage or from the adjacent view. In the above experiment, a is the egocentric position and b and h are the adjacent positions. If the three are combined, it can be seen that twenty-two were made by the child from her own position or those adjacent to it. If the selections made from any of the other three adjacent views are combined, it can be seen that the child's view did not dominate selections:

The positions at e, f, d, yielded 14 selections
The positions at f, g, h, yielded 27 selections
The positions at b, c, d, yielded 23 selections
There is no indication that the child imposed her view on the puppets.

DISCUSSION
Only Tozama chose correctly 75 per cent of the time and can, in Piagetian terms, be considered to have reached substage IIIB (about 9 to 10 years), at which point the mastery of simple perspective is complete. She was the only child who had television in her home. The other twelve children were still in substage IIA (about 4 to 6 years).

During the test, I monitored the children's behaviour and found that their performance was hindered by failures that had little to do with the skill under examination. I offer one example. Very few of the children, despite my suggestions, looked at each photograph in the display before selecting one. Some would take a long time over the selection but their eyes would be glued to one photograph (e.g. Gwali, Peliswe, Togu). They did not scan the available material. Schwantes (1969) studied cognitive scanning processes in children and he offered some evidence that children do not scan as effectively as adults and that their success is tied to reading experience and ability.

Deregowski (1980), reporting on perceptual hypothesis-testing, refers to the work of Mackworth and Bruners (1971) on intracultural data on eye movements in pictorial perception at various ages. He says that,

> They found distinct differences between searching eye-movements of children and adults, the latter being less systematic. On out-of-focus pictures children were less skilful in locating the important aspects of the picture than adults; on clear pictures children identified such elements with ease but made the error of concentrating on one of them to the exclusion of other elements. They seemed to lack, relative to the adults, ability to attend centrally to one element whilst peripherally monitoring others. When they encountered a distinct contour they tended to follow it slavishly with their gaze – a phenomenon not observed in adults. These tendencies make it difficult for children to offer plausible hypotheses and to verify such hypotheses, and hence to construct a trustworthy notion of the visual field.

If the children fail to draw plausible hypotheses because of inadequate scanning techniques, it becomes difficult to accept conclusions drawn from the Three Mountain test that claim to reflect the degree of egocentricity. The Three Mountain Experiment tests a complex of strategies that are closely related to experiences such as reading. Class membership is a determining factor in success on the task. Evidence of parental literacy, attitudes towards reading, experiences in class, availability of books become relevant. Lloyd (1981: 178) observed different scanning and response strategies among Yoruba children in test situations that she linked to class differences.

The test is confounded by a number of issues of great complexity such as those that surround pictorial perception. In a recent review called 'Pictorial perception and the problem of universals', Johada (1981b) concludes that '. . . pictorial depth perception turned out not to be a straightforward entity, but seems to involve a number of component skills whose nature remains as yet somewhat unclear'. On children's ability to make correct size judgements on the basis of depth cues in pictures, Jahoda says that no clear pattern of environmental determinants has emerged. He believes that both the culturally determined degree of exposure to pictures and the amount of formal schooling appear to be involved; but that in such a complex interaction, with the likely addition of other unknown factors, they are not easily disentangled.

Wilberts and Florquin (1977) relate facility in reading to the ability to structure space. From a study of learning they conclude that, 'Although the intellectual factor facilitates learning to read, it progressively loses its importance, and perceptual-motor structuring of space becomes and remains more important.' A child, it would seem, needs exposure to the processes of reading and pictorial perception in order to structure space and she needs to be able to structure space in order to learn to read.

SPACE AND THE UNIVERSE

Finally, on the topic of space on the horizon of their worlds, we looked out at the universe. I asked each child to make the sun, the moon and the earth out of clay so that they were the correct relative size one to another. As the child worked, we talked about distance, size, temperature, movement and light. The results were curious. Of the earth, sun and moon only six were made as balls and twenty-six as flat shapes. Of the latter, sixteen were round and nine were square. One moon was crescent, another a rectangular cube and a third was a flattened ball with moonrays attached as one might see in a drawing. Gedja said, 'The moon is wood *(iinkuni)*', which is a reference to a modern myth known to many of the adults at Crossroads. It is said that if one looks at the moon one can see a woman walking on it carrying a baby on her back and a bundle of wood on her head. She was banished to the moon as a punishment for collecting wood on a Sunday instead of going to church.

Of the three, eight children believed that the earth was the largest, then the sun and then the moon, while two thought that the sun was biggest and another two the moon. Seven thought that the sun was closer to the earth than the moon, and five the reverse. Hintsa claimed never to have seen the moon nor to have been outside at night. The moon was in the sky one day as Cebo and I walked around Crossroads. I asked him what it was and he said he did not know but that the blue part was heaven. Yet he had theories about the distance of the moon from the sun and he believed that it stayed in Cape Town by day while the sun travelled to Johannesburg at night. Children's knowledge is not easily accessible and they enjoy inventing theories to fit the occasion.

Only Gwali thought that the moon was brighter than the sun. Most of the children said that the sun was made of something hot and the moon of something cold. Nine believed that the sun could move and four that it could not; five that the moon could and four that it could not. Only Peliswe said that the earth could while five said it could not.

Eclipses were important as historical markers among the adults of Crossroads and Lungiswa had been told about them but was troubled as to how they fitted into her ideas about movement in the universe. She said:

'The sun and moon both move. Not the world. When there is an eclipse of the moon, the world is moving. I don't know how they move.'

Tozama's belief that, 'Both the sun and moon follow where a person goes,' fits Piaget's notion of egocentric thinking. She was the only one to think thus.

Their ideas as to where the sun goes at night were diverse. Two thought that it went to heaven, one to Johannesburg, one to the other side of the mountain and another that it stayed in the sky but for some inexplicable reason could not be seen at night.

PLAY SPACE

Psychoanalyst Erik Erikson holds that the ground plan of the human body co-determines biological experience and social roles. He believes that experience is anchored in the ground plan and that there is a·male and female experience of space. The theory can be found in most of his major works and he reconfirmed it as recently as 1974 (Erikson, 1974).

Erikson used the term 'inner space' to signify what he considered a prime factor in women's identity formation and he has claimed that 'sensory reality and logical conclusion are given form by kinesthetic experience' such as 'the existence of a productive inner bodily space safely set in the centre of female form and carriage . . .' (Erikson, 1968). His single experiment about the play configurations of pre-adolescents was the data base of his theory of inner space. In that study about 150 children of both sexes were tested when they were 11, 12 and 13 years old. They were given a selection of toys and were told: 'Choose

THE CHILDREN AND SPACE 108

any of the things you see here and construct on this table an *exciting* scene out of an imaginary moving picture.' (Emphasis in the original.)

According to Erikson, the results of the play configuration study indicate, and in fact are an expression of, biological sex differences:

> For it is clear that the spatial tendencies governing these constructions closely parallel the morphology of the sex organs: in the male, external organs, erectible and intrusive in character, serving highly *mobile* sperm cells; internal organs in the female, with the vestibular access, leading to statically expectant ova. (Emphasis in the original.)

He believed that the sex differences in children's play pervaded the life span as 'a profound difference in the sense of space in the two sexes'. He rejected a social explanation for his findings (Erikson, 1950: 101). The theory has a fairly wide popular currency. There have been few attempts to replicate the study. I know of two. Cramer and Hogan (1975) drew the same conclusions and the results of Caplan (1979) run counter to the original findings and suggest that the thetory of 'inner space' be re-evaluated.

I replicated Erikson's study as nearly as possible with thirteen of the children in my sample. I wanted to see how each child would use a space with a given boundary in play (the table); how each would order their use of space and selections of toys; and I was interested in identifying sex differences: I suspected that Erikson's results were largely socially determined and was curious as to whether a different setting would yield similar findings. There was, besides, an aspect of his theorizing that Caplan's competent critique ignored. Erikson held that the scene and instructions that he gave each child were sufficiently impersonal stimulus for an unselfconscious use of the imagination. Over one and a half years, 150 children constructed about 450 scenes – of which not more than six movie scenes and only a few dolls were named after a movie actor. Erikson (1965: 92–93) comments,

> It appears . . . that such vague instructions do accomplish what the encouragement to 'associate freely' (i.e., to let thoughts wander and words flow without self-censorship) effects in a psychoanalytic interview, as does, indeed, the suggestion to play in interviews with children.

His stated aim had been to test the clinical proposition that play observation can add significant pointers to available data from other sources. I was ready to welcome such pointers from a child's unselfconscious use of imagination.

Each child in turn came to my room where the following materials were laid out near a small table: 210 toys including eighty blocks of assorted colours and sizes; twelve vehicles (cars, trucks, vans); eighteen 'people' (six white plastic dolls, twelve wooden figures in various colours); fifty-nine animals (wild and domestic); ten tools (e.g. scythe, spanner, saw); nineteen pieces of furniture and twelve trees of three kinds (wooden). I assumed that my random selection was as acceptable as Erikson's. He provided: 122 blocks, eleven animals, thirty-eight pieces of furniture, eight cars and fourteen small dolls. One significant difference in our selection of toys was in the dolls. Erikson provided dolls identified by their clothes as to age, sex and in some cases, jobs. For example, he provided a Red Indian, a cowboy, a monk and a policeman. The policeman turned out to be the doll most often selected by the boys in his sample. My dolls were unidentified by age, sex or job. Given the political climate of South Africa, I felt that the inclusion of a police doll would weigh too heavily as a symbol and thus invite certain play scenes. It is, therefore, of special note that one quarter of the play scenes made by the children of Crossroads involved policemen or police cars. They will be described shortly. First the child was given the instructions as in the original study, excluding for obvious reasons the reference to a movie scene. Upon completion, the child was asked for another scene set specifically in Crossroads and with the extra instruction: 'Make something, perhaps, that you remember.'

I was aware that the toys were probably unfamiliar to the subjects but I was interested in the children's recognition and use of their symbolic forms and I wanted to compare these play situations with the sketches of those that I was collecting from children at play in the sand of Crossroads. The prime aim in setting up this situation, as for any other, was to allow me access to the child's cognitive processes so that I might describe the world of a 7-year-old.

Seven girls made fourteen scenes and six boys made ten. Two boys made only one scene each: Cebo worked so feverishly, for so long, and used so many items that it was lunchtime when he finished and he declined when invited to make another; Hintsa used only one item for his scene and would do no more.

Erikson (1965: 96–9) concluded that the most significant sex differences in the children's play scenes were the tendency of boys to erect structures, buildings, towers or streets; the girls tended to use the play table as the interior of a house, with simple, little, or no use of blocks.

Taking his summary statements, the results from the scenes made by the sample of children in Crossroads are as follows:

1. *That more boys than girls built towers.* Only two children built anything that resembled a tower: one was a girl, Nomvula, who stacked eight blocks as the windows of a house that was being built; the other was a boy, Mlawu, who made a structure also composed of eight blocks.

2. *That boys built higher towers.* This was not so.

3. *That more boys built structures, buildings, towers or streets.* Eight of the fourteen scenes built by girls contained structures or buildings (57,1 per cent) whereas only three of the boys' ten scenes did (30,0 per cent). In five of the girl's scenes (35,7 per cent), cars were placed as if on a street whereas this was done in only two of the boys' scenes (20,0 per cent).

4. *That girls tended to use the play table as the interior of a house.* Fourteen scenes were of or included a house identified by the child. In three of them, my house was depicted and closely linked to the child's world. Eight of them were girls' scenes (57,1 per cent) and six boys' (60,0 per cent), in which a similar percentage treated the table as an interior without defining walls (girls 42,8 per cent and boys 40,0 per cent).

5. *That more girls than boys built simple enclosures.* Four of the girls' scenes included simple enclosures (28,5 per cent), one of which was a cattle *kraal*. Two boys' scenes had simple enclosures (20,0 per cent); again one of them was of a *kraal*.

6. *That boys more than girls built enclosures only in conjunction with more elaborate structures.* This was not so: the only elaborate series of structures were fifteen hawkers' stands built by a girl.

7. *That girls used more objects and people in their enclosures than boys, that only girls used furniture only, and that more boys made constructions of blocks only.* Girls did use more people in their enclosures, fourteen to the boys' three, and more objects, sixty-nine to the boys' fifty. However, only one child used furniture only and that was a boy, and one child made a construction of blocks only and that was a girl.

8. *That boys used more blocks and used them in more varied ways than girls.* Girls used 270 blocks, an average of 19,9 blocks per scene, and boys used 120, an average of 12,0 per scene. There was no difference in their use.

9. *That boys used more moving objects outside enclosures.* Girls used more cars – sixty-eight with an average of 4,8 per scene to boys' thirty-three, average 3,3 per scene; and more people – forty-four, average 3,1 per scene to boys' twenty-one, average 2,7. However, boys used more animals – 151, average 15,1 per scene to girls' 71, average of 5,0 per

scene.

The data do not support Erikson's claim *that the modalities of height, downfall, strong motion and its channelization or arrest characterize the scenes of boys.* Height and downfall were not features in anyone's scenes. Motion was verbally identified in relation to twenty-one sets of objects by girls and three included cars driving, police chasing, people running away, a man pursuing animals, cattle going to the veld, children throwing stones and using saws as weapons. These actions all occurred outdoors in the nine scenes (64,2 per cent). Boys identified six series of objects in motion including cars driving, an accident, people dancing, police vans coming to raid and a car burning: more girls represented channels of traffic or movement – eight in five scenes (35,7 per cent) to boys' three in three scenes (30 per cent). Police arresting people featured in three scenes made by girls (21,4 per cent) and two by boys (20 per cent). Another boy's scene of a burning car implied that police had been there but they were neither mentioned nor represented.

The modalities for girls that result in their making scenes with static interiors, which are open, simply enclosed, and peaceful or intruded upon as in Erikson's sample did not seem to result in similar patterns for the Crossroads sample. Only one boy and one girl made scenes in which only static interiors were represented. Boys and girls made open rooms equally often (40 per cent and 42,7 per cent respectively) and they enclosed them simply equally often (20 per cent and 28 per cent respectively). Intrusions were outdoors and intruders were policemen or police cars in scenes of both sexes.

The data suggest that no significant sex differences were visible in the play situation of thirteen 7-year-old Crossroads children. The only difference that I could identify was that boys tended to make more scenes that represented outdoors only – five scenes (50,0 per cent) to girls' five scenes (35,7 per cent). All other scenes had features from indoors and out. Girls tended to distinguish inside from outside more clearly.

Given the small sample, I cannot presume to cast doubt on Erikson's theory of inner space, but can only conclude that his technique did not yield sex differences in this situation. If I was a psychoanalyst, I might consider the significance of enclosures (the *kraal*) for boys in one context and structures (the skyscraper) for boys in another.

On refuting possible interpretations for the observed differences in the play scenes between girls and boys based on socialization, Erikson (1965: 102 note) compared his findings with the play constructions of pre-adolescents in India and observed that, '. . . the general character-istics of the play universe differ markedly and in accordance with differences in the social universe, while sex differences are expressed by the spatial modalities . . .' It is possible that the children of Crossroads did not express through their play scenes the same concern with anatomical models as did the pre-adolescents of California. Erikson (1965: 100), however, does not think that age makes any difference. Rather, he claims that '. . . the dominance of genital modes over the modalities of spatial organization reflects a profound difference in the sense of space in the two sexes, even as sexual differentiation obviously provides the most decisive difference in the ground plan of the human body which, in turn, co-determines biological experience and social rôles.'

While the data in this study did not support Erikson's theory of sex difference as it affects the use of play space, individual scenes were instructive as to each child's central concerns and life experience. Erikson (1951) claims that '. . . a play act – like a dream – is a complicated dynamic product of "manifest" and "latent" themes, of past experience and present task, of the need to express something and the need to suppress something, of clear representation, symbolic indirection and radical disguise.' Just as he found that themes tended to appear which on closer study proved to be intimately related to the dynamics of the person's life history, so it happened among the Crossroads children. The children were fascinated by the small pieces of furniture and two of them identified these as the excitement in their scenes. Thirty-one dolls were placed 'sleeping in beds' by the children. A comment on the discomfort of sharing sleeping space with, sometimes, as many as three siblings?

Nine children made two scenes that contrasted one with the other in some obvious way. For some the contrast was an indoor then an outdoor scene; for others a scene of tranquillity then one of confused activity – see Figures 4–4a and b which depict (a) Tozama's house owned by black people in Claremont (a white-zoned suburb) and (b) her re-creation of a police raid in Crossroads. Gwali built a busy, carefully organized scene that incorporated town (Cape Town), Claremont and the Transkei (Figure 4–5a) and then one of silent confrontation in which nine 'speed cop' cars had come to the scene of an accident (Figure 4–5b).

One quarter of the scenes involved the police. One was of an accident (see Figure 4–5b); two were of a police raid into Crossroads; one a scene in which the police had come to shoot the people at the school;

and two were of incidents that occurred during our work on the play scenes, in which two men were killed and their cars stoned and burnt by young blacks. The incidents have been described in Chapter 2. The scenes that they created, apart from the one of the accident, and the children's descriptions follow:

Figure 4–4a: Tozama's Scene of a House in Crossroads

Figure 4–4b: Tozama's Scene of a Police Raid in Crossroads

Tozama (see Figure 4–4b) described her scene thus:

'It is fighting. The people are fighting over Black Power. The people of Crossroads are fighting the police. There are two landrovers with policemen – the brown and blue cars. The residents are escaping: two are in the van, one is running behind. She was to get on but they left her behind. The donkeys are here. The person wants to milk the cow behind the donkeys. He is chasing them and the cow is running away. The brown car wants to knock the child: the child runs away . . . During the Black Power, the police caught the people undressed . . . People are being taken to prison. Crossroads people were defeated by the police in the real fight [1978]. It is also so here. The people who are here who are not police are defeated.'

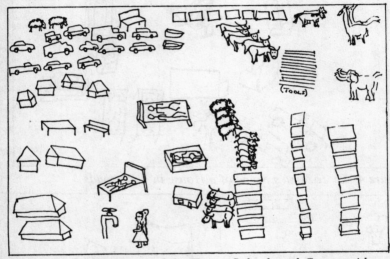

Figure 4–5a: Gwali's Scene of the Town, Suburb and Countryside

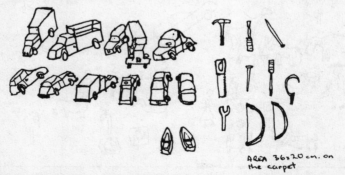

Figure 4–5b: Gwali's Scene of an Accident

For her second scene, (Figure 4–6) Lungiswa sat on the floor and placed some furniture saying that the excitement was the dressing-table with a bottle of perfume upon it. Nearby, twelve cars are lined up side by side facing a building. She said:

AREA 100 x 90 cm on the carpet

Figure 4–6: Lungiswa's Scene of a Furnished House and a Police Raid

'The cars are police coming to Noxolo School to shoot the people. I saw that. The people were singing. It is the Roman Catholic Church in the Green House [next to the school]. Some people are inside, some are outside. The Crossroads people are black. The police are white men.'

Mlawu said of his scene (Figure 4–7):

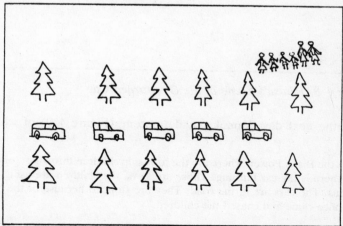

Figure 4–7: Mlawu's Scene of a Raid and a Riot

'It is a raid at Crossroads. The children of the riots burnt the cars. Here are the adults and children of Black Power. They are the people of the shacks. The cars are the landrovers of the Boers.* They have come to raid. They are coming to take people to jail.'

The above configurations were made before the two men died after being stoned and burnt as they drove past Crossroads on 11 August 1980. On the Monday following the week of incidents, Hintsa came to my room and was asked to make a scene. He prevaricated. I prodded a little and he said, 'One thing that happened was the trouble on Monday.' I said, 'All right, make that.' He fiddled with cars, took a blue one and placed it in the middle of the table saying, 'The people have run away. The man has been taken to hospital. Only the car is left with the wheels up.' (Figure 4–8).

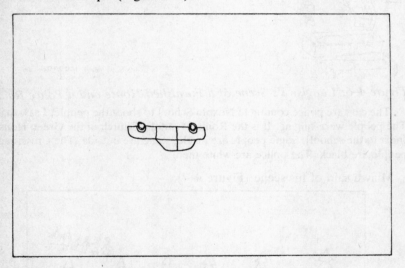

Figure 4–8: Hintsa's Scene of the Overturned Car

On the next day, Yameka made a scene (Figure 4–9) of which she said:

'It is the Black Power. There are the township children throwing stones at the cars. There is the car burning. Those are saws, the children are using them as weapons. The cars are in the road. They are stopped because of the burning. The police came and chased the children.'

* Boers means farmers in Afrikaans but is often used to mean all Afrikaners.

117

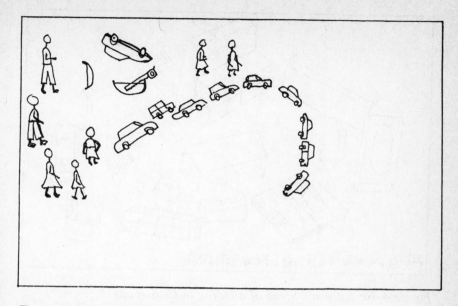

Figure 4–9: Yamela's Scene of the Students of Black Power

Twice Phalo, an *igqira,* visited me just as a child had finished making a scene. On the first occasion, Nukwa had placed fifty-four animals side by side on the edge of the table facing away from him. In front were two giraffes. The *igqira's* interpretation, unsolicited, was that, 'The child has been called [to be an *igqira*]. He should not go to school if he rejects it. His gift lies between the animals: between the wild and the domestic.' He then launched into an hour-and-a-half description of being called. The *igqira* did not know that Nukwa had dropped out of school.

On the second occasion, Saliswa, who does not go to school and whose mother – herself an *igqira* – said she too had been called, had just made her second scene. It was a simple enclosure in the middle of the table with walls made of furniture; there was no entrance and four dolls were lying in bed. Outside, thirteen cars stood beside each other facing away from the house (Figure 4–10). She described it thus:

'It is a small house for the dolls. It is in Crossroads. The dolls are father and mother and children. It is a zinc house. The cars are going to Claremont, past Claremont.'

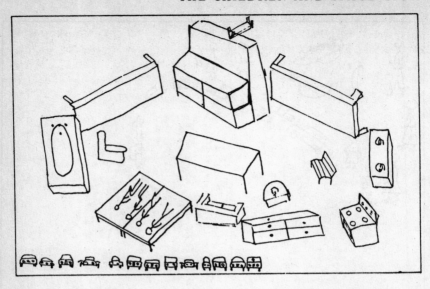

Figure 4–10: Saliswa's Scene of a House in Crossroads

The *igqira* said:

'She should not have used the cars. One of her gifts is to build a house and to put the furniture inside. It is her gift now to be a homemaker. The cars are for fun: they have no meaning. She will be a worker especially in the home. She will not be called; one of her children might. Notice her order. Her soul likes nice things.'

I quote the above to suggest that 'doctors', Erik Erikson in California and Phalo in Crossroads, interpret from within their contexts. There may be more in common between the attitudes of male doctors across continents than differences between the play scenes of girls and boys.

SUMMARY OF THE SECTIONS TO DO WITH SPACE

The tasks described early in the chapter support the observation that children's competence is easily obscured by other factors in any given situation. This seems to be particularly so in a society in which people's attention is not focused on the need to perform to rule on school-type tasks. The maps on felt were fair representations of the children's range within Crossroads and awareness of their environment as shown on guided walks. The children seemed to ignore boundaries, external landmarks, and path destinations and origin points. Their relative freedom to range was not reflected in their walks or maps. In the next section, it was suggested that Piaget's Three Mountain tasks test a complex of strategies that are closely related to experiences such as reading. In the final section, no sex differences along the lines detected by Erikson were found and the impact of current happenings in society was seen to affect the content of children's play scenes.

5

The Children and Kinship

According to Van Warmelo (1935), the Cape Nguni include those groups which have been in the Transkei and Eastern Cape for centuries (Xhosa, Thembu, Mpondo, Mpondomise and Bomvana) and Fingo and other recent immigrants (Mfengu, Bhaca, Xesibe and Ntlangwini).

The following observations about kinship are taken from Hammond-Tooke (1969: 86–7). The social structure of the Cape Nguni tribes is similar in broad outline. Its main features are ideally polygynous families, patrilineal descent groups and the apparent absence of any form of preferential marriage or formal age-regiment system.

Homesteads show a great variety of structure, from nuclear to compound and extended forms, and a feature (since the 1960s) is the high percentage of widows as homestead heads. Marriage is patrilocal with a strong tendency to settle in the neighbourhood of the father's homestead (formerly actually in the homestead) and effects a transfer of both rights *in uxorem* and *in genetricem* to the groom's group.

Cape Nguni kinship terminologies are broadly similar, being of the bifurcate merging type, i.e., the terms for 'father' and 'mother' are also applied respectively to father's brother and mother's sister. Parallel cousins are thus equated with own siblings except that, among the Xhosa, the term *kanina* is used between men only for children of the mother's sister. Separate terms are used for mother's brother *(malume)* and father's sister *(dadebobawo)* and all cross-cousins are referred to as *mza* or *mzala*. Spouses of father's brother and mother's sister are called 'mother' and 'father' respectively: spouses of father's sister are called 'father' *(bawo, bobawo)* and the wife of mother's brother is termed *malumekazi* or 'mother'. Emphasis on relative age is strongly marked. Father's elder brothers are distinguished terminologically from father's younger brothers, elder brothers from younger brothers and elder sisters from younger sisters (between siblings of opposite sex). Generally speaking all kin of the first ascending generation are classed

* A version of this chapter appeared in Burman and Reynolds, 1986.

either as 'father' or 'mother's brother' and all females as 'mother'. Cousins are either assimilated with siblings or distinguished as 'cross-cousin'. Both paternal and maternal grandfathers are termed *bawomkulu* and both grandmothers *makhulu* except among the Mpondo, who do not make a sex differentiation and call both *makhulu*. There is a terminological confusion between father's elder brother and father's father (both *bawomkhulu*). In the first descending generation the terms 'son' and 'daughter' are applied to children of parallel cousins and, apparently, those of cross-cousins (these relationships have not been recorded in the literature). Thus all children in the first descending generation are classified as own children. Great-grandparents are all classified as *khokho* (male) or *gogo* (female) and the reciprocal (grandchild) is the non-sex-denoting *mzukulwana*. The system reflects the lack of discreteness of the nuclear family in Cape Nguni social structure. Among all the Cape Nguni the family is embedded in a wider kinship group, the lineage and, ultimately, the clan.

This chapter focuses on children's kinship concepts. The material comes from a variety of interviews and exercises conducted with thirteen children over a year. The interviews include three replications of studies done by J. Piaget (1928), R. LeVine and D. Price-Williams (1974), and S. Haviland and E. Clark (1974).

My interest in replicating the three interviews was two-fold: one was to test the sample children's ability to handle relational kinship and the other was to use the interview schedules as tools with which to elicit the children's knowledge and application of kinship terms. Besides replicating the three interviews, I recorded at various times the lists given to me by the children of whom they thought were members of their families and of their households. I also noted their use of kinship terms during observation sessions and informal interaction. Finally, I devised an exercise using puppets to test the children's use of kin terms of address. The three replications will be reported on first.

JEAN PIAGET'S TEST

Piaget (1928) reported research that he carried out on a set of relational concepts including the two kin terms *brother* and *sister* (*frère* and *soeur*). In this study, he asked 240 French-speaking Swiss children aged 4 and 12 years a number of questions about brothers and sisters. Among them was 'What is a brother (sister)?' The children's answers suggested to Piaget that there were three stages in the development of what he called the concept of a term like *brother*.

Stage One consisted of the most primitive definitions, e.g., a brother was simply a boy, a sister, a girl. In addition, children at this stage of definition often maintained that adults could not be brothers or sisters.

Stage Two definitions were relational in nature in that the child would maintain that there had to be more than one child with the same parents. The relationship was not reciprocal, however, because the term *brother* was applied exclusively to only one of the siblings involved. In addition, the restriction excluding adults rarely continued to operate at this stage.

Stage Three definitions were both relational and reciprocal in that the title *brother* (or *sister*) was now allowed to apply to all the siblings. In other words, the child understood that in order to *be* a brother, you had to *have* a brother or sister. Most of Piaget's subjects reached Stage Three by about the age of 9 or 10.

The questions that Piaget asked each child were:

1. How many brothers have you? And how many sisters? (Let us suppose that the child has a brother A and a sister B.) And how many brothers has A? And how many sisters? And how many brothers has B? And how many sisters?

2. How many brothers are there in the family? How many sisters? How many brothers and sisters altogether?

3. There are three brothers in a family: Auguste, Alfred and Raymond. How many brothers has Auguste? And Alfred? And Raymond?

4. Are you a brother (or a sister)? What is a brother (or a sister, according to the sex of the child)?

5. Ernest has three brothers, Paul, Henry and Charles. How many brothers has Paul? And Henry? And Charles?

6. How many brothers are there in this family?

The ages at which at least 75 per cent of the children of the same age answered each question (or test, as Piaget called them) were:

Age	Test passed*
5	0
6	**2**
7	2
8	2, **3**
9	2, 3, **4**
10	**1**, 2, 3, 4, **5**, **6**

Piaget's analysis of the answers is focused on the child's growing

* Tests are underscored at the age at which they were first passed.

capacity to take the role of the other person and understand that a term like 'brother' is not a static attribute of a person (like 'boy') but a relation between two persons, and in particular, a symmetrical relation such that if X is Y's brother, Y is also X's brother. The Xhosa term is not symmetrical and therefore cannot be used to indicate the child's development of the capacity to understand the logical concept of symmetrical relations. The term for elder brother is *umkhuluwe* and for younger brother, *umninawe* (Hunter, 1936: 29). The same linguistic term is used for elder and younger sisters. According to Hunter (1936: 34), either *udade wethu* or *umnt'akwethu* may be used for both younger and older sister.

Despite the problems replicating Piaget's study in a society in which the kin terms for brother are asymmetrical, I decided to administer the test to see how the children would handle the logic of relations and to ascertain whether or not they used the traditional asymmetrical terms for older brother and sister, and for younger brother and sister, or whether they used the terms current in Crossroads that had been adopted from Afrikaans, that is *bhuti* for brother and *sisi* for sister.* Besides, I was interested in seeing how the children handled the test format.

The test revealed that children aged 7 and 8 in Crossroads use the terms *ubhuti* and *usisi* as reference and address† to older brothers and sisters only. The rule seemed to be more firmly entrenched for the former than the latter term. Besides, they are used about or to siblings somewhat older than themselves and there seems to be no firm rule as to how much older a brother or sister should be before he or she is deserving of the form of reference or address under consideration. *Bhuti* and *sisi* are terms of respect that recognise the hierarchical ordering of relationships within the family.

For the first question, one could not replace the question, 'How many brothers have you?' with two questions asking 'How many older brothers have you?' and 'How many younger brothers?' as one might assume to be possible given the traditional asymmetrical terms, because the children would have denied (and they did deny) that they had any of the latter. Younger brothers and sisters are simply called 'child of the house' *(umtwanabendlu)* or 'child of my mother'.

The test was thus rendered more difficult. For example, question 1

* Note on origins of the two terms: *bhuti* came from 'boetie' and *sisi* is short for *usisiomdala* (older sister) or *usisiomcinci* (younger sister), so my Crossroads informants said. *Sisi* may be derived from the Afrikaans 'sussie'.

† In the vocative case there is no prefix.

asks how many brothers has one of the subject's brothers (in the following, the same applied to sisters). In order to reply the child must either include or exclude himself as a brother of his brother depending on his age relative to that brother. The question is a more searching test of a child's ability to take another's point of view (decentre) than Piaget's original one.

Question 3 is also made more difficult. The question sets an abstract problem: 'There are three brothers in a family. Sipho, Geza and Malusi. How many brothers has Sipho? and Geza? and Malusi?' According to the children's use of the term brother, there ought, in that family, to be another child to whom all three are brothers. Some handled the problem by disregarding their usual use of the term and some tried to assign seniority and gave answers accordingly. Questions 5 and 6 presented similar difficulties.

Question 4 asks, 'Are you a brother?' Most children replied taking into account their position in the family. Question 4 also asks, 'What is a brother?' and the definitions offered largely concentrated on relative sibling positions not on links established via parentage. For example, a girl defined a sister by describing her own position in the family. 'I am a sister to the young ones. An old girl.' Others used the phrase 'child of the house' assuming it to be an adequate definition of brotherhood or sisterhood.

The test's applicability across cultures is limited because the questions seem to demand a use of number that assumes a conceptual grasp or confidence beyond that possessed by some of the children. The test demands that the child pay attention without the help of activity or material aids through eighteen questions. It is probable that some societies demand and train children to concentrate on intense verbal exchanges more than do others. Therefore, inattention in certain circumstances could be due to an absence of cultural emphasis on its value under such conditions.

The questions were more difficult for those children with large families, especially if some members lived elsewhere. Another source of confusion was the fact that the terms *bhuti* and *sisi* are sometimes used across a broad spectrum that includes cousins and clan members. For example, Togu mentioned as his brother a boy whom I knew was not his brother and when asked who he was, he said:

'He is a boy. His clan is also N–. Our relationship is from the Transkei. I call him brother.'

As a result children other than brothers, as defined in the context of Piaget's test, were sometimes included. As LeVine and Price-Williams

(1974) found among the Hausa, children are often encouraged to address (and categorize) certain persons in the compound with kin terms that indicate a desired social relationship rather than in accordance with accepted definitions of consanguinity and affinity. This occurs among a wide variety of peoples.

As Piaget pointed out, the test is limited in that only children with at least one brother and one sister can answer all the questions. One is not then able to estimate the differences that being the only child in a family may have upon the use of kinship terms. After the study of the use of fifteen kin terms Haviland and Clark (1974) concluded that personal experience had little effect on the results. This is contrary to Piaget's anticipation in 1928. His emphasis on the impact of social factors then was greater than in his later works. For example, Piaget (1928: 71–2) said, 'Social intercourse . . . modifies the structure of thought' and '. . . formal thought is really dependent on social factors.'

According to Piaget's scoring method, no child in the Crossroads sample succeeded on the test. As I knew the children's families well, I could judge as to whether or not they were using terms for brother and sister in strict accord with their own usage. Scoring thus, Lungiswa obtained full marks, Tozama one less, Zuziwe three less and Peliswe four less. The scores are shown in Table 5–1 in the Appendix.

The next interview to be discussed is an adaptation of Piaget's test, using a naturalistic approach among a non-Western group of children.

R LeVINE'S AND D PRICE-WILLIAM'S TEST

The authors' aim was to explore the ways in which individuals, particularly children, use cultural categories to conceptualize their experience. Like Piaget, they selected kinship and family as means through which to explore the topic.

They set out to devise an approach applicable to the study of children's concepts in a society where kin terms are not symmetrical and a nuclear family system is not the norm. Their specific aims were to discover the extent to which children's verbal reports concerning kin relations in their homes would reveal developmental trends in accord with (a) relation thinking, (b) informational accuracy, and (c) the salience for the child of compound residents in certain realtionships to him.

Procedures. A single set of questions was administered individually to fifty-three Hausa children aged 4 to 11 in rural Nigeria. The authors' description follows (LeVine and Price-Williams, 1974: 39):

In the interview, which was entirely taped, the child was first asked who lives in the compound. He would give several names spontaneously. When he stopped, the interviewer asked him, 'Who else?' A distinction was made between the spontaneous list and the elicited list . . . Next, the interviewer went down the list the child had given and asked, 'who is' each person on it; the child could identify the person in any way he chose. A major purpose here was to see whether kin terms were used in identifying persons, and if not, what kinds of attributes were mentioned. The interviewer then went down the list again, this time asking about each person for whom a kin term had not been given already, 'How is he related to you?' If a child had not spontaneously identified the person with a kin term but knew the term applied, he could use it now. We could check the terms he gave against the rules of Hausa kinship terminology applied to the adult census material. The interviewer reviewed the list a final time asking for pairs of adjacent persons. 'How is this one related to that one?' Here the purpose was to tap the child's capacity to view kin relations from a decentered perspective, taking the rôle of the other relative. In the final part of the interview, the child was asked to define three kin terms, including ones he had used (if any) and including a general term for 'grandparent'.

The authors believe that the technique tapped formal aspects of children's thought processes and some of the content of childhood experience, particularly the acquisition of domestic norms of social distance and the emotional salience of certain kin for the developing child. Finally, they say that the approach forms their proposal for a 'comparative phenomenology of child experience, in which ideational data from children of diverse cultures could be brought to bear on issues of broad theoretical significance' (LeVine and Price-Williams, 1974: 42). The exercise confirmed Piaget's major findings.

The set of questions is not ideal for a situation such as the one in Crossroads. In essence, it requires the child to list the members of the household, give each a kin term, describe the relationships of adjacent pairs and define three kin terms. An immediate problem in a squatter camp in South Africa is the shifting nature of household compositions. It is hard for anyone to keep up with changes in membership and even more difficult to keep track of relationships. A new member could be a relation of either the family head or his wife, or a member of their clan, or a neighbour from their country home (a home-man), or simply a lodger. During the year, I would occasionally check household membership and frequently found changes in persons and in number. For instance seven households had the following number of members at different times:

Mlawu's in March, 13 and in May, 15
Togu's in March, 11 and in November, 19 (a new house)

Nukwa's in March, 13 and in August, 6 (a new house)
Nomvula's in March, 16 and in May, 21
Zuziwe's in March, 14 and in June, 18
Gedja's in May, 9 and in November, 12
Tozama's in March, 12 (composed of 3 adults and 9 children) and in May, 12 (composed of 4 adults and 8 children).

Different marital patterns exacerbated possible confusion: one man, Mr Ketshe, admitted to having two wives and children by each; five parents had had children by someone other than the child's other parent; nine families had at least one child living away from home; one child's father had died and his father's brother was head of the household; three others lived without their fathers and one of them without either her father or mother. Not many of the above complications occurred in accord with established norms that could be explained to a child. Two examples of confusion follow:

1. Saliswa's parents each had had children before they met each other and produced progeny together. They did not admit to their former unions to those, at least, outside the family. Saliswa thought that her brother, a few years older than she, was the child of her father but not her mother whereas he was the child of both.

2. Tozama was asked to describe the relationship between two of her brothers (X and Y) who were born of her mother and another man. She said: 'They are not related, they come from the same house. X calls Y *bhuti*.' Her mother did not admit to the early union with a man other than Tozama's father and the child was unable to work out the nature of the kinship ties.

The composition of the household was rendered more difficult for the child to grasp by the nature of work patterns. Some found it difficult to say whether someone was a member of the household or not, because he or she seemed to be away most of the time. Gedja, for example, did not include her grandmother in the list, 'Because,' she said, 'she is working.' Yet she did include her mother, who was away at work all week and only returned for the weekends.

In attempting to clarify the relationship to the family of someone listed, I sometimes found that I was asking the child to discuss delicate issues that were either not common knowledge or not discussed openly before children. This was particularly true of parentage. Lungiswa, for example, claimed that her youngest brother was the child of a different father from the rest of the children while her mother denied this. I was wary of enquiring too closely from certain children as to who an 'uncle' *(malume)* was, as mother's current man friend was often introduced as such to the child. The true parentage of a child must eventually be revealed if only because obligations (for example, the son's traditional anticipation that his father will assist in making his marriage payments) and rights (for example, the father's over his daughter's *ikhazi*) may be later pressed and possibly contested. The question raises interesting ethical issues: traditionally did the child have the right to know who begat her even if the appropriate rites to place her under the protection of her maternal grandfather's ancestors had been fulfilled? What would the modern view be on that issue? It is a thorny topic in Western societies when an adopted child's rights are in question and English law has recently altered, giving the child the right to such knowledge in early adulthood.

In administering the interview I came upon certain problems inherent in this format and acknowledged by the authors. The test varied in difficulty according to the size of the household in which the child lived. With a large household, one could easily confuse or tire the child. I was not sure whether one ought to prompt the child when eliciting household membership. If one did not, the rest of the test would be less searching. For example, Hintsa did not name any children under either question 1 or 2 which asked for a list of members of the household. Early confusion between the child and me as we sought to clarify names and relationships may have led to passive resistance and the effective end of the interview. One source of such confusion was the variety of names by which a person could be known: a man might be known by an English name; a Xhosa name; a clan name or a nickname; a woman might be known by the same range plus a married name.

Question 1 and 2 (who lives in your house?) yielded fairly accurate lists of occupants though, as was to be expected, those from larger households forgot more members than did those from smaller. Table 5–2 in the Appendix shows the number in each household and the figure beneath the name represents the number listed by that child.

Yameka and Togu lived in a single room which was part of a large household with twenty-four and nineteen members, respectively. They could not, nor did they, attempt to list everyone in the house. Yameka lived in one room with her mother's brother, his wife, their child and a lodger. Six people in a room 5 x 4 m. I was not aware of there being a baby but having a lodger live in the same room as the family yet pay rent to the owners of the house probably ensures a frequent turnover of lodgers. I checked the numbers in each household during the month in which the kinship interviews were given, but I could have been out of date on some moves. Togu had six people living in his room: his parents, his younger brother, his father's brother's son and his mother's sister. The last named came only at weekends. He listed his mother, brother, his father's brother's son and three others from the wider household. Children within a household, even adults on occasion, occupy different rooms for varying amounts of time and even sleep in various rooms. I give the two examples above to illustrate the imponderables that can skew even the list of occupants of a single room.

Nukwa and his mother had moved house within Crossroads in May. His brother remained at the first house where his guardians (his father's brother and mother's sister who were husband and wife) lived. In listing the members of his household, Nukwa drew on both houses. None of the houses to which the children in the sample belonged were occupied by members of the nuclear family only. In Saliswa's house there were members of the nuclear and extended family and of her father's clan besides a patient of her mother's and lodgers.

Nine of the children listed their mothers in question 1, which asked for a list of members of their households. Two others included her in response to question 2, which asked who else lived in the house.

Five children included father in the list under question 1 ('the spontaneous list') and two under question 2 ('the elicited list'). Of those without fathers living in the household, Nukwa listed his father's brother and Yameka named her mother's brother, both in response to question 1. Neither Togu nor Nomvula listed their fathers and the latter child referred to her mother as *mamkaZukiswa* , that is, her sister's mother. The term is a traditional form of polite address. Saliswa named her parents by their respective clans.

Wilson and Mafeje (1963: 87–9) found that the extended use of kinship terms indicating seniority was changing in town. *uMama* in 1963 was restricted to the speaker's own mother, though in the country it was still being used in address to mother's sister, and also mother's contemporaries. Traditionally *ma*, rather than *mama*, was used in this extended way, but *ma* was also the formal address to mother. Similarly, *bawo* was traditionally used by a man to his father, formally, and to no one else. However, in town girls were using *tata*, the equivalent of the more familiar 'daddy', rather than 'father,' and *tata* instead of *bawo* was being used in the extended sense, by both men and women, for father's brothers and senior men.

There were incidents among the boys and girls of Crossroads in which the extended use of *mama* could be heard. This happened often in Cebo's home, where his mother and her elder sister shared house: the children of both women called them both *mama* . However, there were indications that in other Crossroads homes the term was used in a more restricted sense. For example, the following conversation between Gwali and his friend John, who was not related to him, was overheard. On an evening in October, Gwali's mother was calling him home for supper.

John: 'Mother calls you, Gwali.'

Gwali (angrily): 'What do you mean, John?'

John: 'I mean auntie, who is your mother.'

The Crossroads children used *utata* much more often in speaking about or to their fathers than *ubawo*. They used *utatomkhulu* rather than *ubawomkhulu* for grandfather.

In the Crossroads sample, if substitute figures for mothers or fathers are taken into account, every child listed a 'mother' and ten of the thirteen listed a 'father' in response to either question 1 or 2. There are data derived from other exercises conducted with the children during the year that show that the two children who omitted to list their fathers (Togu and Nomvula) had particularly close relationships with their fathers.

Questions 3 and 4 will be dealt with together. The former asks the child who each of the persons is whom she has named, and the next question asks how he or she is related to the child (that is, for each name not given a kin term in response to question 3). The most striking feature of these answers was that the children related people through a parent, usually the mother, rather than themselves. The usual kinship diagram looks something like this:

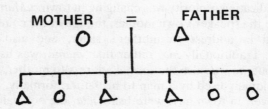

Siblings are tied together, as it were, and then linked to the parents. A diagram that better represents these children's scheme might look like this:

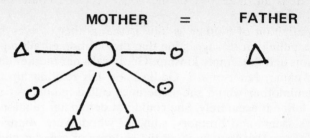

MOTHER = FATHER

in which the children define their relationship to each other through their mother and to the father through their mother.

No child used the words for son or daughter. More often the phrase 'child of the house' *(umtwanabendlu)* was used. The word used for house was *indlu*. In traditional Xhosa households a number of such units make up an *umzi*, homestead, at the head of which would be the senior male relative. *Indlu* was used by these children to refer to the children of one mother much as would be done in a traditional *umzi* in which each married woman would have her own house and property.

Kinship terms for grandchild, cousin, niece or nephew were not used although the opportunity arose. The following ten terms were used by the children during the test: *umama* – mother; *utata* – father; *usisi* – sister; *ubhuti* – brother; *utatomkhulu* – grandfather; *umakhulu* – grandmother; *umyeni* – husband; *umalume* – mother's brother; *udade-bobawo* – father's sister; *umakazi* – mother's sister. Terms such as father of . . ., mother of . . ., were often used.

Question 5 asks of adjacent pairs of persons in the lists given earlier: 'How much is this one related to that one?' Six children did not give acceptable replies but two did, although even here each gave only a one-way definition: for example, Yameka said of the relationship between her mother's brother and his child, 'She is his baby.'

Five children each gave three adequate definitions of the relationship between two family members.

Finally, question 6 asked for the definition of three kin terms, ones used by the child and a general word for grandparents. Only two children, Lungiswa and Tozama, gave meaningful definitions. Tozama's were:

Mother: 'I don't know. A person is a mother because she has children.'

Grandmother: 'A person who has got grandchildren. Mama says *'mama'* to grandmother.'

Brother: 'It is an older boy of the house. At this home there are girls.'

Gedja's definition of mother as 'She is the mother of everybody in the house' is telling for its suggestion that the position entails a position of social status and not simply kinship. Gedja calls her mother either by her English name, Jane, or *sisi*. Gedja knew her relationship to Jane and her grandmother whom she sometimes called *mama*, yet she did not always define it accurately. She could not define her relationship to her mother's sisters and brothers, some of whom were younger than she, except to say that they were all the children of grandmother.

Wilson and Mafeje (1963: 89) recorded the same use of the terms *umama* and *usisi* in Langa among families of migrants, and among town families who send their children to the country to be brought up by grandparents. The grandmother, they note, who has charge of the children may be called *mama*, and the real mother, who only sees them from time to time, *sisi*. They observe that the substitutes are a direct reflection of change in everyday behaviour. In Gedja's case, both she and her mother were born in Cape Town and both live with Gedja's grandparents in the city.

S HAVILAND'S AND E CLARK'S TEST

Another set of questions was asked based on the study of the acquisition of English kin terms. The questions asked for the definitions of fifteen kin terms from fifty children between the ages of 3 and 8. The kin terms were: mother, father, grandmother, grandfather, son, daughter, grandson, granddaughter, brother, sister, aunt, uncle, niece, nephew and cousin. Haviland and Clark (1974: 36) assumed that the relative sematic complexity of the entries would be the main factor in their acquisition by the child. They also wondered whether other factors such as the child's own experience and the child's own rôles might affect acquisition. However, on the last point they concluded that experience with kin does not affect acquisition (Haviland and Clark, 1974: 43). They concluded, too, that children's definitions for all fifteen of these kin terms seemed to go through the four stages outlined by Danziger (1957), with only a few minor exceptions (1974: 43), and their third major finding was that a very important factor in determining the order in which kin terms are learned relative to each other *is* their degree of semantic complexity (1974: 47).

In administering the interviews, Haviland and Clark (1974: 37) found that younger children sometimes showed signs of boredom but that, 'Fortunately, the older children were eager to show off their knowledge. Interviews with children over 5 years and 9 months invariably yielded complete protocols.' It was the reaction of the 7- and 8-year-old children in Crossroads to such an interview format that I was interested in observing. It seemed clear that the responses would not be sustained by many children when requested to define so many terms. Xhosa culture does not encourage children to 'show off their knowledge' especially to strange adults. Besides, the children were not accustomed to systematic questioning by strangers. I was, of course, interested in the problems to which the authors had sought answers, but I predicted a low level of response.

Results. Six children (Hintsa, Saliswa, Nukwa, Nomvula, Cebo and Yameka) gave no replies at all. Togu and Gwali tried to give definitions but none beyond stage 1. Gedja and Peliswe gave one definition each at the level commensurate with their ages, and Tozama, Zuziwe and Lungiswa, all of whom are girls, gave four or five definitions at stage 3 level. Tozama's definition of father's sister *(umakazi)* illustrates the use of some kin terms beyond actual kinship:

'An aunt is a person who stays in the same house and instead of using her name you say *makazi*. Some are related and some are not. If I belong to clan M– and the person is also of that clan, then she is *makazi.*'

The child defined the term as it is used for kin, household members and clan members which, in fact, is quite common in Crossroads. Traditionally (Hunter, 1936: 53–7), father's sister, *udadebobawo,* was distinguished from mother's sister, *umakazi*, and mother's brother's wife, *umkamalume.* Wilson and Mafeje (1963: 87) found that in Langa some informants still distinguished *udadebobawo*, but many did not and that many people used one new term *uanti*, from the English 'auntie', for all three relationships. The term was also extended to mother's contemporaries. I seldom heard the term *uanti* used by children in Crossroads. *Umakazi* seemed to be used instead. This, possibly, reflects a class difference in the use of kin terms in town.

Lungiswa, whose parents live apart, gave a revealing definition of a daughter:

'A daughter is the girl of a mother.'

(Who else can have a daughter?)

'Fathers do have daughters and leave them with their wives. They also have sons.'

Her definition of a grandfather illustrates a point made earlier to the effect that kin relations are often traced through a mother:

'A grandfather is the husband of your mother's mother.'

As predicted, the interview format yielded very little. Performance was poor but this cannot be taken as a true reflection of competence as the technique used was alien to the children's experience.

PLAYING WITH PUPPETS

The three tests so far described have two features in common. They each test reference kin terms and none of them uses material or activity. To examine the use of terms of address and to provide concrete aids, I devised a test using the family of puppets with which the children and I had played during the year. There were five puppets: an old man – Bhololo; his wife, an old woman – Nosipho; their daughter – Thandeka; and her son – Zolani, and daughter – Nopinki. The father was away working on the docks of a small port. They were, of course, black. The children named them. I used them to discuss aspects of the children's experience indirectly such as the journey from the Transkei to Cape Town, the arrival in Crossroads, shopping in the city, fighting in the home.

The following was the format used with each child. We took out the puppets, handled them and reminded each other of their names and kinship. I then said that we were going to play a game in which each puppet in turn was to call each of the others but was not allowed to use their names. It was practice for *hlonipha* (ritual avoidance). One puppet would be placed on the child's hand and Mary and I would have the others on our hands. The child might have the mother. I would say, 'Thandeka wishes to call the family to come and have supper. Zolani and Nopinki are playing on the road; Nosipho is washing in the yard and Bhololo is buying vegetables from a hawker. Thandeka is not allowed to use their names, how does she call Zolani?'

The children seemed relaxed and they enjoyed the game although Nomvula and Hintsa gave up after three puppets had called the others.

There were a limited number of address forms that could be used. They were: mother – *mama;* grandmother – *makhulu;* grandfather – *tatomakhulu;* brother – *bhuti;* sister – *sisi;* my child – *mntwana wam;* my daughter – *ntombi;* my son – *nyana;* grandchild – *mzukulwana;* husband – *myeni (ndoda);* wife – *nkosikazi;* mother of . . . – *mama ka . . .;* father of . . . – *tata ka . . .*

A point was given for each correct address form used in the twenty calls. The above forms are those commonly used in Crossroads. (See Table 5–3 in the Appendix.)

Peliswe got full marks and Tozama two less, five children got over half marks. Fifty per cent of all possible points were scored whereas on

Piaget's test only 36 per cent was scored. Although the range of possible kin terms was limited, just as many were used as in the LeVine and Price-Williams interview where the possible range was far greater. Given the complicating factors in family life for children living in a South African urban squatter camp, I suggest that variations of the use of puppets could prune away some extraneous foliage from family trees and allow a more accurate measure of children's use and understanding of kinship terms to be made. If a list of members of the household is desirable, it could be elicited by using objects such as models.

In writing up his study of kinship, Piaget (1928: 92) remarks on the fact that children handle relational problems on the plane of action long before they do on the verbal plane. This is because the child has not yet become 'quite definitely and consciously' aware of the distinction between membership (we are three brothers) and relation (I have two brothers). Piaget, therefore, warns against using material objects at least for the problems set in his interview. However, although the puppets represent concrete forms and their membership as a family is given as well as their reference kin identities from the point of view of the mother puppet, the subject still has to work out relations within a fairly complex network and so demonstrate an ability to handle the symbolic system. For example, while the subject is told that the puppet called Nosipho is the mother of the children's mother, it is not stated what kin term the grandmother should use to call her grandchild(ren). Further, while Nosipho and Bhololo are known to be Thandeka's parents, the subject is not told what kin terms they use to address each other.

The 1928 study carried one of Piaget's strongest statements on his view of childish egocentrism. He stated that until the age of 7 or 8 the child always takes his own point of view as something absolute and remains ignorant of the habits of relativity and comparison and that his field of consciouness is still restricted. For example, Piaget (1928: 89) says the child 'has always considered his brothers and sisters from his own point of view, calling them brothers and sisters, counting the family only as a whole. But the thought of their individual viewpoints has never crossed his mind . . .' It is this last comment that the play with puppets questions.

There is no ego involved in the puppet kinship play, but it is interesting to see that when either of the puppets representing the children, Nopinki and Zolani, was asked to call, the success rate was high, as is shown in Table 5–4 in the Appendix. The chart shows how many children called the other puppets using the correct kin term when pretending to be each puppet in turn. For example, when the children were holding Nopinki, five of these called all the others and eight called three of the four others correctly. Six of the eight failed to call Nopinki's brother, Zolani, correctly. When holding Zolani seven of the eight failed to call his sister, Nopinki, correctly. This fits in with the particular use of terms for brother and sister noted earlier. I had not defined which puppet child was older than the other, preferring to allow each child to decide for himself or herself during earlier play sessions.

A child holding Nopinki or Zolani (the puppet son or daughter) would use the correct kin term more often in calling the others than when an adult puppet was held. Perhaps a fairer description of Piaget's notion of egocentricity in childhood would be in the term child-centricity. Child-centricity eliminates some of the secondary meanings that have been loaded onto the term egocentricity. After all, how many adults successfully perceive the world from the point of view of the child? In concluding their study, Haviland and Clark (1974: 46) suggest that a child should have less difficulty in taking the viewpoint of another child than in taking that of an adult. They add that 'it is clearly a factor that should be explored further.' The above study lends support to their suggestion.

The puppet test does not demand a firm conception of number as does the Piagetian test.

DISCUSSION
In preparation for a task that involved estimating the relative size of his or her family (see the report in Chapter 4) each child gave me a list of the members of the family. The lists highlighted the number of variables that had to be taken into account. A child may have had to decide whether or not:

a) to include members of the nuclear family whether or not they lived in the same house or area (i.e., parents and/or siblings);

b) to include members of the wider family whether or not they lived in the same house or area;

c) to include members of either parents' clan;

d) to include a parent's 'husband'/'wife' if other than the child's parent and/or their offspring;

e) to exclude other household members.

Seven children listed every member of the nuclear family while six did not, as some members lived away from the Crossroads home. Eight children named at least one member outside the nuclear family. With four children (Togu, Nukwa, Saliswa and Nomvula) it was difficult to establish for certain whether or not they were clear as to who belonged to the nuclear family. It took questioning using a tape recorder, an exercise with clay figures, a life history interview, and kinship interviews to establish that each child did know who was a member of the immediate family group. On some occasions Togu and Nukwa each denied having a brother (the latter denied having any kin on one occasion); Nomvula usually insisted on including her father's brother's daughters as her sisters; and Saliswa was sometimes confused as to exactly which parent begat which child in her large, complex family. The point to be made is that a child's conception of family membership is not easily traced when family composition alters in the face of change. However, comments such as the one made by Seagrim and Lendon (1920: 200) about the cognitive concepts of Aborigine children are questionable in the light of the above findings. Their comment was made as part of their explanation of how the 'Aboriginal mode' affects their (lack of) quantitative thinking. Their first reason for the absence of such thinking is that '. . . the Aboriginal infant is brought up in a society in which the notions associated with personal ownership are largely lacking: his care-takers are numerous and largely interchangeable and even the kinship terms used to designate each equivalent person (mother and mother's sister) are the same . . .' The authors link non-ownership of possession to the number of child care-takers and the equivalence of kin terms. Yet they do not record from the child's point of view just how interchangeable the care-takers are nor how equivalent in value. They fail to plumb the depths of the fiction.

Before concluding, the following conversations recorded during the observations of children at home will be offered as illustrations of points made earlier in the chapter. One such point was that within families emphasis is placed on seniority among brothers and sisters and the respect due from those younger. Van Warmelo (1931) observed that brothers everywhere scrupulously observe the prerogatives of primogeniture. To lack respect towards an elder brother is a great offence and easily leads to blows. The same applies to the relations of sisters among themselves.

Observation on 11 November 1980 at 5.20 p.m. outside Tozama's home:

Tozama: 'I have seen Makhosi kicking my ball. What can I do to find it?'

Friend: 'It is easy for you to ask him to give you the ball for it doesn't belong to him. It belongs to you so he must return it to you.'

Tozama: 'Hey! Makhosi, kindly give me that ball as I want to play with it.'

Makhosi (her brother aged 18): 'I am not your size. You must not call me like that. I am older than you, you must have "respect" for me.' (Respect was said in English.)

Tozama: 'What's that? What's "respect"? Tell me, brother, I want to know that English word that you said to me.'

Makhosi: 'I mean having no manners, a child who is naughty like you is a child who has got no "respect", no manners. Do you hear what I say?'

Tozama: 'Yes, I do understand your explanation of the word.'

In the same family on the evening of the following day, this conversation was recorded.

Tozama's mother upbraids her sister, aged 14, for losing a bottle of Permanganate of Potash which she needs to mix in medicine required by people for a journey to the Transkei at Christmas. The girl, Nomvula, is asked by the *makoti* (her brother's new bride) to wash dishes but she plaintively says that she has to find the Permanganate of Potash although she is not at all certain that her mother gave it to her to keep. Tozama interrupts her plaint, saying:

'Oh, no, Nomvula, stop talking nonsense about Mama.'

Nomvula (angrily): 'What, Tozama, what do you say? I'll hit you if you are naughty. You must not be naughty. You must know that you are a child. I am older than you.'

The following record some instances in which the term 'brother' was used. The first came from Cebo's home and reflects the way in which Cebo uses 'brother' to address or refer to his cousin (his mother's sister's son, aged 14).

At 8.30 p.m. on 10 November 1980, Cebo had eaten and his aunt (mother's sister) was dishing up for her son, Mxolisi.

Cebo: 'I am also going to eat again with Mxolisi. He is my brother, I must eat with him.'

Mother: 'When you eat your own food, he is not your brother, you do not think of him; but when he is having his own food, he is your brother.'

Cebo laughs.

At 6.00 p.m. on the next day, Cebo's mother asked Mxolisi, her sister's son, 'Where is my brother, Mxolisi?' meaning his father, her sister's husband.

And this conversation was recorded on the following day: Cebo's father returned from work at 7.30 p.m. He asked his wife if he could have a fire tin in his bedroom and she said it was a waste to have one there as well as in the sitting-room where everyone was gathered. Father said, in a hurt tone, 'But I am wet.'

Mother: 'Oh! I didn't know that you are wet. Please forgive me then. Let me make a fire for you, my *daddy*.'

Mother's sister: 'Here. Take my fire.'

Father: 'Thank you my *swaer*,* *my wife* was a bit rude to me though she can see that I am a little wet.'

Mother: 'Cebo, go and take the heater from *my sister's* room.'

Cebo: 'Mama, Mama, it is heavy for me to carry.'

Mother: 'Mxolisi, help him please, *my dear son*. Hurry up. Here is a cup of coffee for you, *daddy*.'

Father: 'Thank you, *mama*.'

Mxolisi: 'Here is a chair for you to sit on, *daddy*.'

In the above, kin terms are frequently used and not always in strict accord with nuclear ties, e.g., mother calls her sister's son, 'my dear son' and he calls his mother's sister's husband, 'father.' On 19 November 1980, in Togu's home, a man who belongs to the same clan as Togu's father addressed the boy as 'my brother's son' and Togu addressed the man's son as 'my brother'.

Two examples will suffice to suggest the wide use to which the term 'mother' can be put:

In Zuziwe's home at 8.00 p.m. on 27 October 1980, the lodger, Mimi, is preparing a bottle for Zuziwe's 3-year-old brother, Sonwaba. Mimi teases him lightly because he addresses her, using her name:

Sonwaba: 'Make a bottle for me, Mimi.'

Mimi: 'Who is Mimi?'

Sonwaba: 'My mother is Mimi.'

On the following day at 6.00 p.m., Zuziwe is singing and dancing like an *igqira*. She says to her sister:

'I want to dance for Pamela. I wish to do this so that she can see that I am a tribal dancer. I will do the dances of the Xhosa.'

Her sister bothers her, and Zuziwe asks:

'Why do you come and disturb me? You do not want me to dance for my mother when she comes.'

Many such examples could be given. They support one of the conclusions of the paper that the use to which kinship terms are put by children is not easily ascertained through the medium of formal

* In Afrikaans, *swaer* means brother-in-law and is often used in addressing a friend similar to the English 'mate'.

interviews. Attention must be paid both to their use of the terms in address and reference and to the context.

SUMMARY

One of the features of a changing society is the change of kinship terminology. Among the Xhosa, as Hunter (1963) and Wilson and Mafeje (1963) observed, change is not recent. English and Afrikaans words have been extensively assimilated. This study confirms the changes that were recorded by the last two authors in Langa: that is, changes in the use of terms for father's sister, mother's sister, mother's brother's wife, a man's elder brother, a woman's brother, and different, less extended, use of mother and father. However, terms that were replacing them in Crossroads were different from those in Langa. *Umakazi* was used not *uanti; tata* or *umalume* not *ompie; sisi* not *usister wam;* and *tata* rather than *bawo; usïsi* and *ubhuti* were used in the same extended way in Crossroads as in Langa. The use of *umakhulu* had remained the same. Three points must be emphasized. Seventeen years separated the publication of the research on Langa and my fieldwork; the class composition of the Crossroads population differed from that of Langa – the latter having a larger group with more years of schooling and another of migrants without their families; and, thirdly, my informants were children. The effective time gap may be longer than seventeen years in as much as the Langa informants were adults and the Crossroads informants children. Nevertheless, the trends in the use of terms were similar and the issues they raise worthy of closer study. That change in kinship terms was occurring and that their use possibly varied according to class, age and urban status should caution researchers against drawing hasty conclusions based on set interviews amongst sample groups. Change affects family composition, traditional attitudes towards kin ties and responsibilities. These must all be taken into account in the study of kinship terminology.

The abstract nature of the interview technique and its reliance (in Piaget's version) on number conception make it difficult to administer to some child populations. The complexity of household membership in Crossroads made the gathering of a census through children a task more difficult than the one LeVine and Price-Williams faced with Hausa children.* Similarly, lists of family members were difficult to obtain

* In the context of research in Lesotho, Murray (1976: 54) asks,

By what criteria, then, is the household defined? It is not a co-residential group, nor does it engage in joint activities, for the energies of household

141

from children because of family disbursement and changing patterns of work, residence and marriage.†

It seemed to me that children aged 7 or 8 were aware of the implications behind the use of kinship terms. They understood the emotional nuances that choice among possible terms might imply. Sometimes I suspected, on the basis of the use of kin terms, that a child did not know his or her exact relationship to a care-taker but other incidents demonstrated that this was not so. Imputations about emotional salience and the child's understanding of the kinship system cannot be reliably drawn from single tests based on the use of kin terms.

(continued from p 140)

members are divided between participation in agricultural production in Lesotho and participation in industrial production in South Africa. Nor can it be defined by criteria of kinship for, although its members are almost invariably kin of one sort or another, there is striking variation in actual kinship composition both between households and within households over time. A pragmatic interim approach is to regard the household as an aggregation of individuals within which are concentrated the flows of income and expenditure generated by the activities of its members.

It is difficult, he adds, to distinguish clearly between the house-holder's tangible manifestation as a partially co-residential group and its overall function manifestation in terms of income-generating activities. Murray points out that it is clearly important in assessing the sociological implications of oscillating migration to understand whether a household is discussed in the sense that includes absent members or in the sense that excludes them. He says (1976: 136) that one must take into account criteria of consumption, co-residence, production and reproduction in the analysis of the domestic group. (See also Goody, J., 1972; Gluckman, 1950; and Preston-Whyte, 1974). Spiegel (1980: 8) suggests the need to focus on individuals and their networks, both rural and urban, as basic analytical units.

† Spiegel (1980: 1) gives references to the writings of historians and anthropologists on a body of work that is emerging that deals with 'the manner in which ordinary people, caught up in the rigours of the migrant labour system, have come to cope with the pressures on them and their families.'

6
The Children and Dreams

Like the Mpondo about whom Monica Hunter (1936) wrote, the Xhosa '. . . believe in the survival of the dead, and in their interest in, and power over the life of their descendants. All "old people" *(abantu abadala)* who die become *amathongo* (ancestral spirits), and can influence the lives of their descendants' (Hunter, 1936: 231). The *amathongo* manifest themselves to their descendants in dreams. Thus dreams represent a vital link in the Xhosa system of beliefs.

Dreams also function in Xhosa ritual as the medium for the expression of confession. A pregnant woman, for example, is ritually washed with a particular plant *(isihlambezo)* to help insure that the child in her womb will flourish and, during the ritual, she is expected to confess *(ukulawula)* her dreams (Hunter, 1936: 148). Likewise, a woman who is troubled by dreams of an *izulu* (or *impundulu*), a familiar that is said to be possessed by a female witch, is treated by an *ixhwele* (a herbalist) and an essential preliminary of the treatment is a full confession of dreams, and of relations with the *izulu* (Hunter, 1936: 285). Part of the treatment of a novice undergoing training as an *igqira* is the confession of dreams. She is expected to confess everything she sees *emaphupheni*, that is, in sleeping or waking dreams (Hunter, 1936: 325). The confession of dreams clearly plays a part in cleansing body and mind, implying either the existence of unconscious desires not sanctioned by society or some measure of complicity with forces of evil.

Among the people of Crossroads, it seemed to me, dreams still played a powerful role in the lives of many. In working with the children, I sought to discover to what extent they, at the age of 7 or 8, consciously acknowledge the beliefs held about dreams by adults in their society. I was interested in the content of their dreams, their attitudes towards them and their thoughts about the dream process. I tried, too, to find out their families' understanding of the role of dreams and their reaction to their children's dreams.

Half way through the year, I began to ask the fourteen children to tell me their dreams. In six months, they told me thirty dreams (three of the children never offered any). Once Nukwa said, 'I dream but cannot remember any to tell you', and on another occasion, 'I never have dreams. I know that others have dreams.' Yameka said, 'I sleep without dreams,' and Gedja told me, 'I have never seen a dream.' In view of the fact that father was the person most often dreamt about by the other eleven children, it is of interest that none of these three lived with his or her father.

Half of the thirty dreams seemed to be happy and the other half seemed to instil some fear or distress in the dreamer. From Zuziwe, Cebo, Hintsa and Peliswe I have only fearful dreams and from Gwali I have only happy ones. Together we would discuss the dreams and pursue any associations. Towards the end of the year, I interviewed each child about dreams, structuring the questions around Jean Piaget's (1921) early research on dreams.

That the children told me their dreams indicates that there was some degree of trust between us. It is clear that cultural symbols appear in the dreams of 7-year-old Xhosa children living in an urban environment: themes such as the brewing of beer; the slaughtering of a goat; the entering of rivers and forests; and the use of black cowskins, all occur. Themes that recur in all dream analysis are also represented in the children's dreams, for example, themes of death, birth, the shedding of blood, snakes and nakedness. Some of these themes appear in two of Peliswe's dreams (25 July 1980):

'On Tuesday, I dreamt that I was in the forest with my two sisters. We went and went and went and saw a snake. It pulled me by the leg into a hole. I cried. My sisters cried and ran to tell my mother. While I was crying, I went to a house nearby and while I was there, my mother and sisters arrived carrying my clothes as I was wearing only a pantie. That was the end.'

'I dreamt two nights ago that I was walking with my mother's brother, his child and Tozama in the forest. We were walking on our knees. There were black and white skins on the ground. Then I woke up. It was frightening.'

There are suggestive themes in the second dream. There is a theme of supplication: *We were walking on our knees.* Xhosa girls are taught to kneel when giving something to or when greeting a respected person. Besides, Peliswe's family are Christians and regular church-goers. There is a theme to do with divination: the dream occurs in *the forest* where initiates are secluded to learn about themselves and to receive instruction from animal guides. The forest is an area of secret power and is thus threatening: seclusion in the forest is a trial of strength and stamina and emergence from the forest is a time of triumph. The forest reverberates with symbolism: it is a place where lost spirits wander, where boys are initiated into manhood, where girls collect firewood or wild fruits, and it is a place of the countryside not of a squatter settlement in a city.

There is, in the dream, a theme to do with ritual: there were *skins on the ground*. Animal skins play a vital part in many Xhosa rituals. There is a theme of death: *I was walking with my mother's brother*. Peliswe's mother's brother had been killed in a car accident in the year previous to her dream. After the accident her face had become temporarily paralysed on one side. Peliswe's mother connected the child's affliction to her distress over her uncle's death. There is a theme of racism: *black and white*. Peliswe had lived in four homes that had been demolished on the instruction of white men. She had witnessed violence between blacks and whites. She lived in the shadow of white suppression. There is a theme of fear: *It was frightening*. The themes connect in a stark nightmare. At the time of her dream Peliswe had less than a year to live.

I have drawn out possible themes embedded in one dream in order to suggest how the children's dreams could be analysed. It is not my intention to pursue such an analysis, but the reader may. I simply want to suggest that notions of reality and thus of dreams are culturally informed. Children are initiated into some of the culture's notions at an early age and their understanding of phenomena relates to that initiation in complex ways.

I used to offer my dreams to the *amagqira* with whom I worked to obtain a feel for the process of interpretation. I was impressed by the ingredients for psychological care embedded in the interpretations. (For a detailed explication of the ingredients, see Bührmann, 1978, 1981 and 1982.) There is an intricate detail in the tapestry of dreams as interpreted by *amagqira*. To some extent, it is a matter of choice or need that determines whether or not an individual pays much heed to the detail. The dreams of the children and the interpretations given to them by their kin suggest that they too take advantage of the culture's ideas about dreams eclectically.

THE CHILDREN'S DREAMS
A quarter of the dreams featured the child's father. This is noteworthy because the nature of the present South African system forces fathers

and children to live apart, often for most of the children's growing years. Mother appeared in only one-tenth of the dreams. Gwali dreamt (31 July 1980) that a large shack was being built for him and that only he and his father would live in it. In discussing the dream, he said that his mother, brother and Gedja (his mother's sister's daughter) would stay in the old shack and Gedja's mother would come to cook and clean for him and his father. He added, 'I like my father very much and spend a lot of time with him. We talk together about ordinary things.'

Nomvula had this dream about her father (3 October 1980):

'I dreamt that my father had hurt his hand and was bandaging it. He hurt it in a car accident. I was afraid as there was a lot of blood. Nobody was helping him.'

She explained that, when she is awake, she is often afraid that he will be hurt.

Togu once dreamt (9 September 1980) that his father was stabbing his mother. Later, I asked his mother about the dream and she recalled that he had awoken crying. She had comforted him saying, 'No, you are growing up now, my child.' This was a phrase often repeated to children and it means that it is natural that one should face difficulties as one grows: it is a sign of growing. It is said in consolation.

Saliswa had three dreams in which her father appeared. Once (16 September 1980) she dreamt that he received letters from the Transkei. In the morning she awoke and told her mother the dream. Later that day, a kinsman brought letters for her father from the Transkei. The dream was interpreted by her mother as further proof of Saliswa's having been called to be an *igqira*.

Although Lungiswa had not lived with her father for some years, she dreamt of his sister (30 September 1980):

'I dreamt that we visited father's sister's *(datata)* grave at Fish Hoek. After we came back from the graveyard, there were people fighting outside the house at Fish Hoek. That is all.'

She explained that, in the dream, the people fighting were her uncle, the husband of her father's sister, and a man who was drunk. Her father's sister is still alive and lives and works in Fish Hoek. Lungiswa had never been there. Nor had she been to a graveyard even though her sister and brother had.

Do children who live most of their lives away from their fathers dream of them as much as or more or less than do children who live with their fathers? It might be possible through an analysis of the appearance of kin in children's dreams either to check or to supplement the notion put forward by LeVine and Price-Williams (1974) that the emotional salience of kinsmen can be estimated on the basis of the use of kinship terms by children (see Chapter 5).

Tozama and Saliswa had dreams that were interpreted as being messages from the shades. Tozama had a dream that was interpreted as a prediction of her father's and mother's illness and as the first sign of her having been called to be an *igqira*. Mother and child told me the dream on separate occasions. Her mother said (1 May 1980):

'She dreamt that a man was standing next to her bed saying that she must not look at him and that he was going to kill her. She woke and ran to our room and told us the dream. We said that she must sleep on the couch in the sitting-room. The dream was repeated. The next week, both her father and I were ill. An *igqira* cannot treat her own family so we took her to another *igqira* who said. "The dream foretold your illness. She is called. Whatever she does in the house you must not shout at her. You must allow her to do or say what she likes. You must not beat her nor punish her like other children."'

Tozama's delight at the doctor's instructions have been recorded elsewhere (see Chapter 4). She told me (25 July 1980) another dream that she recalled from the past:

'I dreamt as if the beer had been made and the fathers *(obawomkhulu)* were there. I was sick and a goat was slaughtered for me, and my father's sister *(udadebobawo)* was there.'

Besides telling me the dream, she wrote about it and drew it in her book on her own initiative. She drew herself, her father's sister and a goat beside which she wrote *ibhokwe* (goat).

Figure 6-1: *Tozama's Drawing of the Ritual with the Goat.*

On the opposite page, she wrote the following in two columns:*
ndiPhuphe (I dreamt [*ukuphupha* to dream]); *ingathi* (as if); *Kusiliwe* (with beer brewed [*ukusila* – to brew]); *umqombothi* (beer); *KuKhootata* (at our father's place); *ngenye* (one [by one . . .]); *imini* (afternoon); *ndandigula* (I was sick [*ukugulisa* – to sicken; *gulayo* – sick]); *ndaxhelelwa* (was slaughtered for me [*ukuxhela* – to slaughter]); *ibhokwe* (goat); *odadobawo* (father's sister [*udadebobawo*]).

Mrs Ketshe confirmed her daughter's dream and said that as a result of it the family slaughtered a goat on her behalf in 1979. The ritual was seen as an introduction of the child to the shades. She was 7 years old at the time. The incident affords an example of a child's dream that resulted in the focusing of family and communal attention on the child's needs in a manner likely to bring satisfaction to all parties.

Saliswa's dreams were also seen as signs that she had been called. Two examples were the dreams in which she foretold that letters would arrive for her father from the Transkei and in which dogs bit her. Her mother told me (16 September 1980) that her daughter had dreamt of entering a river and, in another dream, she had been deep in a forest. She commented, 'These dreams have meaning, especially the one of the river: it means that she is called.' All three themes – the river, the forest, the biting dogs – are widely interpreted as calls from the shades. Saliswa would wake crying from the dreams and her mother said that she would listen to the account of them and comfort her.

There is a suggestion that each of the girls' mothers, who were themselves *amagqira,* had chosen a bright, sensitive, strong child from her family and had sought signs, especially in dreams, that the child would follow her profession. I do not mean to suggest that it was wholly a conscious search.

Not all mothers paid attention to their children's dream. Mrs Dyani, Lungiswa's mother, said (11 September 1980), 'She has no nightmares. She tells me her dreams but I always think she is joking. She is too young to remember them.' I recorded six of Lungiswa's dreams, three of which she described as distressing. Mrs Gonya said (8 September 1980), 'Nomvula does not have bad dreams and does not tell me her dreams. She is too young yet to tell them.' Nomvula told me two dreams, one of which, quoted above, was about her father being hurt and the other was a happy one about her sisters returning from the Transkei.

* On this occasion she demonstrated an ability to write that was far superior to any ability she had shown during formal test sessions, including one conducted four months later (see Chapter 7).

Other dreams revealed the characteristics of a child: three examples will suffice. Mlawu's love of little children was expressed in a dream. For the first half of 1980, a woman with twin babies lodged in his house. He often played with them with absorption and gentleness. Soon after the lodgers moved, he dreamt that the twins returned and that he took care of them. Another dream in which he was disturbed at being late for school illustrated his conscientiousness. Zuziwe's fear of violence was shown in two dreams in which an older boy beat her. Cebo's nervousness, which he camouflaged behind a front of bravado, came through in a dream in which children stole his wire car and ran off with it into the forest; he dared not enter because he was afraid of *skollies* (ruffians).

Some of the children's other dreams are reported in various contexts. For instance, Lungiswa's dream of a baby being born is in the discussion of birth in Chapter 2; another of her dreams and one of Hintsa's on violence in Crossroads are given in Chapter 2.

We have seen, thus far, that while the dreams of young children are often ignored some are interpreted as meaningful and portentous. Comfort is offered to a child distressed by a bad dream when an adult gives the dream shape and form and, often, a meaning opposite to the tone of the dream content. We have seen that Togu's mother comforted him saying not that the dream of his father stabbing her was unreal or immaterial or even past but that Togu was growing up, indicating that he must handle conflict such as ambivalence or rivalry and accept the compensations that increased age affords. In the following section, the results of interviews with the children based on Piaget's early work on dreams will be given.

In the interviews the children were confused as to how to interpret questions on the reality of dreams (*kwenyani* – real; *eneneni* – really; *ubuqinisa* – reality). One moment they might see dreams as being real (in the sense that any psychological phenomena are real) and then as unreal because they could not be shared nor seen by others and did not exist except in the sleeping head of one person. We must consider what reality Xhosa culture allows dreams to possess.

THE DREAM INTERVIEW
Jean Piaget (1921: 88) called dreams 'the most subjective of all phenomena' and he was interested in children's understanding of them, for he felt that '. . . the explanation of the dream supposes the duality first of the internal and the external, and secondly of thought and matter' (1921: 88). He described the technique used in studying

children's ideas about dreams as delicate and he focused his enquiry on four points which will be described shortly. Piaget (1921: 91) classified the children's answers into three distinct stages which he summarized thus:

During the first stage (approximately 5 to 6 years) the child believes the dream to come from outside and to take place within the room and he thus dreams with his eyes. Also, the dream is highly emotional: dreams often come 'to pay us out', 'because we've done something we ought not to have done', etc. During the second stage (average age 7 to 8 years) the child supposes the source of the dream to be in the head, in thought, in the voice, etc., but the dream is in the room, in front of him. Dreaming is with the eyes; it is looking at a picture outside. The fact that it is outside does not mean that it is true: the dream is unreal, but consists in an image existing outside, just as the image of an ogre may exist, without there actually being an ogre. Finally, during the third stage (about 9 to 10 years), the dream is the product of thought, it takes place inside the head (or in the eyes), and dreaming is by means of thought or else with the eyes, used internally.

The published results of his early interviews with children have been heavily criticized for being too loosely structured, too anecdotal, too difficult to replicate. He developed a methodology that emerged from this work but one that pivoted around activity on the part of the child. Despite its short-comings, the dream interview offers a format to follow and some basis for comparison. I used it for these reasons although I had a particular purpose in mind: I wanted to see whether or not the children assigned an origin and a meaning to dreams that was in accord with the traditional interpretation of origin and meaning within Xhosa culture. Piaget's loose format was followed in interviews with each child and questions pertaining to Xhosa beliefs were added at the end.

The interviews were conducted in late October and I was curious to see how the children would respond to a set of questions that were unrelated to any material or activity. In the event, I was glad that I had not relied on direct questioning in working with the children as it is surprisingly depressing to hear *andiyazi* (I don't know) repeated many times. That is not to say that nothing was learned, only that the going was heavy. The reason for children's reserve has, presumably, something to do with the place that children are assigned in the adult world. Unlike children in the West, Xhosa children are not invited to express opinions on a wide range of topics or to participate in sustained verbal exchanges with relative strangers. When adults converse, children are not supposed to stay close. Tozama's sister, aged 12, was heard reprimanding her for refusing to go outside to play. She said,

'You do not want to go and play outside because you are listening to what people are talking about, and then you answer whether or not you are addressed.'

Sometimes an adult, perhaps an *igqira* or a Crossroads Committee member or a crèche leader, would come to my room while I was working with a child. It would have been rude to turn anyone away and the children and I had to learn to accept interruptions as part of life's natural hazards. While the visitor and I talked, I would observe the child's reactions. Although she might politely take up some activity and appear not to be involved in the conversation, she would steal quick glances and sometimes react to what was being said; it was clear that some close attention was being paid.

I suspect that children listen more carefully and more often than adults, whether the adult be anthropologist or indweller, care to acknowledge. I had hoped to observe and record children's behaviour near conversing adults but being white in a black community in South Africa made me too conspicuous, too disruptive, to enable me to merge with any background. Observing children's behaviour in my presence, I noted that they would come forward to greet me, hover a while with blatant curiosity, drift off on their own business and return shortly to skirt the arena of my exchange with the adults.

Piaget loosely tied questions on dreams to four areas to do with a) the origin of dreams; b) the place of dreams; c) the organ with which one dreams and d) the reason behind dreams. Among the fourteen children, Lungiswa was the only one who suggested an origin of dreams: she said that they come from God. Cebo said later in the interview that they are made in Heaven. Both children had been told so by their mothers. Gwali's reply was apposite, 'I don't know where dreams come from because it is a long time since I dreamt.' There was no spontaneous suggestion that dreams come from the shades.

In response to questions as to where dreams occur, five children said that they happen inside the head and four outside. The replies of the four follow:

Cebo: 'It is there. It is outside the head. It is in the room near my eyes in the bed.'

Gedya: 'In the house. It is far from me.'

Peliswa: 'The dream, I think, is in the Transkei. It seems as if it is outside the head. It is inside the room.'

Hintsa: 'Outside. It is on the bed. It really happens. I am asleep when the dream is happening.'

The remaining five children said '*Andiyazi*'.

When asked about the organ of dreams, that is, with what does one dream, five said with the head, three with the eyes and one with the mouth. The last was Cebo's reply and when asked:
(What does the dream come out of?)
He replied, 'It comes out of the stomach.'
(How does it get there?)
'Nicely!'
Tozama thought the dream came by air.

There were no answers to any of the why questions: no suggestion that they might bear messages from the shades or from God.

Piaget asked his subjects a number of questions pertaining to the reality of dreams. He asked, While you dream, where is the dream? and if the response was that it was in front of the dreamer, he would ask, Is it truly in front or does it only seem to be? and, Is there really something in front of us, or is it only make-believe? While you are asleep, is the dream there? Can two people have the same dream? Is the dream real?

The children at Crossroads varied in their interpretation of the concept of reality. Five of them were firm in asserting the unreality of dreams: Togu, Nukwa, Gedja, Lungiswa and Zuziwe. The last said, 'It is not really happening. I am in bed while I dream. It happens in my head.' Four others were sure that dreams were real: Hintsa, Peliswe, Tozama and Saliswa. Peliswe, for example, said in reference to her dream of being in the forest, 'Yes, it was real. It seemed as if (ifana bonakala 'ngathi) I was in the Transkei. It seemed as if I was in the forest. I was really in my house in bed. Yes, it was a dream in my head.' Both she and Zuziwe believed that their dreams happened in their heads, yet one asserted the dreams' reality and the other their unreality.

Cebo, Gwali and Saliswa gave contradictory replies. Cebo, for instance, in response to the question, While you dream, where is the dream? said, 'It is there. It is outside the head. It is in the room near my eyes in the bed. It seems to be there but is not really there. It is real not make-believe.' Yet, in reply to a question about the reality of a nightmare, he said, 'No. It is not real. It does not happen. I don't know why we are frightened.'

With reference to a dream of his in which he had chased boys who had stolen his wire car, I asked, 'Where were you, asleep or running?' He replied, 'I was sleeping and I was running. I was really sleeping. I was really running. Mother could not have seen me run.' The children's thoughts on the question of the reality of dreams did not accord with the stages to which they were assigned in accordance with their overall responses.

Every child said that no one could see another's dream. Only Gwali suggested that a dream could be shared but changed his mind after further questioning. Half of the children said that dreams only come at night and not if one sleeps during the day.

According to Piaget's criteria, two-thirds of the children who gave enough replies to allow for a fair estimate to be made were in Stage III (that is eight out of twelve children). Two were Stage II and another two in Stage I. It is of interest that so many of the sample reached Stage III in their understanding of dreams although, on the basis of a Genevan sample, Piaget anticipated that the third stage would only be reached by children aged 10 or 11. The four children whose replies placed them in Stages I and II (Hintsa, Gedja, Gwali and Cebo) were the ones who often achieved the least well on most tasks given them during the year.

Thus far in the interview, only one child had mentioned that dreams could come from the shades or carry messages. This was so despite being asked the questions: Is the dream sent by someone? and What sends the dream? In answer to the first question, each child said 'no' except Cebo, who said that Jesus sends us dreams and they are made in Heaven. Only Peliswe gave a reply to the second question saying that the shades (izinyanya) sent them.

To Piaget's basic set of questions, I added the following: Does the dream come from the shades? Can there be a message in a dream? Can a dream tell about the future? Xhosa diviners (amagqira) believe that it can – are they correct? Eight children allowed either that the shades do send dreams (Tozama and Cebo) or that dreams can bring messages or predict the future (Zuziwe, Mlawu and Nukwa) or that amagqira are correct in believing in the predictive power of dreams. None of them was consistent in replying to these questions.

Tozama said that dreams came from the shades but do not bear messages. We discussed her dream which had been interpreted as having predicted her parent's illness and as a sign of her calling. She looked shamefaced and smiled saying:

'Yes. It is right. There are messages. There are always messages.'

(If you have a simple dream of playing outside, will there be a message in the dream?)

'I don't know.'

(Who knows if a dream has a message?)

'My mother.'

(Does she always see a message or only sometimes?)
'Always.'
(Can you see messages in dreams?)
'Yes. I can see it.'

Cebo, too, agreed that dreams came from the shades but denied that they carried messages or predicted the future or that *amagqira*'s beliefs were correct. I asked him if Jesus was a shade and he replied, 'Yes. He was a black man.'

Zuziwe said, 'A dream can tell about the future. I don't know who sends messages.' Mlawu and Nukwa replied similarly. Gwali responded with negatives to the first two questions yet he said that *amagqira*'s beliefs were correct. Peliswe was similarly confused. Saliswa denied that shades sent dreams or that dreams could carry messages or predict the future. When I asked her if the *amagqira*'s beliefs were correct, I added that her mother (an *igqira*) probably believed as they did. She replied:

'Yes, she does. There are messages.'
(Who sends them?)
'I don't know.'
(The shades?)
'Yes.'
(So they can send messages in dreams?)
'Yes.'
(Have you had a message from the shades?)
'No.'
(Has your mother?)
'Yes.'
(Your mother says that you have been called to be an *igqira*. Is that right?)
'Yes.'

Piaget (1921: 116) felt that suggestion had little effect on a child's thinking even at Stage II. Yet, when reminded of their mother's opinions, Saliswa and Tozama altered their own.

Both Togu and Hintsa had been firm in their earlier denials that there was a source for a message in dreams, yet both replied more cautiously with *andiyazi* to this set of questions. Gedja was sure of her disbelief and Lungiswa reaffirmed her understanding that dreams come from God. Neither Yameka nor Nomvula gave any replies.

The dream interviews support suggestions that have been made in some other pieces of research that maturational processes can be detected in children's understanding of dreams but that they learn their societies' beliefs and adopt them so that they override the former. There seemed to be an effort on the part of some children to switch consciousness when faced with questions that reflected others' actual beliefs. Piaget concluded his chapter on dreams with a call for the repetition of the study in different countries in order that the part played by adult influences may be more definitely separated from the spontaneous and constant conviction of the child. On the basis of a number of studies done in various European centres, Piaget (1921: 122) asserted his belief that the child's conviction maintains a constancy and spontaneity that preponderates over the effect of adult influence. I suggest that the context in which one questions a child, including the manner in which questions are put, that is, whether they are generalized queries or tied to particular beliefs held by adults in the child's world, affects the child's responses. There is, obviously, a need to understand the theories about and the uses of dreams in a society before an analysis of children's conceptual grasp of the phenomena can be undertaken.

AN IGQIRA'S VIEWS ON DREAMS

The third section of this chapter is a resumé of an *igqira*'s views of childhood and dreams. The *igqira*, whom I shall call Phalo, lived in Crossroads but travelled widely across the Republic. He had had very little formal schooling but had taught himself to read and write. He was born in Cacadu, in the Transkei, on 3 May 1933, and as a young teenager he had, he said, spent long periods alone in the forest and with the river people in the process of becoming an *igqira*. Phalo had thought deeply about childhood and its place in the cosmic whole. He was curious about Western notions of child development and medical treatment and had formulated ideas as to how they differ and what aspects of them might be seen to supplement or contradict each other. It is not easy to estimate to what extent one *igqira*'s views represent those of others because it is unethical to discuss the ideas offered to one in trust with potential or actual competitors. In order to do justice to the description of Xhosa theories about dreams and childhood, a full study would be necessary. Phalo's views, which follow, offer a sketch of the kinds of ideas to which a Xhosa child in Crossroads may be introduced.

Phalo told me that:

An infant is born with her fists clenched. In both hands are her gifts. In the right fist she holds her future as an adult and in the left her dreams. Dreams come from the shades. A child dreams because she is the creation of all the people.

Dreams give signs of what the child will be. Every dream is in accord with a person's origin, language and customs. Dreams may even direct the play of a child. The child's life plan is revealed through dreams, even details such as when she will walk. Parents should not, therefore, be concerned about variations in the age at which development occurs. Children have power through their dreams adults do not. Adult teaching can result in the loss of the dreams' strength and revelations. Gifts are diluted when parents teach a child to use their minds. The child must respond to teaching with an inner receptiveness or she will learn nothing. Adults should allow the child space and freedom in which to grow and use her gifts. Too often the will of adults dominates the child's mind.

If a child cries in her sleep, she is dreaming of the shades. The shades are visiting the new person in the family. They are strangers to the child and she is naturally afraid. Laughter in a child who is asleep is a sign of the child's love of people. As an adult, she will have peace among people and never be lonely. Troubled dreams may signify that the child has been called to become an *igqira*. These dreams are often of animals. In order to interpret the dreams accurately, the child's origin must be known. This should include her position in her mother's womb and the strengths and weaknesses of her parents when they formed her. Throughout the process of her initiation, the child will dream. When she is old enough, she will tell her dreams.

The interpretation of dreams varies. Some themes recur. For example, if a child dreams of flying like a bird, Xhosa custom says that it is a dream of growing up. A dream of being bitten by a dog represents recognition by the shades: that child will keep the customs [see Mrs Qasana's interpretation of Saliswa's dreams in this chapter]. Dreams come through difficulties and reflect the child's needs. If a child dreams of water and wakes crying and running, it is a sign that as an adult she will be alone, unloved and uncared for.

SUMMARY

Earlier sections of the chapter recorded that some children by the age of 8 had had their attention drawn to facets of the detail in dream interpretation within Xhosa culture. It was suggested that there may be different levels of consciousness among children in their understanding of dreams. Sigmund Freud said,

for a child, like an adult, can produce phantasies only from material which has been acquired from some source or other . . . (Freud, 1925: 529)

and

. . . a child catches hold of his phylogenetic experience where his own experience fails him. He fills in the gaps in individual truth; he replaces occurrences in his own life by occurrences in the life of his ancestors. I fully agree with Jung in recognizing the existence of this phylogenetic inheritance;

but I regard it as a methodological error to seize upon a phylogenetic explanation before the ontogenetic possibilities have been exhausted (Freud, 1925: 577).

Freud wanted us first to explore the ontogenetic possibilities, that is, the mechanisms of growth (or the origin and development of the individual being). The *igqira*, Phalo, is closer to Jung in holding that the mechanisms of growth cannot be understood unless the 'origin, roots, language and customs' of the people are known. Jung and Phalo would agree that these inform the unconscious and are expressed through both action and dreams. Piaget (1970b: 166) exhorts us to formulate 'a solid third position' that explores 'the mechanisms of growth (ontogenesis) in their relation with heredity and above all the phylogenetic relation between heredity and milieu.' The dreams of children in different cultures may offer a format for such an exploration.

7

The Children and Order

The chapter reports details of the way in which the children ordered their thoughts and actions. It describes what tools they could muster in making sense of the world; what vocabulary they had in store; what control they wielded over their perceptual and physical powers; what mastery they had achieved over pen and paper; what confidence and experience they brought to their initiation into the world of reading, writing and number. Piaget once said (1947), 'Life is a creator of patterns.' I sought to discover what patterns the children of Crossroads were making out of the pieces life had, thus far, seen fit to provide.

During the year, I set out to document what skills the children possessed in ordering their conceptions of the world. I observed how the children acted during test sessions: the attention they paid to the matter in hand; their span of concentration; their need for encouragement; their resistance, either passive or active; their interest or lack of interest; their response to instructions; their attitude towards a task, including the bewilderment, efficiency, anxiety or caution with which they set about it. I sought to document minutely interfering factors (obstructions not related to actual ability) in test behaviour. With a small sample I was able to notice when a particular situation troubled a certain child and to link that concern to other facets of the child's life.

I also recorded the children's level of skill displayed over time and in a variety of situations. On many occasions during the year the children had to do tasks such as counting, writing, adding or sorting objects. I have combined these in giving the results. Tests were administered to each child at different intervals during the year. Most of the tests took only a few minutes to administer to each child. These tests included sorting, writing, counting, drawing of a person and Piaget's tests of the conservation of number and class inclusion. The results of tests given over time are useful in estimating the impact of schooling or of my work with the children and in demonstrating whether or not cognitive ability rather than experience on a particular task is being measured.

The aims outlined above affect the style in which the findings are reported. While I paid close attention to the rules that psychologists have formulated for the administration of tests, I shall not give the results according to the format used by psychologists, because it is the individual's response to the whole situation and the link to environmental factors that I wish to emphasize. As a result, the following sections demand that the reader pay close attention to small items of behaviour. In order to persuade the reader that the children in the sample are not atypical of the population of 7- to 8-year-olds in Crossroads, I compared their test results on five Piagetian tasks with the results of a control group of twenty-five children in Crossroads who attended the same two schools.

I administered a series of Piagetian tests including those that tested conservation concepts, relational concepts (seriation), classificatory concepts (class inclusion) and special concepts (projective imagery) to the sample children and the control group. The data confirmed that the sample children were representative in terms of experience and home background of 7-year-old children in Crossroads. And the test results confirmed that they were alike in terms of developmental maturity.

The Piagetian tests were used for other reasons. Two of the tests (the conservation of discontinuous quantities and the class inclusion tasks) were used as a form of pre-test against which change among the sample group could be measured after a year. The tests were also used in order to offer some base upon which to compare levels of skill between the Crossroads and other children. I used Piaget's tasks because they offer a way to probe the nature of children's rediscovery of the fundamental operations of thought and their re-invention of them through their own activity. The somewhat hallowed *méthode clinique* uses probing questions that attempt to reveal the underlying reasons for a child's initial statement or judgement, by presenting counter-suggestions to the child's arguments, and by providing conflict situations that enable one to discover cognitive functioning (Ginsberg and Opper, 1979: 235). The use of this method among children in non-Western societies can be problematic for obvious reasons. I followed Piaget's test procedure and scoring criteria although some allowance had to be made when children did not explain fully the reasons for their actions.

PIAGETIAN TESTS

The Control Group

A control group of twenty-five children was chosen from the same four classes in the two Crossroads schools that the ten sample children attended. The average age of the sample children was then 7 years and 5 months. There were thirteen boys and twelve girls. All the children had seen me frequently walking or driving around Crossroads and collecting the sample children from their classrooms. Many of them had visited my room and played with my balls, puzzles, marbles, etc. Wherever children were gathered they would chorus *umlungu* (white person) on catching sight of me and later *Nosapho* (mother of children: *usapho* the family) which is the name that the residents gave me.

Each child was tested individually on all seven tests. Care was taken to imitate Piaget's technique, to make each child feel comfortable and relaxed and to anticipate problems.* The tests are described in Appendix D.

Results. The results have been presented as percentages of those who succeed on each test in Figures 7–1, 7–2, and 7–3.

The tests performed on the data are for the samples of ten school-going children and of all the fourteen children versus the control group of twenty-five children. No significant difference between either sample group and the control was found. The results were similar in pattern for all three groups. Out of the seven tasks, the sample children scored slightly better than the control group on six of the seven tests. On the pre-test of the conservation of discontinuous quantity and the conservation of number, the sample children did less well than did those in the control group. However, in the mid-year and post-tests, the sample did better. The poor results of the pre-tests relative to later scores suggests that psychological tests administered by strangers in novel situations may yield scores that do not accurately reflect actual ability.

On all the five tasks to do with conservation ability, the sample of ten conserved on 62 per cent of them; the sample of fourteen on 57 per cent and the control on 52 per cent. Piaget's conservation criterion is 75 per cent. The sample of ten does not fall far below it. See the results of the tests administered to the sample and control groups in Table 7–1 in Appendix G.

The results of the test on class inclusion were much poorer than the results of the conservation tests and have, therefore, been analysed in detail in the following section. (See Appendix D for a description of the test and its variations.)

* For a careful account of the technique followed in administering Piagetian tests in a non-Western society see G.W. Seagrim and R.J. Lendon, *Furnishing the Mind. A Comparative Study of Cognitive Development in Central Australian Aborigines*. Sydney: Academic Press, 1980, p.63ff.

Class Inclusion

On the basis of his studies in Geneva, Jean Piaget (1966: 103) said that 'the understanding of the relative sizes of an included class to the entire class is achieved at about 8 and marks the achievement of a genuine operatory classification.' Each of the three groups that were tested (the sample, the control and fourteen illiterate women of Crossroads*) performed noticeably less well on the class inclusion test than they did on the four conservation tests. The first test administered was the original bead test and the second was one using small plastic animals – three horses and seventeen sheep. The protocol was the same for both except that I added a market question to the second task. Having clarified with the subject that the horses and sheep were all animals, I asked: if your father took you to market and upon showing you these animals in a *kraal*, he asked if you would like to take home the sheep or the animals what would you answer?

As might have been expected the scores on the latter set of materials are better than on the task using beads. Not much better, however. The protocols mirror those quoted by Piaget. The same apparent understanding is belied by the answers to the questions. For example, subject 16 (Mxo), in the control group, agreed that the sheep and the horses were all animals. In reply to the question: Are there more sheep or more animals?, he said:

'More sheep.'
(Show me the animals.)
'All of them.'
(Are there more sheep than animals?)
'Yes.'
(I gave the market problem and asked whether he would take the sheep or the animals.)
'I would take the horses.'
(I pointed out that his father had not offered him the horses but all the sheep or all the animals.)
'I would take them all.'
(Then are there more sheep or more animals?)
'More sheep.'

Occasionally, I would add another task in an attempt to understand why the subjects found it so difficult. I presented seventeen drawings of

* A group of women met with me one afternoon every week for six months: their stories of their past and present provided a background against which I could set the experiences of children. Seventy-five per cent of the women conserved on tests 2, 3 and 4a.

children to Nukwa. He identified five as boys and twelve as girls. He sorted them accordingly and agreed that they were all children. In response to the question as to whether there were more girls or more children he said,
  'More girls.'
  (If a man came to your school and asked you to call the children together so that he could take them to the circus, whom would you call – the girls or the children?)
  'I would call the children of Noxolo.'
  (Would you call all the children or all the boys?)
  'I would call all the children.'
  (Now, tell me, are there more girls or more children here?)
  'More girls.'
  Gwali's reply was similar.

The women also failed to score as well on this problem as on the conservation tests. Before using the beads, we discussed colour terms.
  Every woman could name the basic colours, some in English and Xhosa; some used only one or the other language. Many of them knew the more common Xhosa names and specific names used only for beads. They said that their mothers had taught them the names while threading beads. At about the age of 6 or 7, little girls would pick up beads that had been dropped and learn to create patterns on blades of grass. The mother would correct them and teach them to count at the same time. The women no longer teach their children in like manner, if only because beads are too expensive to buy. When I could afford it, I would provide beads at our weekly meetings and the women would make necklaces and other items while we talked. They took the completed items home.
  The intricacy of the women's bead work, the complicated use of design and colour, the incorporation of geometric figures, the use of line and space and the speed with which a pattern would emerge leaves one wondering at their failure to achieve an operational level on Piaget's class inclusion test. The women all counted to seventy in the conservation test using either English or Xhosa. Five could not count in English. Two could count to 10; three to 200 and three to any number, in English. In Xhosa one woman said she could only count to 20 and two to 40 whereas they counted the beads to 70. Two claimed to be able to count to 70; three to 100; one to 500 and four to any number. None had learnt to count in a formal situation.
  Regina Twala (1951) wrote a treatise on the use of beads among the

Zulu to code messages. The code could form a good base for Piagetian-type tests in an area where it is still learned.

In learning beadwork from women, girls were taught to count, sort, order, organize patterns and manipulate small objects. I had hoped to use such training in devising tests but poverty and family disruption, among other factors, have broken the tradition of work with beads among these women.

Only two women scored on an operational level (Stage III); another's performance was marked as transitional (Stage II). The text of their replies is similar to the children's. I repeated the test using different objects. In one series, I used one-rand coins (large and silver) and one-cent coins (small, brass) and a story about ironing. First I explored with each woman the words she used for coins, rand and cent. A surprising variety was used: for coins amatye (stones), losgeld (Afrikaans for change), imwangalala (change) and coins (English); for rand either rand, or white money in Xhosa; all the women used the word cent.

I put the Piagetian questions to Notyhefu, asking her if there were more cents or more coins (17 cents + 3 rand) using the words familiar to her. She was firm in her decision that, 'There are more cents. They are more in number than the rand.' I said, 'Now suppose I am a white lady in a private house and you have done my ironing. I say, "Notyhefu, thank you, you have finished. Go to the table and take either the cents or the coins." What would you take?'

Notyhefu replied, 'I would take the three rand.' She thought a moment then said angrily, 'I would take it all, and I would ask for more. It is not enough for the ironing.' On being asked the original question she returned to her earlier position.' With the other women, I took care to say that each had done a little ironing.

Colette's response was similar. In response to the ironing question she said:

'I would take the rand.'
(Why would you leave the cents?)
'I must choose.'
(You were told to take the cents or the coins.)
'Then I would take it all.'
(You mean you would take the coins?)
'Yes.'
(Then are there more cents or more coins here?)
'There are more cents.'

Nokoyo gave similar replies but when asked a question to do with ikhazi using small plastic animals, twelve sheep and eight horses, she replied differently. The problem set was as follows: Nokoyo's daughter was to marry. The father of the prospective son-in-law offered Nokoyo's family his sheep or his animals. What would the family choose? Nokoyo said, 'The animals' and kept to it on the repeat of the formal questioning using the plastic animals.

The women did better with these problems than on the task using beads, but not remarkably better.

Three points that are worth pondering emerge from the testing of the women. One is that it seems unlikely that, outside the test situation, the women had not yet gone 'beyond the initial prelogical level' (Piaget, 1966: 184) of a 6- or 7-year-old on class-inclusion, especially as Piaget linked it to the seriation of relationships and operational generalization of number and so to the level of reversible operations. Piaget (1966: 157) claimed that '. . . the concept of class does not precede that of a number, but is acquired simultaneously, the two concepts being interdependent.'

The second point that emerged from the tests given to illiterate women is that problems of language are much easier to discuss with adults. As demonstrated above, the women were familiar with different words from the ranges that referred to colours and coins. This is, no doubt, a phenomenon of fairly recent migration from country to city and of dialectical differences in their speech. The performance of children in similar circumstances is possibly handicapped by the absence of common word coinage even within their own language.

The final point is that as I administered tests to the women, I became aware of a sense of unease. I felt like a charlatan. The women and I had been meeting for four hours every week for over four months and a strained atmosphere was easily detectable. A few days later, Mary reported that the women were grumbling. They felt that during the tests they were being tricked and they did not like it. At the next session, we discussed it and I admitted to having felt foolish administering the tests. I laughed with them about their underground rumblings and explained more clearly the reasons for giving the tests. They were content. That is the kind of feedback one seldom gets in psychological testing. How often, I wonder, do children feel that they are being duped, especially in Piagetian tests where the correct answers are neither apparent nor offered at the conclusion of the experiment?

The women's greater facility with words and, therefore, explanations made me wonder if the children were not hindered by unease as often as an actual lack of understanding.

The rest of this chapter gives the results of a variety of tests administered to the children in the sample during one year.

SORTING TASKS
Two relatively simple tasks were given to each child in March and November. Each child was asked to sort eighteen cards according to colour and size. The cards were commercially produced for a 'Learning to Reason' activity; each card had either a large or small triangle or circle or square in either red, blue or yellow. I used them as a starting point for discussions of shape and colour and as an exercise during which I could observe the child's response to instructions and attention to order.

Every child could do both exercises, although some needed encouragement. The tasks were given to the children in our first session; everything was, of course, strange and a little threatening. The next occasion was towards the end of our working relationship. Two points of interest emerge from the sorting tasks: many children did not follow the directions and some did not attend to the matter in hand unless pressed to do so.

A strong tenet of Xhosa culture is that children must be obedient and respectful to their elders. Equally strong is the tenet of middle class Western society that children must pay attention if they are to succeed. Many formal tests (including, I would claim, Piagetian) measure, at least in part, the ability or willingness to devote undivided attention to the parameters and detail of any given situation.

Colour
Nine of the children could name six colours each, including black and white, five could name only three. None had a sizeable vocabulary nor could anyone identify many colours given their names. There was no discernible increase in their vocabularies during the year. Many of them used the Xhosa word *luhlaza* for either or both blue and green. Some used a few words adopted from English like *ipinki*. In the light of Monica Hunter's (1936: 70) record of there being 57 terms used to name the colours of cattle, the paucity in these children's colour vocabulary is significant. (See Appendix F for a brief report on conversations recorded with herd-boys about their knowledge of the traditional colour vocabulary and the names of trees and birds.)

Shapes
No child in the sample had in her vocabulary either an English or a Xhosa word for circle, square or triangle, either at the beginning or the

end of the year.

Writing

Thrice during the year, the children were asked to write their names, and twice to form their names using letter blocks. None of those who did not attend school could do either, nor could they recognize any letters. Three of the school-going children could neither form their names with block letters, nor read or write them on any occasion.

The other six children could each write their first names and three of them could write their surnames at the beginning of the year. Most used upper case letters but none consistently nor accurately.

The fourteen children made little progress over a year in sounding letters, recognizing letters, forming their names with letters on blocks or in writing their names. Whatever impact schooling had made or whatever it had taught them, it was not apparent in the measures made of their concepts of number, colour vocabulary, or writing ability. Experience in school had not necessarily equipped the children with a good rudimentary base with which to learn essential skills or trained them to use techniques useful in ordering and organizing learning situations. Nevertheless, in comparing children who did with those who did not attend school during the year, it was clear that some of the school-going children acquired skills in addition to writing that the non-school-goers did not possess. On cross-cultural research on cognition Scribner (1977) suggests that the impact of even a small amount of schooling on test success is dramatic. The need, now, is to go beyond this level and examine the impact of schooling in terms of its quality.

READING

In an earlier section of this chapter, the children's ability to handle a test on classification (class-inclusion) was examined and some possible reasons for their failure were put forward. Let us now turn to a less structured examination of their ability to classify, that is an analysis of the skills involved in learning to read.

J. F. Reid (1966: 61) published an informative study of children's conception of the reading process. She says that the process involves '. . . an understanding of hierarchical structure in its simplest form (that of a notion of a class with two or more sub-classes). In short, the children had to come to see that language and pictures are two kinds of symbol, that letters and numerals are sub-classes in the class of written symbols, that "names" form a sub-class in the class of words, and that capitals form a sub-class in the class of letters.'

Using a structured interviewing technique, Reid studied twelve Edinburgh school-children from families of varied socio-economic backgrounds. The children were 5 years old and in their first year of school. Her interviews were loosely structured and the questions were worded in ways that left the children free to use, or not to use, terms like 'word', 'letter' and 'sentence', and free to mention the features of standard orthography. Her purpose was to encourage the children to talk and not, in any narrow sense, to obtain information on specific points.

What emerged as important for Reid (1966: 58), 'was the general lack of any specific expectancies of what reading was going to be like, of what the activity consisted of, the purpose and use of it, of the relationship between reading and writing; and a great poverty of linguistic equipment to deal with the new experiences, calling letters 'numbers' and words 'names' . . . It was also found that the children did not mention that books contained stories.' The fourteen children at Crossroads were similarly in the dark.

Four children replied to the query as to what the spaces between words were for, with the following: Peliswe, 'To read well'; Togu, 'So that the words must not be mixed'; Lungiswa, 'It is because the words must be absolute' *(pheleleyo)*; and Tozama, 'They are to separate the words from each other.' Their replies are more explicit than those given by the 5-year-olds in Edinburgh but more of the latter gave an explanation.

My immediate concern was to describe the skills that each child had at her disposal to marshal as necessary in a variety of situations. Her stock of conscious understanding of the symbols and their connecting fabric that make up reading and writing was low. Apart from Hintsa, the children who did not go to school and the 'drop-out' gave far fewer replies to the interview questions and did not use vocabulary such as 'words', 'numbers' or 'letters' (one child said that her father read 'words' to her). The others seemed to learn during the interview. The children exhibited similar linguistic and conceptual uncertainties about the nature of the material that they had to organize as did the 5-year-olds in Scotland. Reid (1966: 61) says that, 'The resolution of these difficulties lay in learning difference between pictures and written symbols, as two modes of conveying information, and then learning to discriminate between two classes of symbol, the alphabetical and the numerical. They had to discover what "words" are, and that almost all language, written or spoken, is composed of these, though written language also contains marks of other kinds. They had to learn, furthermore, to think of a "sound" and to realize that written words are spatially ordered groups of letters bearing a systematic relation to the temporally ordered sounds of speech. To achieve effective understanding at this level, it is probably necessary to be able to use correctly "letter" and "number" (or, better, "numeral") and to associate these with reading and counting respectively; also to use the term "word" in some sense which will distinguish it from "letter" in writing and "sound" in speech.'

There is a room for confusion in the Xhosa vocabulary. The children did not know the word for alphabet: I do not think that there is one other than a phrase or an adaptation of the English word. The word for vocabulary is *isigama,* the root of which is used for a word or a name. A word can also be called *ilizwe* which can, too, mean a voice. *Inani* refers to a number, or numeral, or figure. While *ukubala* can mean to count, enumerate, calculate, compute, reckon or number. A sound is *isandi.*

Appropriate basic research is needed on children's cognitive development, especially among those denied easy access to experience with the written word.

COUNTING

The ability to count is a culturally learned skill. To discover whether or not the children in the sample could count and how firm their ability was across situations, we played with numbers on different occasions during the years. Table 7–2 in Appendix G sets out the measurable results.

I want to suggest that the relationship between counting and number conservation must be carefully researched before Piaget's tests of number conservation are administered cross-culturally and that more attention should be paid to actual number conception before mathematical skills are introduced. I shall give the findings briefly as, while the matter is important, I tested neither systematically nor extensively enough to reach firm conclusions.

Of the fourteen children, five could count as high as they were asked to do throughout the year; two seemed to regress; two remained as poor at the end of the year as at the beginning and five improved. There was no improvement during the year on the recognition of numerals up to 20. There was some improvement in the addition of small sums.

Three points that are related to the above will be considered. One is that the findings confirm Piaget's statement that counting verbally is not the same as the ability to conserve number.

The second is that a child who could not count to 10 could not conserve. This was true for the sample of fourteen and the control group of twenty-five. The final point is that no child conserved unless she first placed the counters in one-to-one correspondence. Again this was true for children from the sample and the control.

On the basis of the exercises across the year, I have concluded that the ability to count is a necessary but not sufficient skill in being able to conserve on Piaget's number test for this population. And that the ability to place objects in one-to-one correspondence is also necessary but not sufficient. Not the recognition of numerals, or the ability to write them, or facility in adding small amounts is necessary to success on the conservation of number task.

The table is perhaps useful for one other purpose and that is as a rough guide to the amount that the children did nor did not learn during the year. Learning among the school-going children was certainly not uniform. The effects of the school boycott should be kept in mind. By the end of their first year of formal schooling, two of the ten children could not recognize numerals up to 10 and one could recognise only a few; three could not add small sums; four could not write the numerals 1 to 20; and one could not count accurately even up to 12. Some of the children could recognize numerals up to 10 (five); add small sums (three); write numerals 1 to 20 (six) and count to 12 (six) at the beginning of the school year. Of the four children who did not go to school one failed to improve his counting ability, one seemed to regress and two improved. Only one conserved and none learnt to recognize, write or add numerals.

In February, I played dice with each of the fourteen children. We had one large dice each, about three centimetres square with clearly marked, symmetrically arranged dots. First the child counted each face and we talked about dice and their existence in Crossroads. It was a common sight to see a group of men, usually young, playing dice in the dust of the streets. Each of the school-children could count each face except Cebo who did not count accurately each time and insisted on counting the 3 and 3 of the 6 separately. The children and I played a simple game: one of us would select a number and the first to throw it would win a point. Each could play although Cebo and Nukwa laboriously counted the face before they could recognize the number and call it out. Two girls (Lungiswa and Nomvula) attempted to determined the fall of the dice and two boys (Mlawu and Togu) played with relish, Togu clicking his fingers as the dice rolled.

Only one non-school-going child (Gedja) could count each face and play. Saliswa could count the faces but not recognize them in play.

Neither of the other two could count or play.

In November we played dominoes using firm white cards 7,5 x 15 centimetres divided by a black line and marked by large black dots arranged asymmetrically. Again the child would count the dots and we would discuss the rules and the fact that only half the card was to be considered at a time. Then we played. I dealt the starting domino, a double 6, to the child. Dominoes caused more problems than did dice for obvious reasons of complexity, and, no doubt, unfamiliarity.

Seven of the school-children played adequately and three never quite mastered the game. Two of the non-school-going children played fairly well and two did not. Interestingly, Gwali, who only ever counted to 6, played pretty well apart from having some difficulty with 6; and the two who had been able to count since March were not very adept.

My findings on the children's ability to play with number suggest that for these children the concept of number (despite the ability to count and for some of them to conserve) is not yet a tool to be wielded with full confidence. The implications for school learning are obvious.

To conclude, I shall relate an incident that was told to me at Crossroads. A young Xhosa man in the Transkei had gone on a bike with his school mates and a master. Upon their return, he was amazed to see that the master *counted* the boys in order to check if they had all returned. Furthermore, the master went through a process of elimination in order to determine who was missing. When the storyteller had been younger, he and other boys would herd animals. They would gather them together in large groups to guide them home. Each herdboy would look at them and know at a glance if all the beasts belonging to his herd were there and, in the same glance, which one(s) was/were missing or slow.*

It reminds me of the story of the 'Six Fishermen' each of whom, at the end of the day's fishing, counted his brothers to ensure that all were safe but each forgot to count himself and so they mourned the loss of one of them.

While in the Transkei, I played some games with the herdboys, trying to reach such abilities. I was impressed by their ability to scan the herd in a valley from quite high up a mountain and to point out and name individual beasts, and by their discussion on the size and composition of each other's herds. More work needs to be done on traditional ways of handling number, its comparison with urban experience and the implications for schooling.

* Mary Douglas refers to this ability among shepherds in *Evans–Pritchard* (1980), Glasgow: Fontana, p.76.

PERCEPTUAL-MOTOR CO-ORDINATION

In May I administered to the sample children the Purdue Perceptual-Motor Survey that was compiled and standardized by Drs Roach and Kephart (1966). It represents a direct action approach to non-achiever problems and the normative data were developed with children between 6 and 10 years of age in the USA. In administering the test, I hoped to identify major physical or perceptual problems that the children might have or, conversely, to affirm their normality on this score. I was also keen to see if such a test would pin-point areas of inadequacy that could be related to differences in cultural expectations or socio-economic status.

It is an extensive survey and yields 36 scores plus a score derived from the Human Figure Drawings and records of eye movements and the use of a dominant eye, hand or foot. The results are discussed in five sections that scored the child's ability to copy geometric shapes; to write her name; to imitate rhythmic writing; to make lines and circles with chalk; to perform physical actions. The survey was designed to identify non-achievers between age 6 and 10 and the testers expected most children to perform successfully on almost every task, taking age into consideration. There is no doubt that, according to the norms, none of the sample children performed perfectly overall. See Table 7–3 in Appendix G.

Physical Activities

I was surprised by the children's lack of control over their bodies in the physical activities. The scores in section 5 seem high but the execution left much to be desired. No pattern of difference between boys and girls was detectable. The children found it difficult to obey verbal instructions, particularly for skipping, change of rhythm and rhythmic hopping. There was much confusion over the Angel activity in which a child lies on her back and moves her arms and legs in turn according to aural, visual or tactile instructions. Nothing remarkable here except that such difficulties were not anticipated by the testers for USA children. Once again, the children's failure to attend closely to particular instructions impeded their performance. The children's weight and height are given in Table 7–4. Only Nukwa was undernourished and Peliswe's weight was low. On tests of physical ability, Nukwa scored well and Peliswe poorly.

Geometric Shapes

Seven geometric shapes had to be copied from cards. The first three

(a. ○; b. +; c. □) presented few problems although my marking was lenient. Only two children could not form an acceptable cross. Three could not copy the next shape (d. △) and performance on the final three shapes was poor (e. ▓ ; f. ◇; g. ◇). Only three children copied (e) and five copied (f) and (g) fairly well.

Chalk

In the use of chalk, each child had to draw a circle on a blackboard with one hand and then two circles simultaneously with a piece of chalk in each hand. Two points had to be joined by a line first laterally then vertically. Eight children had difficulty with the two circles.

Rhythmic writing patterns

A series of patterns was presented to each child, who had to copy them in the shape provided. The results were barely acceptable from any child because the children either had just begun to attend or did not attend school and few had much access to pen and paper.

According to those who formulated and standardized the test, there are five pointers to the existence of non-achievement: if a child is unable (one) to balance well; (two) to change rhythm on instruction; (three) to copy 'e'; (four) to copy 'g'; and (five), to make chalk circles using both hands. If a child is unable to do these tasks then it is likely that co-ordination is affected by the perceptual–motor deficiency.

In retrospect, it can be seen that the seven children (Mlawu, Peliswe, Togu, Tozama, Yameka, Lungiswa and Zuziwe) who performed well on the Purdue Motor–Perception Survey also performed well on most of the year's exercises.

The same relationship between this test and others held for the five who did poorly. I would suggest that, ideally, the administration of tests across cultures be preceded by motor–perception surveys and physical examinations. Health and physical control must be linked to test performance. Both may be assumed to be in order in wealthy communities; neither may be assumed among the economically oppressed. We should know the constraints in any testing situation.

SHOPPING

Let us consider how children order shopping, an activity in which each of them is involved almost daily. During the seven evenings that each child was observed at home, each was despatched by an adult to the shops at least once an evening. Some went gladly and some, like Zuziwe, reluctantly. In some homes, a child was sent three or four times in one evening, each time to make a single purchase. Sometimes the child would be sent only once the need for the item was obvious such as for a candle after dark, or sugar when the tea had been prepared, or bread when supper was ready. The frequent trips and late purchase are, no doubt, the result of poverty: little cash, sparingly spent. Children often went to the shops for sweets. A number of fathers were greeted on their return from work by excited displays of warmth and the request for a few cents with which to buy sweets.

There were many tiny shops in Crossroads. Some of them were no larger than cupboards. The quantity of goods varied but the range was not very great. Prices varied sometimes by as much as 5 cents for the same item and one of the arts of a good housewife was to know which shopkeeper cut his price on which item in order to attract customers. Shops provided meeting grounds where news and gossip were exchanged. For children, excitement tinged with fear often accompanied excursions to shop at night.

It was suggested to me that while young children in Crossroads might not perform very ably on formal tests, they carried complicated messages and shopped reliably and efficiently. I decided to investigate with the sample children by giving each child R2,00, a basket and a verbal list of eleven items that fell in seven categories, with the request that she purchase them for me.

Another purpose behind the exercise was to check whether or not the children had difficulty in following instructions in a familiar task. Such difficulty seemed to have hampered performance on other tasks, in particular the Purdue Motor–Perception examination (see previous section). I was curious to see what techniques of ordering the children might use in recalling a list and with what success they could remember it.

For the exercise, three shopkeepers agreed to co-operate. Two shops were near the schools and the third near the homes of the children who did not attend school. The shopkeepers were asked to give each child the incorrect amount of change. The list and prices follow:

Categories	Number of Items	Price
1.	1 packet of sugar	30c
2.	1 bottle of milk	25c
3.	1 box Omo soap powder	28c
4.	2 boxes of matches	4c
5.	1 packet of beans	28c

6.	4 lollipops	8c
7.	1 packet of tea	20c
	TOTAL	R1,43

Prices varied in the shops, for example:

Item	Shops:	I	II	III
Omo		28	16	15 cents
Beans		28	30	30 cents
Tea		20	18	15 cents

In shops II and III, we substitued a candle for milk as the latter was not stocked. One candle cost 9 cents.

Each child was given the money, the basket and the list (verbally), which was repeated once. We chose a quiet time of day so that the shops were not crowded.

Results

While it must be seldom, if ever, that the children are given such a long shopping list, the success of two of them in purchasing every item suggests that the task was not too difficult. The exercise was not meant to be a formal test of memory. Nevertheless, certain points of interest emerged. Not one child asked for clarification as to size or brand name. All the children used English words for the money. No child visibly attempted to count the number of categories or items read out nor classify them into groups such as edible/inedible. Nor was it suggested that they do so. Peliswe and Tozama voluntarily repeated the list to me after the first reading – the two who were always the most confident in seeking clarification on task directions. Both scored well. Togu, Hintsa and Gwali returned shortly after leaving to make the purchases and asked me to read out the list again.

This task seemed to stir up more emotion and reluctance than most other exercises. It was September and the children were used to our sessions: perhaps the length of the list, the task itself or the involvement of others (the shopkeepers) bothered some of them. Peliswe, Lungiswa, Tozama and Cebo were noted as being confident. The last two were also cheerful as was Mlawu, despite the fact that he twice predicted that he would forget things. Peliswe was harried and had trouble concentrating because her teacher was annoyed with her for having got 2/10 for her sums and was exasperated by having her called out of the classroom by me. I had to make peace later. She was the only teacher who was sometimes hostile towards my interruptions. So little was achieved in some classes during the year, partly as a consequence of the school boycott, that I did not feel too guilty.

Two children came to this particular session reluctantly. Nukwa was brought crying and resisting by his mother. As she led him through my door, she was saying to him, 'Do you know that those people who are not educated work hard in the mines? Sometimes the mine collapses on the heads of a thousand or a hundred people. I am thinking of you. You do not want to be educated. What will happen to you?' The child did not reply. She left and I talked to him saying that he did not have to come (Bateson's double bind in view of his mother's tirade?) but I would miss him if he did not as I was fond of him and enjoyed working with him. He laughed and looked happy and set about his shopping in good spirits. He did well.

Hintsa was the other reluctant participant. He came unwillingly. His mood was not lightened by Mary who asked, 'Why are you so very dirty and ill-dressed? Why did you not wash and change from the clothes in which you slept?' Hintsa said that not his mother or his grandmother (father's sister) or the young bride who was staying in the house were at home when he awoke. Mary was dissatisfied and rebuked him saying, 'Can you fetch water from the tap and wash yourself?' He did not reply. I quote the incident because it shows how any adult assumes the right to rebuke a child for unseemly behaviour. Hintsa and I drew for a while until he seemed more cheerful.

I shall mention the mood of just two more children. Togu looked anxious and asked for the list to be repeated a third time: his shyness had waned but this task seemed threatening to him. Zuziwe was unusually cautious and passive. She took a long time in the shop and did not shop well. From observations made of her at home, it later became clear that for her shopping was an onerous job. Twice in one week she was reprimanded for not having shopped well. At 7.20 one evening, her aunt (mother's sister) complained as follows:

'I have asked Zuziwe to go and buy Sunlight soap for me and she has brought Holsum (margarine) instead.'

Teenager lodger: 'It's because Zuziwe is naughty; her mind runs quickly, not thinking of what she is being told to do.'

Aunt: 'She was thinking of something else or thinking of her cousin's money that she received from her mother to buy sweets.'

Zuziwe: 'Not at all, auntie, I had forgotten what I was sent to do.'

Aunt: 'Yes! Zuziwe, get away from here.'

The child danced and sang around her aunt, and her mother, who had just returned from work, joined her.

The second incident occurred as follows:
It was 7.10 p.m. a few evenings later and Zuziwe was sitting with her father's brother in his car. Mother returning home saw her and said:
'Why are you quiet, Zuziwe? What's wrong with my girl? Are you sick?'

Mother enters the house grumbling about not having time to care for her children. She is greeted by her sister who says:
'What does this child [Zuziwe] always think of? Why does she not do what she is told to do? I told her to go and buy salt for me and she has brought me matches instead.'

Zuziwe (entering): 'Yes, Makazi, you did tell me to buy salt but there was none. That is why I bought matches.'

Mother: 'Stupid child. What is the matter with you? Are you mad?'

Zuziwe: 'No, I am not mad.'

Mother: 'Why do you always do things that you like? If you do it again I will hit you.'

Aunt: 'She is always thinking about something else or about playing with her friends.'

Zuziwe: 'No, Makazi, it is not that I want to play. I always forget for what I was sent.'

She began to dance and sing.

Lodger: 'Come, Zuziwe, let's go to the shop again and buy salt.'

Zuziwe: 'I don't feel like going to the shop because they take a long time to sell to us and then I forget what I was supposed to buy. So then I am not going at all.'

Ten minutes later Zuziwe was hungry and as supper was not ready she asked for 'Pronutro' and her mother said they needed milk. Zuziwe quickly reminded her that she had said the girls must not go out in the evening so Mthetheli (her mother's sister's son) would have to be sent. Her mother laughed and her aunt said:
'I have never seen a child who is as clever as this one. She is quick-tongued like her mother.'

In response Zuziwe's mother teased her sister: 'It is good if she is clever like me. Even if I am not here, you must beware of what you do: this clever girl will tell me.'

Zuziwe was a clever child but she chose to apply herself only to certain tasks. That she could shop efficiently was demonstrated during an observation of her behaviour in July. She was sent to buy a pint of milk. She knew that she had 30c and that milk cost 23c and that she must bring back 7c change. She checked the change upon being given it.

With a large sample, moods and circumstance that affect performance on a particular day or task are balanced out. However, it is interesting to see their effect on children in a small sample.

The exercise enabled me to test their familiarity with the use of money. Sometime during the year, five children hawked: Lungiswa, clothes; Yameka, fish; Peliswe, offal; Tozama, chicken and Mlawu, meat. Each of them shopped relatively successfully. Here is the record of one occasion upon which a child hawked in Crossroads:

On 28 July, Lungiswa and a girl friend spent from 10.00 a.m. to 5.00 p.m., without lunch, selling clothes for a neighbour. Each item sold at 30c or 40c. Lungiswa sold six items of clothing and did not know how much money she had collected. The neighbour gave her 20c for her labour. She added it to her savings in a SPAR box and now has R1,25. She is going to buy clothes. She hawked on another occasion recently and earned 50c. She intends selling every day as she is not currently attending school because, she says, she was expelled for not having paid her fees. This is unlikely since the school is being boycotted.

The above children and Nukwa returned with the most number of categories from the list. Yameka forgot only the beans but she brought two instead of four lollipops. She was the only non-school-going child to shop well. Nukwa's mother sold beer and sweets and it is possible that he helped her.

The children who hawked during the year and who did well on the exercise did well on most other tasks. It is difficult to determine whether they were allowed to sell because their families encouraged initiative and enterprise or because they were seen to be able. A chicken and egg problem that is hard to unscramble.

In observing at a number of stores in Crossroads, I noticed that many adults did not ask the price of goods that they purchased and, as the prices varied, could not check their change. No doubt they knew within a few cents what it ought to be. None of the children in the sample asked for prices and so none were told them. They simply accepted the change even when it was incorrect by a rand or more.

To conclude, the five children who sold goods in Crossroads during the year shopped well. It was a familiar task for every child and the shopkeeper to whom the child went was known to the child. Yet, for some it was a threatening exercise. All the children named the coins in English and could identify most of them. Only five, all of whom went to school, could add up amounts under two rand. The instructions seemed to cause no bewilderment except that three children asked for the list again. The two items most frequently forgotten were those least often purchased in reality by the children.*

SERIATION

In his examination of fundamental reasoning capacities, Piaget observed the development of the ability to seriate objects that differ quantitatively on some dimensions such as length. He believed that the ability to seriate and to classify objects on the basis of various attributes is fundamental to an adequate understanding of number, representing its ordinal (seriation) and cardinal (classification) aspects.

In setting out to find a psychological proof of the interdependence of ordination and cardination, Piaget sought to analyse the child's reactions when presented with a problem involving counting aloud with the aid of concrete material that could be both seriated and evaluated cardinally. Piaget (1941: 123) described the seriation task as follows:

The simplest (task) consists in merely getting the child to seriate sticks representing the steps of a staircase and to estimate the number of steps already climbed and then, after breaking up the series and picking out one of the steps, asking him to estimate how many steps would have been climbed when that one was reached . . . The technique used is the following: The child is given a set of ten little sticks of varying lengths and is asked to form the series from the shortest (A) to the longest (J). When this has been done, he is given, one at a time and in any order, nine more sticks (which we shall call a – i). He is told that these had been forgotten and are now to be inserted in their right places.*
We then get the series: Aa Bb Cc Dd Ed Ef Gg Hh Ii J. The child is then asked to count all the elements of the series, including the inserted sticks, and then a number of elements corresponding to a figure with which he is familiar is left in front of him. If, for instance, his counting became hesitant after ten, eight sticks would be left, and so on. Pointing to one of the sticks we then ask the child how many stairs† a doll will have climbed when it reaches that point (the actions can either be indicated by a gesture or by making a little doll go from one stick to another as though going upstairs). We also ask how many steps are

* These results should be compared with those found by Gustav Jahoda in interviews with children during which he sought to clarify their understanding of basic economic principles. His findings are published in 'The Construction of Economic Reality by some Glaswegian Children' in the *European Journal of Social Psychology*, Vol. 9, 115–127, 1979; and 'The Development of Thinking About Economic Institutions: The Bank', in *Cahiers de Psychologie Cognitive*, Vol. 1, 55–73, 1981.
* 'The sticks A, B, C, etc. differ in length by about 0,8 cm, and the sticks a, b, c, etc. differ from A, B, C, etc. by about 0,4 cm, the complete set ranging from 9 to 16 cm.' (Note that the use of letters to identify the sticks is incorrect in the 1965 edition of *The Child's Conception of Number*, Norton Library).
† Xhosa has two words for a step – *ibanga* and *inqwanqwa*. Many children used an adaptation from English – *isteppe*.

behind the doll and how many it will need to climb to reach the top of the stairs. Finally, the series of sticks is disarranged and the same questions as before are put to the child, who is then obliged to reconstruct the series before replying.

Piaget asserts that the children who failed ·to make any regular seriation without help were at a pre-serial level as regards this particular problem. Piaget (1941: 126) points out that 'numeration implies ordination' and where a child fails on the counting task, there can therefore be 'no possible relation between ordination and cardination'. He claims that success on the task implies a '. . . grasp of the operations involving both the logic of number and that of seriation of asymmetric relations . . .' (Piaget, 1941: 133). That is to say, 'He has therefore grasped the close correspondence between ordination and cardination, and coordination in the case of particular elements is the sign that this level is operational' (Piaget, 1941: 153). He anticipates that, on the concrete plane, a child will attain operativity between the ages of 7 and 11 (Piaget, 1941: 155).

I gave the children three seriation tasks. I administered Piaget's stick series first in each case to avoid 'contaminating' the exercise with possible practice effects from the other tasks. The second task was intended as an easy test to simple seriation using familiar materials and obvious size relationships. The following animals were each drawn on a piece of strong paper some 30 x 20 cm in size: an elephant, cow, dog, cat, mouse and ant (here called an animal for convenience). On one side each animal was drawn the same size as the others: on the reverse, each was drawn in correct (approximate) size relative to the others. This task was for the child to place the animals in order from largest to smallest using the side on which they were drawn of equal size. Once the child was satisfied with the order, the cards could be turned over and the size ordering checked.

The third task, which I shall call the figure task, was to order 10 cut-outs representing a child increasing in size at regular intervals from 5 cm to 45 cm. No gender was indicated on the cut-outs. No child had difficulty in recognizing a cut-out as representing a child. In administering Piaget's tasks, I concentrated on identifying differences in reactions or approach among the children. I was particularly interested in each child's facility with number in relation to the task at hand. As we saw earlier, numeracy varied.

Scoring

In order to be scored as having achieved an operational level on the stick seriation task, a child had to display Stage III behaviour on both sections of the exercise as described by Piaget. Table 7–5 in Appendix G gives the results. Mlawu had gone to live in the Transkei so there were thirteen children in the sample. Three main categories were used in scoring. An A was assigned to those children who were classified as being at the operation level, a B to those at an intermediate level, and a C to those at a pre-operational level. The same symbols were used to score the Animal and Figure tasks: A equalled success in forming a series without hesitation or correction; B success with discussion; and C failure.

Results: Piaget's Stick Task

No child scored at the operational level (A) on the stick task. (See Table 7–5 in Appendix G.) On the first part of the task, no one made a stair without hesitation or inserted the extra sticks immediately in the correct place. On the second part, no child counted the number of steps to stick N only and derived the number left to the top. Four children scored at the intermediate level (B). The rest performed at a pre-operational level (C). The same patterns noted by Piaget among children who performed below the operational level were observed in the protocols of the Crossroads children. For instance, children below Stage III(A) often separate the material into a smaller series, which is what three of the sample children did. Piaget noted too that at this stage children would often select one among the longest or shortest sticks when asked to pick the longest or shortest. Among the sample children only four chose the smallest and the longest stick when asked to do so. In tackling the second part of the stick task, Piaget observed that children below Stage III frequently included stick 'N' in counting how many steps have been climbed and how many have still to be climbed, i.e. A – N and N – J. Both Yameka and Gedja did so. Piaget also noted that children below Stage III often count *all* the steps when asked to find the number climbed up to a certain point. Five of the sample children did that on either the stick or the figure task. It was a pattern of behaviour that I observed on a number of different occasions.

During the exercises, nine children counted accurately to 20. Most of them counted in English. Some could not count in Xhosa beyond 5: Mary was shocked. One reason may be that the higher numbers are longer in Xhosa than in English. It should be noted that two of those who could not count to 20 were school-children although one had stopped attending school in July and it was then October. The four who failed to count accurately were the only ones to fail on all three seriation tasks. The results suggest that for this population the ability to count is a necessary but not sufficient skill for success on Piaget's full seriation task.

Piaget (1941: 161) held that a sound conception of number '. . . can be regarded as being necessary for the completion of truly logical structures . . .' He made much of the observation that number use in addition, subtraction and multiplication tables is frequently merely verbal and does not necessarily imply a firm conception of number. The ability to count is a culturally learned skill. The seriation test does not purportedly set out to test the ability to count. It is unlikely that many school-children in the West cannot count efficiently up to 20 by the age of 7. I suggest that before the seriation task is accepted as a culture fair test the implicit assumptions made within it about subjects' ability to count be carefully researched and that before the test is administered the ability of subjects to count be documented.

Results: The Animal Task

No more than nine of the thirteen subjects could order the animals on the basis of relative size. I had included the task assuming that it would be a simple means of confirming the children's ability to place familiar objects in a series on the basis of one dimension: in this case, relative size. Three children succeeded at once with no discussion. Six succeeded with discussion and one of their protocols follows.

In each case, the child and I talked about the animals and the task did not commence until I was certain that she could demonstrate through word or gesture that she knew their approximate relative sizes.

Nukwa was asked to place the animals in line from the largest to the smallest. He placed the elephant and then the cow. Some distance away he put the ant, cat, mouse and dog saying:

'They all look the same.'

After discussion, he agreed that in reality they are not the same size. When he was asked to place them according to their size in reality, he placed the elephant, cow, cat, dog, mouse and ant in a line. When asked to demonstrate with his hands the size of a dog and a cat, he did, making the latter smaller.

(Is the order correct?)

'No.'

He reversed the cat and dog, turned the cards over and confirmed the series. Four children failed to place the pictures in a series. They also failed on the other two seriation tasks. Given that each of them could explain with word or gesture the size of the animals, their failure is puzzling. It may have involved some perceptual confusion, perhaps a lack of understanding of the instructions and a refusal or inability to attend only to the rules of the game. One of them, Cebo, attended school while the others, Gwali, Gedja and Saliswa, did not.

Results: The Figure Task

Four children placed the figures in a correct series without hesitation or discussion, three did so after some trial and error and discussion and six failed to do so.

During the administration of all three tasks, significant aspects of behaviour were observed: one, only two children asked any questions about the tasks; two, there were clear signs of inhibition in altering series even though errors had been identified and commented upon by the child following dicusssion; and three, five of the sample children failed to take full advantage of the base line as a guide.* For example, Gedja placed one figure on the opposite side of the base line although in the right order; Zuziwe made a correct series but with the heads rather than the feet of the figures in line; Togu tilted the last two figures off the line; and Yameka placed one figure horizontal to the base.

The children's performance level was probably obscured to some extent by a variety of factors including: their inability to count accurately; their shyness in asking questions and in changing the products of their actions and their unfamiliarity with the use of symbolic representations. Possible also is that a lack of practice in manipulating small size differences, as existed in the stick series, hindered the display of real competence. Cuisenaire rods were not used in the classrooms and I only used them as blocks in the Eriksonian play scene.

The results of the three seriation tasks are much poorer than those collected by Seagrim and Lendon (1980) among Aborigine children and Serpell (1976) among Zambian children, although both sets seem to have been exposed to better schooling than were the Crossroads children. The results are closer to those collected by Opper (1977) among rural Thai school-children. However, according to Ginsburg and Opper (1979), children in Western countries usually succeed on the test at age 6 and 7.

Much has been written recently in the literature on cross-cultural studies about the need to take into account different situations or contexts, including the familiarity of subjects with material, experiments and the testing process, when evaluating test results.† Piaget

* See, for example, Cole and Means (1981).

† When a Genevan child failed to achieve a series, Piaget would suggest the use of a base line.

(1941: 149) drew attention to similar facets when he wrote,

It is obvious that in each test a considerable number of heterogeneous factors intervene, e.g. the words used, the length of instructions given, their more or less concrete character, the relationship between the instructions and the individual experience of the child, the number of elements involved, the intervention of numbers the child knows, etc., etc. We noticed wide differences in the results of the various tests of cardinal correspondence, showing that we never succeed in measuring understanding of this correspondence in its pure state and that the understanding is always with respect to a given problem and given material . . . The calculation of the correlation between the levels of cardination and ordination, without the accompaniment of an extremely thorough qualitative analysis, could therefore give only misleading results unless our experiments were transformed into 'tests' in which statistical precision could no doubt easily be obtained, but at the cost of no longer knowing exactly what was being measured.

Having carefully observed the behaviour of a small number of children in doing the seriation test, I suggest that Piaget's seriation test should be accompanied by a thorough qualitative analysis of the children's socio-cultural context. Without additional analysis, the test may be useful as a diagnostic tool or as a teaching vehicle but it has doubtful value as a comparative test across cultures. Too many extraneous factors obscure competence.

No child achieved an operational level on seriation whereas at least half of the same children did on the conservation of continuous and discontinuous quantity, substance and number.

DRAWINGS

On three separate occasions in March, May and November, each child was asked to draw a man. The draw-a-man test has long been in use in cross-cultural research and has been claimed by many to be culture fair in that a minimum of verbal exchange is demanded. I administered a form of the test in order to see how the children drew figures, how their drawings compared within the group and to determine whether each child's score over time would be consistent. (See the line copies of a selection of the children's drawings on pages 279 and 280. Compare these drawings with those of the children of Elsies River, Cape Town, reproduced in Pinnock, 1980.)

A large body of literature exists on the test but I shall refer to only some of it here. A fair amount of scepticism is currently expressed in academic journals about the value of the test; however, it is still used widely in research, in psychological evaluation and in school entrance examinations. I have scored the drawings according to Elizabeth Munsterberg Koppitz's (1968) scoring manual for developmental items, emotional indicators and school achievements. Her ten-year study of almost two thousand children's drawings has yielded norms apparently valid for a broadly based USA population of 5- to 12-year-old children. Koppitz claims that the Human Figure Drawing Test (hereafter called the HFD) is one of the most valuable techniques for evaluating children because it can be used both as a developmental and as a projective test. Her hypothesis is that:

HFDs reflect primarily a child's level of development and his inter-personal relationships, that is, his attitudes towards himself and towards the significant others in his life. It is further maintained that HFDs may reveal a child's attitudes towards life's stresses and strains and his way of meeting them; drawings may also reflect strong fears and anxieties which may concern the child, consciously or unconsciously, at the given moment . . . the HFD is not regarded as a portrait of the child's basic and enduring personality traits nor as an image of the child's actual appearance. Instead, it is believed that HFDs reflect the child's current stage of mental development and his attitudes and concerns of the given moment, all of which will change in time due to maturation and experience. The HFD's particular value is seen in its very sensitivity to change within the child, and these changes may be developmental and/or emotional. The HFD is regarded as a portrait of the inner child of the moment (Koppitz, 1968: 1).

I resolved that if I could glimpse such a portrait through the children's drawings I should be most happy, and I set about an analysis of them.

In the test, the child draws a 'whole person' in the presence of the examiner. The drawings should be a product of an interpersonal situation. According to Koppitz, the HFD is a graphic form of communication between the child and the examiner and as such differs from spontaneous drawings children may make when they are alone or with friends. She claims that a child's HFD shows both a basic structure and a certain style which is peculiar to that particular child. The structure of a young child's drawing is determined by his age and level of maturation, while the style of his drawing reflects his attitudes and concerns (Koppitz, 1968: 5). She thinks that one drawing is sufficient for screening, quick evaluation and research. I asked each child simply to draw a person. In Xhosa, the word *umuntu* can mean a man or a woman. I felt that further instruction might confuse or overwhelm the child.

The drawings are scored for two types of objective signs: one set is related to children's age and level of maturation, and these are called *Developmental Items;* and the second set is related to children's attitudes and concerns, and are designated as *Emotional Indicators*. Particular studies conducted by the author convinced her that artistic ability, school learning and the instructions given or the drawing medium used do not affect the presence of *Developmental Items*. It is only fair to point out that Koppitz does not claim reliability for her scoring methods across cultures. For instance she (1968: 26) suggests that 'school learning at the KG level does not affect the drawing of a human figure to any appreciable degree when the children come from middle-class suburban homes. Whether this would also apply to the drawings of culturally deprived *(sic)* children who never had much opportunity to draw prior to coming to school is not certain. The only items on HFDs that seem to be influenced by training are clothing and the correct number of figures and possibly, two dimensions on the arms and legs.' Her items were selected from the Goodenough–Harris (1963) scoring system and her own experience. Many of the finer details on drawings, which were included in the Goodenough–Harris system, were omitted from this list since her investigation was limited to the HFDs of elementary school-age children.

Developmental Items

Out of the thirty signs selected, four frequency categories emerged from the normative per cent study; they were, the Expected Items, the Common Items, the Not Unusual Items and the Exceptional Items. The first includes all items which were present on 86 per cent to 100 per cent of the HFDs in the normative study at a given level. Since they were present on the HFDs of almost all normal children, they constitute the basic minimum of items one can expect in figure drawings of children of a given age. The fourth frequency category includes all items shown on 15 per cent or less of the HFDs and these are considered unusual. It is the Expected and Exceptional Items that are used to assess a child's general level of mental maturity even though no definite IQ score is given. In scoring each HFD, each Expected and Exceptional Item is given a value of 1. Omission of an Expected Item is marked as -1, while the presence of an Exceptional Item is called $+1$. In order to avoid negative scores, the value of 5 is added to the sum of all positive and negative scoring points a child receives on his HFD. The results of Koppitz's (1968: 30) study and correlations made with the WISC Full Scale IQ scores and the Stanford–Binet IQ scores lead her to conclude that '. . . the Expected and Exceptional items in HFDs can be used with some confidence as a guide and easy method of assessing the level of mental maturity of groups of children.' The results compare favourably with the correlations between Goodenough DAM test scores* and IQ test scores.

The human figures drawn for me by the sample children on three different occasions were scored according to the above format. Koppitz (1968: 327) used her Scoring Manual for 30 Developmental Items on HFDs of Children and (1968: 330) her Expected and Exceptional Items on HFDs of Boys and Girls Age 5 to 12 to analyse the drawings of 1 856 children for her normative study. Table 7–6A gives the scores for the Crossroads sample and Table 7–6B (both in Appendix G) is a summary of the results.

According to the HFD scores of the fourteen children tested on three occasions over a span of nine months, no child could have been considered to have a High Average to Superior Intelligence (a score of 8 or 7 on the HFD) or an Average to Superior Intelligence (a score of 6) and only one child (Togu) on all three of his drawings achieved a score that suggested an intelligence of Average to High Average (a score of 5). On the other hand, six children on at least one HFD were shown to have Borderline IQs (a score of 2) and four were marked as being Mentally Retarded (a score of 1 or 0). Although age was controlled for, only two children had a consistent score on all three drawing tests.

Four children improved their scores from the first to the third test, four scored less well, the scores of two were consistent and the rest fluctuated.

Sex Differences in Developmental Maturity
Koppitz found:

. . . minor but consistent differences between the occurrence of Developmental Items on the HFDs of boys and girls. The findings accord with the observations of Goodenough (1926), Harris (1963) and Machover (1949), all of whom emphasize that the drawings of girls in the primary grades are superior to those of boys. There is also a consensus that this difference between the sexes diminishes gradually. By age 8 or 9, boys not only catch up with girls but often surpass them in the quality and details of their drawings. At all age levels, there appear to be some drawing items which are more 'Masculine' or 'Feminine' and which occur more often on the HFDs of boys or girls respectively (Koppitz, 1968: 19).

Koppitz found that the 'masculine' items included drawings done in profile and of knees and ears, while the 'feminime' items included hair,

* See Goodenough (1926), (1928), and Goodenough and Harris (1950).

pupils, eyebrows, two lips and clothing. She feels that because these particular differences have been reported so often they cannot be attributed to chance but must be accepted as real differences between drawings of boys and girls in the USA. Koppitz does not believe that the differences are biologically determined but that they reflect values and attitudes that are generally accepted and fostered in the middle-class Western culture. Koppitz (1968: 19) explains that:

From infancy on, girls watch their mothers fuss over clothes and hair and facial makeup. A little girl's interest in these things is reinforced by her natural desire to imitate her mother and to gain parental approval by displaying feminine charm. Girls' drawings tend to reflect their awareness and interest in feminine attire and beauty. By contrast, the boys in our society are expected to be more independent and outgoing than girls. The profile drawing is often associated with a turning away from others and a striving towards independence. And, finally, a young boy's short hair makes his ears quite conspicuous and focuses his attention on them. Girls, who are more concerned with the drawing of hair, tend to omit ears from their HFDs, especially when they draw girls or women.

She concludes that specific 'masculine' and 'feminine' items on HFDs reflect attitudes in children that have been learned unconsciously in early life from the social and cultural environment in which they live. Further, she assumes that the frequency of occurrence of such items will differ in different cultures and she adds that a child's drawing can only be evaluated if the mode of dress and grooming in her environment is known.

The HFDs of the Crossroads sample offered some confirmation of her assumption, but with some exceptions. Contrary to Koppitz's findings, only two boys drew ears while six girls did. Xhosa children have curly hair that seldom grows very long and is, in any case, kept short. It is not surprising that girls should be as aware of the need to add ears to the drawing of a person as are boys. The presence or absence of ears makes no difference to the scores of the HFDs among children aged 10 or less. Hair, however, is an Expected Item for girls though not for boys. While current fashion among Xhosa women in Cape Town included dressing hair into plaited designs (sometimes with beads), girls were not allowed to wear their hair thus to school and only Gedja, in the sample, sometimes had hers dressed. Hair was no more a feature or a culturally fussed-about facet of dress for girls than for boys. Therefore, it is unfair to make hair an Expected Item for girls and not boys from age 6 onwards as does Koppitz on her scoring manual. If, for the Crossroads sample, hair is dropped as a scoring item, the girls' results alter from A to B (as shown on Table 7–6A, column A and column B).

| | A | | | | B | | |
	Test I	II	III		Test I	II	III
Peliswe	3	4	3		3	5	4
Lungiswa	3	4	3		3	4	4
Nomvula	4	3	4		5	4	5
Zuziwe	4	4	4		5	5	5
Tozama	4	3	4		4	4	4
Gedja	2	2	4		3	2	4
Yameka	4	3	1		5	4	2
Saliswa	2	1	3		2	2	3

On the new set of results, four girls attain a score of 5 on at least one drawing, that is, equal to an Average to High Average I.Q., and there are no longer any scores suggesting mental retardation. Based on the findings that the drawings of girls in the USA are superior to those of boys under the age of 10, girls are penalized at ages 6, 7 and 8 if they fail to draw two, two and one (respectively) more items than the boys. Besides, boys at age 7 and 8 are awarded scores for two extra items than are girls. We might wonder if, in a squatter camp in South Africa, girls do develop more rapidly than do boys. Are they expected to devote the same attention to detail and obedience to the intricacies of rules as is expected of girls in the West?

If we accept, for the moment, the suggestion that 7- and 8-year-old girls in Crossroads may not develop more rapidly than boys on the sorts of skills that the HFD measures, and remove the Expected Items (hair, feet and legs drawn in two dimensions), for whose absence girls are penalized whereas boys are not, then the scores alter from A to C (as shown on Table 7–6A).

| | A | | | | C | | |
	Test I	II	III		Test I	II	III
Peliswe	3	4	3		3	5	4
Lungiswa	3	4	3		4	4	4
Nomvula	4	3	4		5	4	5
Zuziwe	4	4	4		5	5	5
Tozama	4	3	4		4	4	4
Gedja	2	2	4		3	3	4
Yameka	4	3	1		5	5	2
Saliswa	2	1	3		3	3	4

According to the results under C, no child has a score equal to that of a mentally retarded child and only one score indicates a Borderline IQ and it comes after two scores of 5 which indicate an Average to High Average IQ. Three children now have consistent scores across the three tests. The above analysis offers evidence to support Koppitz's contention that the mode of dress and grooming in an environment must be known before tests based on human figure drawings can be administered. It also suggests that the relative ability of boys and girls at particular ages should be tested under different socio-cultural conditions. If evidence is found to support the hypothesis that girls develop more rapidly on the skills that HFDs measure then the assumption, as to why, do need to be carefully examined. Assumptions based on middle-class parent–child relationships and culturally appropriate roles and patterns of play will not necessarily hold. If data drawn from tests administered to a small sample of children across nine months throw doubt on certain aspects of the scoring system that concerns sex differences, then we might wonder what other cultural differences have similar effects.

Emotional Indicators

Koppitz devised a scoring manual to test emotional problems using the HFDs. On the basis of her results, she concluded that, when an HFD shows none of the 30 Emotional Indicators (EIs), then it seems likely that the child is free from serious emotional problems. The presence of only one Emotional Indicator on an HFD appears to be inconclusive and is not necessarily a sign of emotional disturbance. However, two or more are highly suggestive of emotional problems and unsatisfactory relationships.

Once again, it is fair to quote Koppitz (1968: 55) before using her scoring manual in a situation for which it was not designed. She writes:

There appears to be a consensus among the experts on HFDs that no one-to-one relationship exists between any single sign on HFDs and a definite personality trait or behaviour on the part of the boy or girl making the drawing. Anxieties, conflicts or attitudes can be expressed on HFDs in different ways by different children or by one child at different times. This writer can only underscore what others have emphasized again and again: it is not possible to make a meaningful diagnosis or evaluation of a child's behaviour or difficulties on the basis of any single sign on a HFD. The total drawing and the combination of various signs and indicators should always be considered and should then be analysed on the basis of the child's age, maturation, emotional status, social and cultural background and should then be evaluated together with other available test data.

With that caution firmly in mind, let us see how the sample children fared. The Scoring Manual for 30 Emotional Indicators on HFDs of Children and List of Emotional Indicators on HFDs of Children were taken as valid for the ages of boys and girls from 5 to 12 years. Table 7–7A in Appendix G gives the results of the three tests of human figure drawings. According to the USA norms, on the first, second and third drawing respectively, eleven, eight and ten children showed signs of having emotional problems and unsatisfactory relationships. From my own experience and the testimony of family members, school staff and neighbours no such sorry pattern of problems existed. According to Koppitz's (1968: 54) norms, about one-fifth (19 per cent) of good students can be expected to show more than one Emotional Indicator.

Three of the Emotional Indicators appeared often on the figure drawings of the Crossroads sample. The first to be discussed are tiny drawings, that is, two inches or less. Thirteen children (92,9 per cent) made at least one tiny figure on twenty (47,6 per cent) of the total number (42) drawn on all the tests. According to Koppitz (1968: 59), who quotes other studies, the drawing of tiny figures indicates extreme insecurity, withdrawal and depression.

It seems unlikely that this EI was picking up individual problems. Perhaps the children found the test situation threatening: the first occurred on each child's second formal encounter with me in my room at Crossroads. It is also possible that the item reflected the emotional trauma of being a black child in a South African squatter camp. Possibly, the evidence simply reflects inexperience with the use of drawing materials. If we remove it as an Emotional Indicator, then the scores are as in column B in Table 7–7A.

Ten children (71,4 per cent) did not draw a nose on half of all the figures. The omission of the nose is associated with shy and withdrawn behaviour and a lack of overt aggressiveness (Koppitz, 1968: 66). Perhaps one of the arguments given above applies to the omission of the nose. The omission may reflect the children's anxiety in a strange situation (although, in this case, each test produced seven figures without noses and it is unlikely that the same discomfort was felt at the end as at the beginning of the year). Insecurity and inexperience may account for it. Column C on Table 7–7A shows the scores once the omission of the nose has been removed as an Emotional Indicator.

A final item that occurred so often as to suggest it was not measuring individual problems, or not solely, was for a figure that slanted 15° or more. Nine children (64,3 per cent) drew at least one slanting figure and thirteen HFDs (31,0 per cent) slanted more than 15°. Koppitz feels that the item does not seem to be associated with any specific type of behaviour or symptom but rather suggests a general inability and lack of balance. She (1968: 59) adds, 'A slanting figure on the drawings of a child seems to indicate an unstable nervous system or a labile personality: above all, it suggests that the child lacks secure footing.' They live, perhaps, in houses built on shifting sand. I was told that when people first moved to Crossroads, it was hard to walk across the dunes as the sand was soft. By 1980 the sand had been beaten down by the tread of feet. During the year, one of the central topics of conversation was to do with the Government's proposal to move everyone to another site. Many people expressed fear and distrust at the prospect of another move and it exacerbated deep political divisions amongst them. I often heard the matter discussed in front of the children. Oddly enough, the first houses were being demolished and their occupants were moved to New Crossroads on the day that the children and I had our farewell party. As we cut a cake on which a tin shack had been etched in icing, one mother commented, 'We demolish this shack as the Government demolishes our own.'

It has been noted in the section on seriation how few of the children made good use of base line guides in ordering the sticks or cut-out figures. I suspect that in most cases inexperience with similar tasks yielded the slanting figures. One may be tempted to explain the phenomenon in terms of the absence of a 'carpentered world' as is currently fashionable, but at Crossroads there was no lack of lines and angles on the zinc sheets that made up the shanty town. Serpell (1980: 8) points out that the orientation of a drawing on a page, the representation of depth and consistency of angle or view, are all problematic features of drawing. He adds that they have little or no importance in modelling, which presents problems peculiar to the clay medium.

Column D has done away with the slanting figure item. Column E gives the scores minus all three items discussed above. Table 7–7B and 7–7C summarize the results of Table 7–7A. I do not mean to suggest that one should arbitrarily play with tests as I have just done. I am, in truth, making two points. One, that socio–cultural conditions seem to have clear effects on even non-verbal tests, and, the other, that once the items in question have been set aside, an interesting and, I feel, worthwhile pattern emerges in the scores for Emotional Indicators on the HFDs of the fourteen children. Six children are now seen to be clear of emotional problems on all three of the tests. Of the six, four score consistently. Three children show signs of having problems (a score of

2) on one test each and two others show the same signs on two tests. Only three children consistently score 2 or more on all three tests: Cebo, Nukwa and Hintsa. The results are consistent with Koppitz's finding, referred to earlier, that up to 19 per cent of good students show signs of emotional disturbance on the human figure drawings.

School Achievement

Koppitz (1968: 53) devised and validated a test that relates scores on Emotional Indicators to School Achievement. She found that seven of the EIs had high predictive value on school success: poor integration of parts, slanting figure, omission of mouth, body or arms, monster or grotesque figures and the drawing of three or more figures. These indicators appeared significantly more often on the HFDs of special class pupils, that is, children with emotional problems and/or brain injury. She claimed that they can be used with some degree of confidence for predicting difficulty in learning and adjustment in kindergarten and the first two grades. Table 8A gives the results of the three tests administered to the Crossroads children and scored for School Achievement.

The numbers who scored 2 or more of the 7 indicators and could, therefore, be considered to be low school achievers on the first, second and third test were 7, 4 and 1 respectively. Despite the fact that the scoring method takes age into account, the improvement across the tests is noteworthy. Five children's HFDs showed no sign of poor achievement. If, on the basis of my earlier argument, we do not penalize the nine children who between them produced thirteen slanting figures, then three more children have all clear scores. Column B on Table 7–8A gives the results with the slanting figure penalty removed.

Koppitz holds that the drawing of three figures or more on an HFD is always associated with poor school achievement. She asserts that, 'This Emotional Indicator is found almost exclusively on drawings of children of limited ability who come from large, culturally deprived families and/or who are brain injured . . . It was also observed that some who draw multiple figures lack a feeling of identity, of being a person in their own right.' Such children, Koppitz continues, are frequently one of a crowd of children at home and have never received a great deal of individual attention. They tend to be lost in school since they have not been taught to function independently. Children who draw more than three figures usually require special help in school if they are to become individualized human beings (Koppitz, 1968: 65).

The above description did not fit the five children in Crossroads who drew multiple figures. Each of the five drew three or more figures on the first test only. Three of them did not attend school. Unlike the children about whom Koppitz wrote, two were only children and another had but one brother. The other two children had been singled out as precious and admired members of their families. Three of the five succeeded well on many other tests. As the analysis of the item did not apply to Crossroads children, it is likely that the item is culturally biased. Perhaps it scores individualistic values not held so dear in Xhosa society in Crossroads. It is probable that some children's failure to attend to specific instructions, in this case to draw a person, resulted in their drawing more than one. Had only one test been given, the results may not have been questioned. Column C on Table 8A in the Appendix gives the results with the penalty for drawing more than three figures removed. Column D gives the results after both items have been removed.

Table 8C illustrates the improvement across time of the test results with all the relevant items scored (A) and without the two items analysed above (B). The decrease in the number of Emotional Indicators that relate to poor school achievement is marked. If the test was measuring achievement that was not related to either maturation or school learning, improvement across the three tests should not exist.

That this particular test was unreliable is important for three reasons. One is that a version of the draw-a-man test has been and still is used fairly frequently in cross–cultural research. The results suggest that tests across time might undermine faith in its reliability. The second reason is that some private schools within South Africa use the test as part of school entrance examinations. Certain groups in the population may perform badly for reasons other than true inability. If private schools wish to accept children from advantaged backgrounds only, then the test may serve their purpose. If that is the case, it ought to be consciously and publicly acknowledged. Finally, the unreliability of the test for this population is important because it means that there is yet another area in which Xhosa children are at a disadvantage as even their need for accurate diagnosis cannot be met. I recall a senior government official saying that there was no centre for mentally retarded black children in Cape Town because there were not enough of them to warrant it. Apart from any other fact, how did he know how many retarded children there were in the population in question?

To conclude the discussion of human figure drawings, I shall compare the results with rank scores among the fourteen children. If we take an average of the positions achieved on the tests which were administered to the children during the year, we arrive at a rough estimate of success among them. The tests included two scores based on the Purdue Perceptual and Motor Co-ordination Survey; eleven scores derived from Piagetian tests of conservation (some of which were repeated); the score achieved on Piaget's Seriation Tests and the score achieved on the Shopping Test. I am aware that Piagetian task success does not correlate closely with school success but the above scores were the only ones available to me. It was a rough measure of rank order that I sought. The children succeeded in the rank order shown in Table 7–9 in Appendix G.

Let us look at the analysis according to Koppitz of the drawings of the three school children who showed signs of having emotional problems on all three of their HFDs and who showed signs of being low School Achievers on two of their drawings (Cebo and Nukwa) or on the third drawing (Hintsa).

Case 1: Cebo was ranked last among the school-children and second last among them all. His Development Indicators were 2, 2 and 4: his Emotional Indicators were 4, 5 and 4; and School Achievement scores were 2, 3 and 1. The scores on the final test show improvement on DIs and School Achievement. His protocol suggests shyness, some aggression, feelings of intellectual inadequacy, withdrawal and inhibited impulses, anxiety, insecurity, imbalance, unco-ordination and instability. The whole caboodle. His mother was concerned about a nervous tic of his that caused him to nod his head lower and lower onto his chest. He was aggressive among his friends and twice fought with courage and pride in front of me. His neighbours frequently complained about his aggressiveness. He was often in trouble at school for playing in class and his teacher expressed dissatisfaction with him in front of adults. His low score on the Purdue Motor Co-ordination Test re-affirms the signs of imbalance and uncoordination. On three of his figures, Cebo left off arms, which Koppitz interprets as a sign of aggression and, often, of stealing. He stole twice from me, once making a quick profit in the classroom on the stolen marbles that he sold for 2 cents each. The incidents seemed to illustrate no more than his naughtiness and opportunism.

Cebo is a lovely child with winning ways and a warm, laughing personality. His low achievement on almost every test puzzled me and his inattention and mischievousness augured ill for a school career. His parents seemed to provide a solid home and both had relatively good educational qualifications. His mother had nervous symptoms. He is a child who could possibly benefit from a full physical and psychological examination.

Case 2: While Hintsa's School Achievement scores on the three tests, 1, 0 and 2, did not suggest particular problems, his rank position on other tasks was low – ninth out of the school-children and eleventh out of them all. His Development Indicators, however, yielded an IQ score never higher than 80. He showed signs of emotional problems on all three tests – 4, 4 and 5. His scores grew worse across time on all three measures. On two figures, he drew long arms and one had arms that reached the ground with hands that turned in towards the feet like a baboon. Coincidentally, a conversation between Hintsa and members of his family was recorded on 3 November 1980, in which he was told by his father that he had been bought from the baboons. The conversation is recorded in Chapter 2 in the section on children's understanding of birth.

Hintsa's protocol, as interpreted according to Koppitz, showed signs of both aggressiveness and extreme shyness, insecurity and withdrawal. I noted on a number of occasions during the year that Hintsa was deeply disturbed when teased by other children. Once he was heard complaining to his mother that other children teased him for wearing old clothes and for being poor. Life at home was not easy: his mother was always away at work for long hours as was his father. The latter had been orphaned early and had had a tough life. There was little daily care for Hintsa, his brother and his sister. The following incident illustrates the kind of hardship which the children often faced. As I sat with the family at 8.00 one Friday evening, I wondered at the lack of activity in food preparation but assumed that they had eaten early. After a while, Hintsa's 7-year-old sister, who was sitting on her mother's lap, began to cry silently. She had recently been diagnosed as having tuberculosis so I asked if she was feeling ill. Her mother replied, 'No. She is just hungry. My husband was ill this week and has not received his pay. There is no money with which to buy supper.'

Case 3: Nukwa's IQ, according to Koppitz's measures, ranged from retarded to 90, yet he ranked seventh among the school-children and eighth among them all. Although he was small and thin (his weight was below the Boston Third Percentile), he scored top marks on the Purdue Motor–Co-ordination tasks. His father was dead and his father's brother was responsible for him. That man's burden was heavy as he had three large families – his own, Nukwa's and another disabled brother's – to care for on R35,00 a week. Nukwa's mother was often in disgrace with her husband's family. Nukwa dropped out of school in July.

On two of his figures, Nukwa omitted the mouth. Koppitz (1968: 66) describes this indicator thus,

> Omission of the mouth appears to be always clinically meaningful. It reflects feelings of anxiety, insecurity and withdrawal including passive resistance. This Emotional Indicator reveals either the child's inability or his refusal to communicate with others.

It is the passive resistance that interests me. More than half of the children omitted a mouth on sixteen figures. In a society like South Africa's and among the Xhosa, a people whose adults demand politeness and obedience from children, passive resistance by young ones may be a way out. An *igqira* interpreted Nukwa's play scene, reported in Chapter 4, rather in that light.

South African black psychologist Abigail Tukulu (1979) wrote a fine paper (unpublished) questioning the possibility of real communication between white psychotherapists and black clients in South Africa. In detailing her doubts Tukulu (1979) writes, 'Blacks have learnt to show indirect rather than direct aggression, to respond rather than initiate and to read the thoughts of other persons while hiding their own. Psychotherapy and counselling methods which encourage discussion of thoughts, feelings and problems in an open manner with a white person would therefore have to eradicate a lifetime of conditioning in the opposite direction.'

The case studies illustrate that these children's HFD scores accurately identified emotional and School Achievement problems only when all three drawings were taken into account. In my opinion, they were the three most troubled children. The point that I wish to underline is that to identify the children's need for help or attention more than one drawing had to be analyzed. The results for the whole sample initially yielded scores that were high on emotional problems and low on School Achievement. The scores fluctuated and improved across time.

In conclusion I must reiterate that Koppitz's HFD scoring manuals do not give results that are acceptable as accurate measures of developmental maturity, IQ or emotional problems for the group as a whole. Nor, except in a few instances, are the results a safe measure of a particular child at one point in time. Poverty, discrimination, lack of access to appropriate materials and experience seem to skew the pitch. It is my subjective opinion that more than one child had an IQ of 85 to 120 and that none of the four children who were measured as being mentally retarded, were so.

On the basis of the above inspection of human figure drawings across time, I suggest that they be used in cross-cultural research with caution. Serpell's (1980) task of making a person in clay offers an interesting alternative for use in parts of Africa. In my opinion, validation of the existing scoring techniques among a non-Western population is of little value. Hunkin (1950) validated Goodenough's Draw-a-Man Test among Zulu children in South Africa and concluded thus: 'The results of the present investigation show a striking similarity to those of other investigations into Bantu intelligence, in that Bantu children make a relatively lower score than do white children and that discrepancy becomes greater as chronological age increases.' While Hunkin (1950: 52–63) pointed out that, 'The relatively low score on the test may . . . be due to culturally determined characteristics of personality and interests and may therefore not be taken to indicate a generally lower level of ability,' the new norms suggested continue to contribute to the deficit-culture school of thought. I hope to have demonstrated above some of the ways in which certain items fail as measures amongst individuals in a Xhosa sample of children in Crossroads, and that there are value assumptions embedded in the scoring technique that do not necessarily apply across cultures. What is called for is a re-analysis of each scoring item in relation to children's particular situation and context.

It is probably not possible to use a variation of human figure drawing as a culture-fair test unless experience with and access to the relevant materials including exposure to pictorial representations are first established.

SUMMARY

In searching for evidence of the skills that children could marshal when ordering their ideas about and approach to the world, I found the following. Children were often hampered in their performance by failing to pay attention to the matter in hand. They failed to respond to the detail of instructions and some had difficulty in obeying verbal instructions, particularly in motor-coordination exercises. While all the children could do simple tasks such as sorting cards according to one or two features, some needed encouragement and others did more than was requested. That their failure to pay attention to the minutiae of instructions was neither an inability to concentrate nor an inability to attend when the matter was of interest or importance to them was made obvious by their behaviour on a variety of other exercises during the year. They seemed not to realize that paying close attention to instructions and the task, however banal or futile they may seem, is the first rule in succeeding in the growing-up game as conceived in the modern world.

The children made little progress on most learned skills during the year. In an economically oppressed area such as Crossroads, one cannot assume that children are provided with a good rudimentary base for the learning of skills or the techniques needed for ordering or organizing learning situations of the sort met with in the context of schools or tests.

For most of the children, the concept of number was not a tool wielded with confidence. Their reading skill seemed to be hampered by the lack of a vocabulary with which to organize the learning experiences. Progress in learning to write and count among the school-children was not uniform and minimal progress was made in the recognition of the letters, their sounding, the acquisition of a vocabulary for colour, and the use of number. Improvements on measures of school achievement and developmental maturity were revealed in human figure drawings across the year.

There were some signs that particular experience had an impact on performance. For example, I administered an extra test of the conservation of discontinuous quantities to the children in the sample and control groups but this time I adapted a game with stones that is played in Crossroads. The game is described in Chapter 3. Instead of using beads and beakers, half the children used stones and holes in the ground. The children who used those materials seemed to perform more confidently and, the results suggest, more successfully. I have not reported the results in detail beacuse it was not a carefully controlled experiment. It does, however, suggest that familiarity with tests' materials may affect results among children in Crossroads.

With a small sample, it was possible to observe the impact of mood on performance. This was detailed in the report on the shopping exercise and it was seen to affect performance appreciably in certain cases. Two aspects of behaviour were seen as limiting: the children never asked questions about instructions nor sought clarification and they did not allow themselves to alter an action already performed even when a move was discussed and error recognised. Their lack of familiarity with symbolic representations including the use of pictorial representations hampered performance. Lack of access to books, pictures and the codes common to story-telling in a literate world clearly hampered the children's ability to succeed on tests.

Schools need to foster classification, order and regularity in the way that children perceive and describe the world and, in particular, learning occasions. Opportunities for exercise in classifying, ordering and regulating the environment exist within the children's cultural heritage, play, games and work yet few of these are built upon in the formal class setting.

I suggest that tests devised in other cultures be used with caution and that Piaget's type of qualitative analysis combined with careful research of the child's physical and social environment are essential accompaniments. I suggest, further, that the children's health, perceptual and motor co-ordination be assessed and taken into account in analysing results. Appropriate basic research must be done on the acquisition of skills such as reading, on the relationship between counting and number conservation and on the children's use of and access to an appropriate learning vocabulary in South Africa. Within cross-cultural research, there is a need for a theory of data collection.

Quite clearly, some training-on-the-job occurred among the children during the test situations. This fits Piaget's theory of learning in which conflict stimulates the search for resolution. The issue as to whether children can be trained to handle Piagetian-type concepts competently prior to certain levels of developmental maturity is an area of disagreement between learning theorists and Genevan psychologists.

In elaborating a theory of learning we ought to pay attention to the kinds of problems that Foucault (1966: xiii) tackles in describing the 'immense density of scientific discourse.' He describes his attempt to explain the order of things thus:

I do not wish to deny the validity of intellectual biographies, or the possibility of a history of theories, concepts or themes. It is simply that I wonder whether such descriptions are themselves enough, whether they do justice to the immense density of scientific discourse, whether there do not exist, outside their customary boundaries, systems of regularities that have a decisive role in the history of sciences. I should like to know whether the subjects responsible for scientific discourse are not determined in their situation, their function, their perceptive capacity, and their practical possibilities by conditions that dominate and even overwhelm them. In short, I tried to explore scientific discourse not from the point of view of the individuals who are speaking, nor from the point of view of the formal structures of what they are saying, but from the point of view of the rules that come into play in the very existence of such discourse . . . It seems to me that the historical analysis of scientific discourse should, in the last resort, be subject, not to a theory of the knowing subject, but rather to a theory of discursive practice.

The rules that come into play in the discourse between adult and child and between child and child and how they are determined need the kind of consideration that Foucault gives to scientific discourse. In considering how a classification is established, he says that

There is no similitude and no distinction, even for the wholly untrained perception, that is not the result of a precise operation and of the application of a preliminary criterion (Foucault, 1966: xix).

He is concerned to describe the 'conditions of possibility' of knowledge. We need to discover with what operation and criteria the child is introduced to the order of things. Foucault's intention is to describe:

how a culture experiences the propinquity of things, how it establishes the *tabula* of their relationships and the order by which they must be considered (Foucault, 1966: xxiii).

We need to know how and when the child is introduced to that order.

8
Conclusion

It has been said that the South African system of apartheid is bad, cruel, unfair, oppressive. It has been said often and loudly yet to little effect. Only now as children rebel and, as a consequence, die and are beaten and imprisoned does the beginning of the end – not yet in sight – appear. However, even when the current regime has been toppled there will be a need to consider the lot of children whose lives have been disrupted, uprooted, shredded by an evil system. It will take time and conscious effort and commitment and understanding to cancel the effects of apartheid. Families must be re-constituted, wealth re-distributed, education overhauled. There is a danger that the interests of children will be overlooked. There is a danger that divisions of ethnicity, class, religion and sex will obscure their interests. Who will be the children's advocates?

It is easy to sentimentalize childhood. It is easy to summarize in glib generalizations children's experiences. It is difficult to record these experiences in detail and in relation to a socio–historical moment. The book has attempted to do just that for fourteen Xhosa children living in 1980 in an urban squatter settlement on the dunes of the Cape Flats. Each child's experience, as with every child anywhere, is like a freshly baked loaf of bread: the ingredients derive from the past (or, in the words of an *igqira* in Crossroads, from 'the child's origin or roots, the customs of her people, their language and their actions') and the present, and the yeast is the child's own.

The book documents the impact that apartheid has on each child's life – it records that their families are forced to build shacks in the sand; that their shacks are demolished before their eyes; that their parents are imprisoned for being in white man's territory; that their education is grossly inadequate; that their mobility and opportunities are rigidly confined. Those facets of the children's lives are visible and relatively easily measured and recorded. The book does more. It documents the impact of the system on the children's fantasies, dreams and play. It links current social mores to the children's ideas (for instance about birth and the origin of dreams), their use of kinship terms, and their behaviour. It documents the inequalities of poverty as it affects children's opportunities for learning. Some psychological tests have been shown to be culturally biased in small particulars so that not only are the children deprived of a sound learning environment but the development of their cognitive abilities cannot be reliably traced.

In the past, using psychological tests, it has been concluded that the mental age of South African blacks was substantially less than that of whites (Fick, 1939) and that the mean social environment of South African blacks lies 'more than three standard deviations below the mean European social environment' (Biesheuval, 1943: 223). Fick's opinion is a classic example of the inferior innate ability approach to intelligence, and Biesheuval's of the deficit culture point of view. In the South African context, both are worth recalling as both are still represented in academic and public life. In 1980, for example, Minister of Posts and Telecommunications Mr Hennie Smit said in the all-white Parliament that the 'thought processes (of blacks) are slower than most of us here,' that they do not have 'specific concepts' and that because of their psychological background blacks reacted more slowly than 'we do here' (Acott, 1980: 1).

Methodologically, I was interested in tracing the links between child thought and the states of consciousness represented in adults' formulations about society. There is no one consciousness to which adults introduce children. Anthropologists, particularly in South Africa, have sometimes distinguished between a 'western' (urban) and 'tribal' (rural) consciousness and have implied that people switch from one to another depending upon circumstances. Kiernan (1980: 12) criticized that view saying,

It has always seemed unsatisfactory to suppose that the migrant cognitively shuttles between two separate universes of meaning, only one of which is deemed to be his own. The more likely options are that he either extends his own world outlook to cover his new circumstances . . ., or he constructs afresh a single model which caters for the real expansion of his social horizon.

It seems equally likely that there is no single model or outlook but that connections are made and re-made among a vast network of notions. Therein lies the possibility for both individual and social creativity.

That the mind houses a number of states of consciousness and that connections among ideas can be made and re-made fits Sahlins's proposed reversal of the mode of discourse that gives mind all the power of 'law' and 'limitation' thus placing culture in submission and dependence. He ponders on another conception of mind in which,

The structures of the mind . . . appear not as the imperatives of culture but as its implements. They constitute a set of organisational means and possibilities at the disposition of the human cultural enterprise, which remains at liberty to variously invest them with meaningful content (Sahlins, 1977: 179).

Mind does not determine culture; therefore, the constraints of a particular culture cannot be taken as representing the limitations of mind. Cultures may variously facilitate access to the structures of mind as implements but membership of a particular culture does not bar one from using the tools of another. The question for society then becomes: How best can children be introduced to the structures of mind that are valued and rewarded in current society?

In South Africa, there is need for much more work on excavating the reality of children's experience. We ought to know what the real impact of discrimination, migration, re-location and repatriation are on children. We ought to know how many childhood years each child spends with his or her mother and father. We ought to discover what access they have to the props of Western society; the physical conditions under which they live; their mobility; the continuity of their school experience; and the quality of their education in the classroom. We ought to enable the children to speak. The problems in the country compound the difficulty of research.

A review of the lives of the fourteen children in December 1982 follows. One was killed by an ambulance as she played in the school grounds; one had pellagra; one had tuberculosis; and one had scabies. Six of their families still lived in shacks in Crossroads and seven had houses in New Crossroads. Gedja and her mother were both living with her maternal grandparents in Nyanga East. For most of 1982, the thirteen children were not all living with their parents. Whereas in 1980 only one child was living without either of her parents, in 1982 five were. Whereas in 1980 only four were living without their fathers, in 1982 ten were. In 1982, five of the children were living in the Transkei; one with her mother; one with her mother's brother's wife; two with their father's mothers, and one with her mother's mother. One child (the fifth living without either parent) was staying in New Crossroads with his father's brother and his mother's sister. Three of the children were living in the city with their mothers and three others with both parents.

Since 1980, the Hlekes have divorced and the Qasanas have separated. Two of the children did not attend school in 1982, nine were in either Sub A or Sub B for the year and two completed Standard 1. The above review reminds us that the children continue to change residence, caretakers and schools. In terms of health, they remain at some risk.

In April 1988 I traced all but one child (who, since 1980, has lived in the Transkei). This is the eighth year since we worked together: each child has lived as long again as he or she had in 1980. Apart, that is, from the child who was killed. How different one from another are their lives now. For example, Cebo is a herdboy in the Transkei; Lungiswa is a mother in Old Crossroads; Yameka is a domestic worker in Johannesburg; and Zuziwe lives in a 'white' suburb in Cape Town during term time and attends a private school.

Of the twelve children (apart from the one who died and the one whom I failed to trace) only four live with both parents. Nine of the children live with their mothers and five with their fathers. The mother of one has died from diabetes and the parents of two children have divorced. Of the ten fathers who are alive, eight have jobs and another is self-employed as a tailor. Some have experienced prolonged spells of unemployment. Of the mothers, seven have jobs (four as domestic workers) and two continue to earn as healers; two do not earn.

Ten of the children live in Greater Cape Town: three in Old Crossroads, six in New Crossroads and one in Khayelitsha. One child lives in Johannesburg and another in the Transkei. Four of the children have, since 1980, spent three or more years living in the Transkei. Of these two returned to their mothers in Cape Town because of ill-health. Nukwa, who is still small and thin, suffers convulsions. He is only in Standard One at school. The families have ten new members, that is, babies born since 1980. Lungiswa's child was born in 1987. She is not married nor is her elder sister who has a baby. Lungiswa's eldest brother was killed in 1986 in a shebeen fight.

Between them the children have passed only one fifth of the grades at school that they 'ought' to have passed. Three have left school having passed no more than two or three grades each and another two attend fitfully. Only one child, Tozama, is in Standard Seven and a boy, Togu, is in Standard Six and two girls are in Standard Five. School boycotts, especially in 1986, explain some of the lag but not all of it. The children in the higher grades are doing very well and have high ambitions.

Most of the children have been embroiled in the trauma that blacks have experienced in the last eight years. They have had, they say, to grow accustomed to seeing casspirs (armoured vehicles) in the streets, white armed troops, death, fear and danger. Zuziwe's cousin (her mother's sister's only son) was killed in 1985 in a battle with police near Crossroads. Saliswa was living with her father when their house burnt down during a faction fight and, in January 1986, she was caught in a street battle and her ankles were so severely hit with a stick wielded by a man that she had to be hospitalized. In one of the early faction fights within Old Crossroads, Tozama's house was burnt down and her father was seriously injured. She only just escaped injury. Having lost their home, the family took refuge in the men's hostels. While their parents were out, the police arrested the children, including Tozama, and held them first in a police cell, then at Pollsmoor Prison. Tozama now lives in the Transkei but, her mother says, she still suffers from headaches and nerves as a consequence of these experiences. She cannot bear to see violence even on the television screen.

Four of the families have, at various times, been in great danger as a result of their involvement in community affairs. Adult members of these families enter Old Crossroads at the risk of losing their lives. This is not the place to document the internal fighting nor the role that the South African Police and the South African Defence Force played in it. Suffice to say that in May and June of 1986 a war raged in Crossroads and neighbouring settlements resulting in the death of an estimated one hundred people. Tens of thousands were left homeless. That was but one, albeit the worst, period of trauma.

I spent an afternoon with a group of the children and, again, was deeply impressed by their vigour, understanding and humour. Those living in brick houses still take pleasure in having running water, toilets and electric lights in their homes. Some even have telephones and television sets. They point with pride to the smooth roads that pass their doors and say, 'Even our letters are delivered'. There was not time enough to record carefully their political opinions but one mother said of her daughter, 'She is now able to differentiate between the life of a squatter and a non-squatter. She does understand a little about a black man's struggle in this country and how life should be for us all.'

In considering the nature of the children's lives, it is worth recalling what Piaget (1935: 173) said on the question of environment influence on development. He said that characteristics of the various stages of cognitive development 'are always related as much to the particular surroundings and atmosphere as to the organic maturation of the mind.' Erikson (1965) said that society must learn to minimize trauma in childhood. South African society seems neither to care about the surroundings and atmosphere that it offers children nor to attempt to minimize their trauma.

DATA ON THE PARENTS AND GUARDIANS OF THE CHILDREN (APPENDIX C-1)

Every parent or guardian of the fourteen children was Xhosa except Gedja's father who was Mpondo and Togu's father who was Mfengu. Ten of the children lived with both their parents. Of the other four, Lungiswa lived with her mother's brother and his family; Nukwa lived with his mother and father's brother and family; Gedja with her mother and either her maternal grandparents in Nyanga East or her mother's sister and family in Crossroads; and Yameka lived with her mother's brother, his wife and child.

Lungiswa's father had separated from her mother in 1976; Nukwa's father had died in 1975; Gedja's father had left her mother when she was a toddler; Yameka's mother had taken her away from her father's home when she was a baby because he had failed to fulfil his lobola* obligations. In 1979, Yameka was brought by her uncle to live in Crossroads and to help care for their baby. I have no data on Yameka's father. Her mother's brother jealously claimed the child as his and either knew very little about her father or chose not to tell me.

FATHERS

Table 2-1 in Appendix G charts some of the basic data on the children's parents and guardians. Thirteen of the fathers were born in the Transkei and the other one on a white man's farm in the Ciskei. They all grew up in the country.

None of the men had educated above Standard Six: three had Standard Five; two Standard Three; one Standard Two, and four men had no formal education. In 1980, Thiso Bhurhu was attending his second year of night school and said that he was in Sub A. The men seemed to have attended school for many years

---

*uku-lobola - to give cattle to the group of a girl taken in marriage.

and to have passed few standards. Kobe Jwara passed Standard Six after ten years schooling; Dakada Cira Standard Five after eleven years; Jali Qasana Standard Five after eleven years, and Duma Paya Standard Three after five years. Obvious reasons such as poverty, herding duties and poor educational facilities do not seem to warrant so many years to achieve so little. On average they had 3,3 standards of schooling and there was no difference in the amount of education achieved by the men over forty-four years of age and those under forty-four.

Except for Khanda, who left home at age eleven, the men left in search of wage employment between the ages of sixteen and twenty-four. Thenceforward, they would return for spells varying from three to twelve weeks a year, occasionally for longer periods in order to be circumcised or married or to build a house or if they could not find contract work or other employment in the cities.

Half the men began as wage-earners on the mines. Among the Xhosa, work on the mines was often seen as part of a young man's initiation into manhood. The attitude was reported by Hunter (1936).

The fathers' ages ranged from thirty to fifty-eight; four were in their fifties; six in their forties and three in their thirties. Mr Feni died in 1975 and his wife did not know his age. Their average age was forty-four years. Twelve of the men on whom I have reliable data from birth and movement to town had, by 1980, spent an average of 56,5 per cent of their years in a city or mine in the so-called white man's territory, with an average of 52 per cent of their years in Cape Town. This was so despite the fact that two of the men were in their early thirties. The four men in their fifties had, on average, spent 62 per cent of their lives in a city or mine and 58 per cent in Cape Town.

After 540 man-years in a city or mine, twelve men had no claims on that territory and owned nothing except some rights in a shack on the sand dunes of the Cape Flats. The land and stock they owned in the Transkei could not yield sufficient income to sustain their families. None of them fit the Government's notion of men living in the countryside with occasional forays into the cities to earn supplementary monies.

MOTHERS

Eleven of the women in question were born in the Transkei, one on a farm in the Ciskei, one on a farm in Stellenbosch near Cape Town, and another in Cape Town. In 1980, their ages ranged from twenty-four to forty-six years: four of them were in their forties, eight in their thirties and two in their twenties. The average age was thirty-five years, nine years younger than the average age of the men. They had on average 6,9 siblings, which is higher than the figure for their husbands. They had, on average, passed 4,1 standards in school compared to 3,3 for the men. Two were illiterate : Thandi Feni and Nozolile Qasana. Three had passed Standard Six; one Standard Seven and two Standard Eight. The seven eldest women, with an average age of forty, had passed an average of 4,6 standards, while the seven youngest, with an average age of 30,1, had passed an average of only 3,7 standards. Is this another symptom of South Africa's growing poverty? In 1980, the older group earned an average of R4,00 more a week.

By 1980, the women had spent an average of 14,5 years living in Cape Town. If the figure is representative of a wider group, as other data collected in Crossroads suggest (see the Introduction) then it belies official belief that squatters are recent immigrants to the city. For most of their years in town, the women did not have passes. Only the 'Cape Borners' were invulnerable to arrests, fines or deportations for being in the city without official permission. In 1980, ten of them had Crossroads passes, two had 10(1)(a) passes, and two, Thandi and Noncumbe, had none. As a consequence of pass offences, six women had been to prison at least once.

MARRIAGES

Five men and two women had had spouses other than the one with whom they were living in Crossroads in 1980.

Of the fourteen couples, two were married, including Yameka's guardians; one couple was unmarried but lived as husband and wife; one was single and lived with her family; one woman was separated from her husband and lived with her brother and his family; and one woman was a widow. Of the twelve married couples, including the widow, the woman who was separated from her husband and Yameka's guardians, all had married according to customary rites (that is to say, their families had received ikhazi* for them), five had married in church and three before a Magistrate. Four had married only according to customary rites.

IN THE CITIES

Prior to their move to Crossroads, the families had lived as lodgers in the townships, or the Bachelor Quarters, or squatter camps such as K.T.C. Modderdam, Browns or The Airport. All the men and the women, except Thandi Feni, were living in Cape Town prior to the creation of Crossroads in 1975. The women gave a variety of reasons for having come to town: three came to their husbands to conceive a baby; two to be with their husbands; two to work; two because of ill health; one to visit a kinsman; another because she had been kidnapped from the Transkei and brought to the city by the man who intended marrying her and the last because she and her family had been sent off a white farm.

Passes

In terms of the Blacks (Urban Areas) Consolidation Act (No. 25 of 1945) as amended, still in force at the time, blacks were subject to being charged or repatriated unless they

---

*i-khazi, pl. ama- cattle given by groom's group to bride's group on the occasion of marriage.

could satisfy authorities that they had permission to be in areas outside the territory that was assigned to them by the government. Xhosa people needed passes to work and live in South African cities, including Cape Town. The Act was abolished in 1986.

A Crossroads pass refers to special permission that was granted to all registered residents of the settlement, allowing them to live and work in the Peninsula. The pass was similar to a 10(1)(d) permission under the Act, and was gained as part of the struggle for urban rights in the 'Koornhof deal'.

Although all of the fathers or guardians of the fourteen children had lived in a city for more than ten years, only five of them - Thiso Bhurhu, Bhuqa Hleke, Dakada Cira, Ngalweni Dyani and Faku Ketshe had 10(1)(b) passes.

Arrival at Crossroads

All but two of the families came to live in Crossroads in 1975 or 1976. Thandi Feni came from the Transkei to consult city doctors in 1979 and Jane Ntinde came to live with her elder sister in 1978 because her mother's home in the township was overcrowded. All but one of those who owned their own shacks arrived and built in 1975.

It was, in 1980, important in terms of permission to remain in town and possible future house ownership for Crossroads' people to establish and prove early residence in the squatter camp. Some of the families may have pre-dated their arrival by a year but no more. The women gave different reasons for their move to Crossroads from those given for their move to Cape Town: four families were sent by the Divisional Council officials from other squatter camps (Brown's, Retreat, K.T.C. and The Airport); three other families said that they had come seeking a place to live as a family; three came because they were tired of lodging; one came because the price of fines in the townships was too high; and the last couple came to find their own home as they had been living in Nyanga East with the woman's parents and that, she explained, is against Xhosa custom. In effect, all but the widow and the unmarried women sought homes in which to live as families.

Kin and Other Networks

Only one couple, the Payas, did not have relatives living in Crossroads. Kin connections were important to new arrivals at the camp, because they helped them establish and build a home and, later, to handle community fines or disagreements. Clan membership and 'home-people' groups served similar functions.

Residence

Eight of the families owned their own homes. That is to say, they held the rent card and were responsible for paying the R7,00 a month rent. Government had undertaken, as part of the Crossroads settlement package, to provide brick houses for every family registered under the surveys of 1976 and 1980, whether the residents were house owners or lodgers. Neither group was supposed to move residence within Crossroads. Many complications ensued.

Rent for a Crossroads house was R7,00 a month and lodgers paid R2,50 or R3,50 per family per month depending upon the amount of space they occupied. Two or three families would often pay the full rent in rotation. The Paya family of four, including Yameka, shared a 4 x 3 metre room with another woman. Mr Paya and the women each paid R3,50 a month to the house owner. The room held two beds, a rough dresser, a small table piled with kitchen utensils, a primus stove and a bucket. The walls were papered with tin covers, newspapers and reject studio photographs of white children. The six-roomed house was occupied by nine women, four men and eleven children. It was located in an area in the middle of Crossroads that was wryly dubbed 'the inner city slum.'

In contrast, in the Bhurhu house seven people shared four rooms. The house was immaculately kept with cacti in pots on the shelves and lace covers on the table, fresh curtains at the windows and a fine kitchen with a Dover stove. It was set in a spacious yard which had an orange metal arch over the gateway.

Among the sample families, an average of 12,4 people lived in a house with an average of four rooms; the range was from seven to twenty-four people in three-to six-roomed houses. On average, there were 5,4 adults per household and 7,0 children. I did not count short-term visitors. The composition of households fluctuated during the year, sometimes by as many as eight people, more or less. During the fifteen months of my field research, four of the children and their families changed residence, three within Crossroads.

Employment

In 1980, six of the fathers were labourers and one each was occupied as one of the following: tailor, driver, time-keeper, scaffolding builder, electrician, and messenger. The eleven fathers of the sample children earned on average R35,50 per week, the range being from R25 to R66. Until he lost his job in May, Dakada Cira had earned R66,00 a week as a driver after seventeen years with the same company. For the rest of the year he lived on unemployment pay of R15,00 a week, and the average income per week of the eleven fathers was then R32,90.

Long service did not seem to be rewarded. Mr Bhurhu earned only R35,00 a week after thirty-five years of service to the same company. His firm deducted R1,50 a week from his salary in order to pay the Divisional Council for his Bachelor Quarters rent despite the fact that he had not lived there for over five years, and despite official legislation that exempted Crossroads residents from having to pay double rents.

Figures derived from data collected from the parents or guardians of the twenty-five children in the control group, are very similar to those given above. Twenty-one of the children in the control group lived with their fathers, all of whom were employed, earning from R15,00 to R64,00 a week, with an average of R34,00. Thirteen of the children's mothers were employed, some part time and almost all as domestics; ten were unemployed and one was self-employed. One child lived with her father's sister. The earnings of the thirteen women who were employed ranged from R5,00 (as daily char) to R30,00 (as a cleaner in a hotel) per week, with an average of R12,00.

Four children had no father living with them; one child only saw her father at weekends; and of the other twenty, father was away from home for an average of 12,5 hours every working day.

Thirteen children did not have the daily care of their mothers. Two of the working mothers returned home only at weekends and a third returned for only one weekend every month. The others were away from home an average of 9,4 hours every working day.

The social costs of the system reverberated down on the children. A sentence written by Lawrence Durrell in Justine comes to mind: 'It is the city which should be judged though we, its children, must pay the price.'

Among the mothers of the children in the sample of fourteen, four of them did not work, and two of them were not healthy; Zanele Cira had a bad hernia and Makaziwe Gonya had serious diabetes. The latter helped her husband to sew when she was well enough. Noncumbe Paya hawked occasionally and fried fish which Yameka sold. The other women earned an average of R16,20 a week or, if we exclude Thandi Feniz whose earnings of R4,00 a week brewing beer could not be checked, the average was R17,50. The highest earnings were R25,00 a week, which is what Pumza earned, as a nutrition research worker, and the amount the two amagqira said they brought in. Kin and neighbours said the latter earned more but I have no data with which to dispute their figures. Income among amagqira varied in Crossroads depending upon individual reputation; the figures quoted most often were R10,00 to 'open the bag' that is, begin discussion and R50,00 for a full cure.

Three women were full-time maids in the homes of whites; two earned R12,00 and R14,00 for a five-day week plus bus fare. Three others were chars;

one worked four days a week, another twice and the third, once. They earned R5,00 a day plus bus fare. One of them also earned R10,00 a week as a literacy tutor in Crossroads. During the one year, one woman stopped working as a domestic servant in October and hawked clothes far afield. Another only began to work in September.

The wage income of the fourteen families averaged R48,20 per week (or R44,20 when Dakada Cira was drawing unemployment pay), ranging from R25,00 to R75,00. These figures hide a great deal of variation within the families and between families. Economies were achieved by sharing houses or by renting space to lodgers. Elasticity in sharing arrangements enabled families to help members in times of need. Sharing among kin, neighbours and clan members was a system of mutual insurance. Some of the elasticity that conditions in a squatter settlement allow, will be lost once a permanent township has been created.*

Remittances

Nine couples had fourteen children who were living in the Transkei, and another who lived in Guguletu, for whom they were financially responsible. All of the children were staying with relatives; four with mother's mother; three with father's mother; and seven with brothers or sisters or their parents.

Seven families sent money to support children in the country-side and two families sent money to support their parents. The nine families sent an average of R35,00 a month to kin in the countryside. Four men sent money to their mothers and one man sent money to his sister, while three women sent money to their mothers, one to her brother and one to her sister. That is,

---

*The average income of the sample families was higher than the average found by Maree and Cornell who recorded an average income for men of R24,30 per week (sample – R32,90); for spouses R9,50 per week (sample – R11,60).

ten women and one man living in the countryside received some money from their
kin in Cape Town each month. I did not record occasional monies sent nor
money spent on the upkeep of land or homes in the countryside. I recorded
nothing which suggested that regular contributions were sent from rural to
urban family members.

SUMMARY

The reasons why men leave the countryside and come to town are clear:
they have no choice for only in town can they earn an income. The reasons why
women come are more complex : many come to find work to support dependants –
parents, siblings, children; many come to escape the poverty and despair of
life in the homelands; many come to be with their husbands, to claim him (and
his earnings) from other women, to conceive children and to share with him
their care and rearing. Many of the men and women build shacks in the sand in
order to create homes in which to live as families. However, that is not the
only reason for squatting in Cape Town. Economic necessity, the housing
shortage, police harassment and the disruption of family life force some
people to seek alternatives to living as nuclear family units. There is
fluidity among husbands and wives and other kin in the care of children, and
administrative attempts to define the family unit that is most deserving of
housing security may not serve the best interests of the children.

SKETCHES OF THE CHILDREN'S LIVES
(APPENDIX C-2)

Yameka Paya

Soon after Yameka's birth, her mother was recalled to her natal home because Yameka's father had failed to pay any <u>lobola</u>. As her parents' union had not been sanctioned in a culturally acceptable fashion, Yameka was not protected by the ancestors of her father's family. Her mother's family ought to have propitiated their ancestors and asked them to accept the child within their ambit. Yameka's guardian in Crossroads, her mother's brother, said that the appropriate ritual was planned.

In 1979, Yameka was brought by her mother's brother to Crossroads to help his wife care for their small child. Yameka was called a 'child of the family' and seemed happy enough. She was expected to accomplish many tasks efficiently and quickly. Her tasks included child-minding and the selling of fish cooked by her uncle's wife. The family of four shared a small room with another lodger. The room was part of a rambling shack that housed twenty-four people. Neither Yameka's uncle nor his wife had permits to live and work in the city and, as a consequence, he was often without work. His wage was seldom more than R25,00 a week. Yameka owned very few clothes and little else apart from a black plastic bangle and a mug. Occasionally she attended church in another township with the family but went on few other excursions beyond the boundaries of the settlement.

Yameka had many friends who lived in the neighbourhood and she was frequently to be seen playing, singing and dancing in a group. Nevertheless, she is a reticent child. She watches life closely and absorbs a great deal. She had, in 1980, never been to school and has lived in greater poverty than have most of the children in the sample and was less secure in having neither her father nor her mother living with her.

Nukwa Feni

Nukwa grew up in the Transkei. His father was killed in an accident
when he was five years old and in 1979 he was brought by his mother to
Crossroads to stay with his father's brother. She came to the city, she said,
for medical treatment. Nukwa is a thin, small child (he weighs below the
Boston Third Percentile). He has a quiet charm. His father's brother
supports three families on his earnings of R35,00 a week. Nukwa's mother sold
sweets and brewed beer in Crossroads. For most of 1980, she ran a small
shebeen with a friend. Nukwa was left to his own devices for much of the time
and he dropped out of school half way through the year.

Zuziwe Hleke

Zuziwe is the third child of Pumza and Bhuqa Hleke. Her mother, a tall
and beautiful woman, was kidnapped by her father at the age of seventeen.
Theirs was a stormy marriage, and in 1980 Pumza was seeking a divorce from
Bhuqa. Zuziwe was the second of four live children. Her younger sister had
cancer of the eye which meant that the family had to live near a large city
hospital to secure her adequate treatment. Zuziwe is a clever and sensitive
girl.

Mlawu Anta

Mlawu is the third child and first son of Nocululu and Sipho Anta. He
is a child of gentleness and dignity. His father holds to traditional values
of discipline and order and is strict with him. His mother is devoted to her
family and works hard, long hours on their behalf. In 1980, Mlawu was always
carefully dressed in school uniform and only the potatoes (holes) in his socks
suggested poverty.

Saliswa Qasana

Saliswa is the twelfth of the fourteen children born to her mother. Four of the children died and six had another father (see the data on the Qasana family in Appendix CI). Her mother is an _igqira_. She described Saliswa as being sweet, happy, quiet and a hard worker. She thinks that the child will be too sensitive to handle marriage, as 'There is no good behaviour in marriage; there is too much force and too many rules to obey.' She hopes that Saliswa will live with her when she grows up. She says that Saliswa has been called to be an _igqira_.

In 1980, the Qasana home was a merry one. A mock fight involving adults and children is described in the test and so is a morning of dance and song in their home. Saliswa suffered quite severely from asthma as a small child; she was frequently hospitalised. Her asthma condition is aggravated by tear gas that is used periodically to quell trouble in Crossroads. Like Hintsa and Zuziwe, Saliswa did not talk about trouble that she had witnessed in the settlement. All three had been tied on their mothers' backs as they ran from the police across the dunes of Crossroads. As a toddler, Saliswa had been imprisoned with her mother. All three children had lived in the settlement since its inception.

Gwali Maqoma

Gwali is a comic. He is always full of laughter. He is short and has a large head and a huge smile. He achieved the least well of all the children on almost every task. In 1980, he did not attend school but spent his time roaming across the sand dunes of the settlement with his brother and their friends. His brother is slightly retarded: Gwali's care and love for him are recorded in the text. I observed many incidents of his kindness and generosity to others.

His father is careful, serious and religious and his mother is jolly and hard-working. The children were left largely unsupervised during the week days as both parents worked outside Crossroads.

Nomvula Gonya

Nomvula is one of five girls in her family. Her father is a tailor and works at home. Her mother, an attractive, slim woman, is often weak and ill with diabetes. Her husband treats her and the children rather harshly. She is not a talkative child: she sits quietly and watches. She is cheerful, though, and has many friends.

Togu Cira

Togu has a round, cheerful face with small scars on his forehead. The scars resulted from razor cuts made during the treatment of an eye infection. He had double pneumonia as a baby and spent the first five months of his life in hospital. His father used to visit him every day. Togu often expressed his love for his father and his jealousy of his young brother, whom he felt had stolen his place in his father's affections. His father had recently lost a relatively well-paid job and was unemployed for much of the year during which I worked with Togu. His mother had had a number of operations.

Togu is shy. It took some time for him to trust me but, once he did, our relations were easy and fruitful.

Tozama Ketshe

Tozama is a lovely girl with a dimpled smile and dark, laughing eyes. She is warm and responsive and moves with dignity, yet there is a touch of humour in all that she does. She is articulate and observant: she gave me detailed accounts of a ritual in Crossroads and of a white man's death (both are reported in Chapter Two).

Her father is very dear to her and she often expressed her love for him
and her fears for his safety. When he returned dusty and tired from work,
Tozama used to fetch a bowl of water and wash his feet. She once said to him,
'Daddy, if you die, I will die too.'

Both of her parents were prominent community leaders. Her mother is an
igqira and a woman of strength, courage and great charm. She gave an
interpretation of Tozama's dream and lassitude as the first signs of her
calling to be an igqira (see Chapter Two).

Hintsa Lusizini

Hintsa is tall and thin. He has large, soft eyes that make him resemble
a frightened deer. He is often teased by other children. His parents are
both away from home during working hours and there is not much supervision of
the children. Hintsa was with his mother when one of their shacks was
bulldozed. He was extremely upset when his mother was imprisoned for a night
because she had no pass, and when he was caught in a clash between Crossroads
settlers and the police at the school (see Chapter Two).

There was frequently insufficient food to feed all the family members in
Hintsa's home. I recorded (see Chapter Seven) one instance when there was no
supper because Hintsa's father had been ill and had no money with which to buy
food.

It was difficult to draw Hintsa out: he refused to talk about events
that had troubled him but he admitted to being afraid of elephants and police
and, initially, me.

Lungiswa Dyani

Lungiswa, like Tozama, is a bright and articulate girl. Her maternal
grandfather, who was an igqira, lived in Crossroads. Having seen the distress
resulting from his eldest daughter's arranged marriages, he resolved to allow

his younger daughters to select their own husbands. Lungiswa's version of the
family history (the date of her parents' separation and the paternity of her
younger brother) differed from her mother's: the child firmly asserted the
truth of her version. At the age of seven, she had already lived apart from
her father from three to five years.

Sometimes Lungiswa had asthmatic attacks (in Chapter Two there is an
account of a dream of one attack). She recounts another dream (see Chapter
Two) in which she is burnt during a riot. One of her play scenes was of a
police raid on Crossroads. Lungiswa is quick, extrovert and enterprising. To
earn money, she hawked old clothes for a neighbour. An aspect of her nature
is revealed in the following. One day in November 1980, she took some crayons
from my room and distributed them among her friends. I said to her that she
ought not to have done that and told her to clean the windows of my room as a
punishment. After school, Lungiswa arrived with Tozama, Peliswe and another
friend in tow. She had informed her friends that I had ordered them to clean
my windows. The girls were armed with buckets, window cleaning soap and
cloths and they set about their task in a festive mood. Upon completion,
Lungiswa said, 'Last Friday I had planned to clean your windows but you were
not here.' Not only had she, like Tom Sawyer, inveigled her friends into
completing a job assigned to her, but she had even assumed initiative for the
punishment.

Cebo Jwara

Cebo is small and stocky. He has a winning smile and delightful ways.
He is often in trouble and causes his parents much anxiety : they are torn
between the need to curb his naughtiness and their desire to shield him (see
Chapter Two). He frequently wets his bed and has some nervous mannerisms.

I recall being a little impatient with him once but I have forgotten why - perhaps he had stolen some marbles or bullied another child. On the following day, I was walking through the settlement berating myself for having been short with him when I felt a hand slip into mine. On turning, I saw Cebo with his huge, apologetic grin.

By age seven, Cebo had lived apart from his parents for three years. He spent most of that time with his mother's mother in the Transkei. He enjoyed life in the countryside and had persuaded his grandmother to conspire with him against the need to attend school regularly.

Gedja Ntinde

Unlike the other thirteen children in this survey, Gedja grew up in Cape Town. Since her birth, she has lived with her mother and her maternal grandparents in Nyanga East. In 1978, to relieve the overcrowding in the Nyanga East home, she and her mother moved to Crossroads to stay with her mother's sister. According to both her mother and herself, she has few fears and has been little troubled by disturbances in either the township or the squatter settlement. She did not attend school in 1980.

She is a cheerful and confident girl and is allowed a greater range of freedom than are the other girls in the sample. Gedja's parents are not married. Apart from the first two years of her life, she has spent little time with her father.

Peliswe Bhurhu

Peliswe was a slip of a girl with a pretty, fine-featured face. She was delicate in her movement and always neatly dressed. She was full of fun and had a number of close friends. She was the much loved youngest child in the family and her movements were carefully monitored by her mother.

Her mother made the family shack into a very attractive home, despite having watched four of her shacks demolished by bulldozers. The demolitions must have contributed to her high level of anxiety. She articulated her

bitterness about the black man's fate in South Africa. In 1979, her brother
had been killed in a car accident and her son injured. She attributed the
paralysis that temporarily afflicted one side of Peliswe's face soon after the
accident to the distress that the child had felt.

Peliswe was generous: on receiving a gift of an angel puppet, she ran
to my room to give it to me to add to the collection of puppets with which we
played. I recall with delight her curiosity and surprise in exploring my home
and sharing in my children's exploits when she and Tozama visited for a
weekend.

In 1981, Peliswe was run over and killed by an ambulance as she played
outside her classroom. What cruel irony that the most carefully tended child
in Crossroads should be killed.

PIAGET'S TEST DESCRIPTION
(APPENDIX D)

TEST 1: One of the most familiar Piagetian tasks is the <u>conservation of</u> <u>quantity</u> (liquids), which is considered to be a marker of the beginning of the concrete operational stage. In this task, the child pours the same amount of water into two identical glasses; once the initial equality is well established, he is asked to pour the water from one container into a glass of a different shape, say long and narrow (or wide), so that the level of the liquid changes. Then the child is asked whether the amount of water is less, more or the same as in the other container. The child at the pre-operational stage will answer 'No, there is more (or less) because the water comes up high (or low).' In other words she is attending to only one of the dimensions and is not able to carry the invariance of quantity across the transformations of the display. At a second stage, the child exhibits hesitations, changing her mind either in the same situation or between situations. At the concrete operational stage (conventionally called 'stage 3'), the child is convinced that the amount of water does not change, and she is able to justify her answer in various ways.

TEST 2: <u>The conservation of discontinuous quantity</u> is the same as the above except that beads (or similar items) are used instead of liquid.

TEST 3: The task of <u>conservation of weight</u> follows the same scheme but the materials are two identical plasticene (or clay) balls, one of which is rolled out (or flattened) by the child during the experiment. The question asked is whether the ball and the rolled out (or flattened) pieces are still of the same weight. A balance is used to visualize the concept.

TEST 4a: This is a test of the <u>conservation of number</u>. It examines a child's ability to place single rows of objects in correspondence and to keep the notion of necessary and lasting equivalence of the corresponding sets despite rearrangments in their spacing. It studies how the child makes two sets of equal value. A row of counters (or similar objects) are placed before a child who is asked to make another row the same in number. Once this is done and the child agrees to their correspondence, one row is spaced out and the child is questioned as to whether the row now has more, less or the same number of counters in it as are in the other row. A reverse operation is performed.

TEST 4b: A variation of the test using eggs and egg cups was also administered as there was less chance of verbal misunderstanding than in the former test. A row of egg cups was set before the child who was asked to select from a cluster of eggs sufficient to correspond with the number of egg cups. She either put one egg opposite each cup or made a more or less compact row the same length as the row of cups. She was then asked to check her result by putting one egg into each cup, thus obtaining one-one correspondence. The eggs were then taken out and clustered together (or the cups grouped) and as before the child was asked whether there was still the same number of both.

TEST 5A: Piaget described his test of <u>class inclusion</u> as follows:

> To study the formation of classes, we place about twenty beads in a
> box, the subject acknowledging that they are 'all made of wood',
> so that they constitute a whole, B. Most of these beads are brown
> and constitute part A, and some are white, forming the complementary
> part A.[1] In order to determine whether the child is capable of
> understanding the (Boolean) operation $A+A^1=B$, i.e. the uniting
> of parts in a whole, we may put the following simple question:
> In this box (all the beads still being visible) which are there more

of - wooden beads or brown beads, i.e. is A[B?

Now up to about the age of 7 years, the child almost always

replies that there are more brown beads 'because there are only

two or three white ones' (Piagetian, 1947:133).

A question relating to the length of necklaces made from the beads was

also asked.

TEST 5b: A variation of the above test was given using small plastic animals

- horses and sheep. With the women, coins were used, that is rand and cents.

According to Piaget (1966:103), the understanding of the relative sizes of an

included class to the entire class is achieved by about 8 years old and marks

the achievement of a genuine operatory classification.

Scoring For the purposes of a chi-squared analysis, the results were assigned

to two columns of non-conservers (NC) and conservers (C). Children judged to

be in a transitional stage were included among the non-conservers. For the

purpose of the Mann-Whitney test, each performance was scored on a three point

scale that was related to actions and replies relevant to each test. Nought

was equal to failure and three to success with the identification of all

criteria. Chi-squared tests were computed on the results (see Table 7-1)

using the following formula:

$$x^2 = \frac{N(AD - BC - \underline{N})^2}{(A+B)(C+D)(A+C)(B+D)}$$

crit. x^2 for 1d.f = 3,84

PONDOLAND HERD BOYS' COMMENTS ON THE LEARNING OF THE NAMES OF THINGS (APPENDIX F)

Of the ninety children whom I interviewed in Pondoland, twenty-eight were girls. On each occasion there were three or four children and we usually spent some hours together. There were five children aged five; seventy-five aged six to fourteen; and ten over age fourteen. The children told me their ages and Nozizwe and I checked what they said against our own estimates.

Most of the children were boys because we spent much of our time in the veld amongst herd boys. This was intentional as I wanted to obtain a rough idea of how much they knew sbout birds, trees and colours. Traditionally, it is the boys who learn more about these things. I was particularly interested in discovering from whom they learnt to classify. The seven-year-olds in Crossroads knew the names of very few trees or birds and could identify only four or five colours: they did not know the colours specifically used to identify cattle, of which Monica Hunter recorded fifty-seven in the 1930s. However, I wanted to obtain an idea of how much of such traditional learning still occurred in the country and how it was transmitted.

From talking with herd-boys, I learnt thirteen names for colours that are used to distinguish cattle; fifty for birds and thirty-four for trees. That was from casual enquiry during conversation, prior to which none of us had met. It was the ten-to-twelve-year-olds who knew most names, but younger boys took pride in displaying their knowledge. I quote below conversations held with some of them because the conversations support my thesis about child learning, that both the teaching and the learning are more ordered and more formal in a traditional world than is usually allowed.

Near Enkodusweni on 7 January 1981, we met a seven-year-old herd-boy named Kholikile in Sub B, who named twenty-three birds and twenty-three

trees. He could describe them and gave many uses for the latter. I asked him
who had taught him. He said:

> 'I hear from the older boys, the herd boys and our parents. From
> my father - I listen when they talk. I listen while we are at the
> fields.'
>
> (To whom does your father talk in the fields?)
>
> 'He talks to us. He is not actually teaching us but we hear while he
> talks. He is telling us. He does not teach us about plants or trees.
> I know about trees. I hear from the other boys.'

This characterizes, for me, the whole problem of listening and hearing
and teaching and learning. The Xhosa say that they do not teach; the children
watch and listen. Yet it happens that young children are in the fields with
their fathers and there is no other adult and he talks about the birds and
they listen. He does not teach and they do not learn, but he talks and they
know.

On the same day, another boy gave me a good answer. I had, in an
attempt to make some boys articulate their thoughts on change, asked whether
they thought that they, as herd-boys, knew more or less about the veld than
did the people of long ago. A child replied:

> 'We know more about the veld than those of long ago because we
> are still learning and they have forgotten.'
>
> (Touché)

On 8 January 1981, we spent much of the day with four herd-boys at
Mpotsholo in Mpande Bay. The boys were: Cebisile, aged twelve in Standard 2;
Notani, aged ten in Sub B; Andile, aged seven or eight, going into Sub A; and
Nomlitili, aged five and the brother of Cebisile. They named thirty-two
birds, seven trees (I rather interrupted their list) and twelve colours. On
learning the names of birds, Cebisile said:

'No one special teaches these names. We were born and these birds were
here already and people were calling their names. And by seeing these
birds we get to know their names.'

(Who calls these names?)

'It is the older boys.'

(When ....?)

'Sometimes you go out to hunt and you catch a bird and they will tell
you what you have caught.'

(Do fathers tell you?)

'Yes.'

(When?)

'Sometimes you ask when you see the bird and then they tell you.'

(And mothers?)

'Mothers are not so good at telling the birds, but they know the kinds
that catch the chickens.'

(He named three.)

I pressed the conversation further in relation to learning the names of
trees. Cebisile said:

'Sometimes we learn from the adults. We go to chop wood and then we
hear the name of that wood. The adult tells us especially. They tell
us which trees to use for sticks.'

Again, the language belies the incident. He said that they 'hear' the
word, whereas it is most specifically being taught to them. In listing the
names of trees, the boys mentioned umthathi (Pleroxy Pon 'sneeze wood') which
recalled a saying to Nozizwe's mind: Umthathi uzala umlotha. (Ukuzala – to
produce, give birth. Umlotha – ash.)

The phrase, as she explained it, means that you may give birth to
someone who does not believe in Christianity whereas you do. The person may
be a fine product of the parent who is of poor mettle, or vice versa. I was
interested in discovering what characteristics the boys assigned to the tree
and asked for a description. All four immediately pointed to a tree some way
off, even the five-year old. One ran off and returned with a sprig and
another sprig from the umsimbithi (Milletia) tree from which good sticks are
carved. They told me that the leaves of the former are fed to cattle sick
with gall. They give them diarrohea which expunges the gall.

The leaves of the two trees were similar in size, in arrangement on the
stalk and in colour. I asked how they told them apart. Cebisile said:

'The leaves differ from each other. You can see that this is a darker
green than the other one. And these are bigger than those and you can
watch the bark of this tree peeling.'

(Who taught you to look so closely at the differences?)

'Seeing that we are used to the trees, we can easily tell the
difference.'

(Can this child - the five-year old - tell them part?)

They laughed and said no. The child in question took umbrage and
pointed,

saying:

'There is an umsimbithi tree.'

Cebisile shrugged, saying:

'Aye, I don't know who teaches. There is no specialist.'

(I understand that but I think the older ones teach the young one
carefully!)

'I agree.'

(You see, what I need to know is who teaches and when.)

'We get to know the names from the older people. Sometimes you go to
the forest and you are told not to destroy that tree or the foresters
will make trouble.'

I left off just a little and asked a silly question. Sometimes one
must. I asked:

(Who is the lucky child: the one whose father is at home or the one
whose father is making money in Johannesburg?)

'I would say that those who are always with their fathers are lucky
because, as a boy, one goes to the veld or the forest with one's father
and learns. Those who do not have a father with them do not get a
chance.'

Nozizwe asked:

Your name means to advise. Would you like to be a magistrate?

'No. I would not like to listen to people and sentence them.'

In the Transkei I learnt more about the pattern of children's days,
their play and their ability to tell stories. Most important, however, was
that I learnt that children in the countryside or, as Holden called them in
1866, 'these denizens of the wilderness', are not very different in many ways
from those in town. Besides, I found hints to confirm the hypothesis that the
traditional learning process has a plan, a rationale behind it that is formal
if not consciously expressed. This matters because I believe that when
traditional processes fall away, the modern educational process often fails to
replace it in terms of the quality of tutorial relationship, the amount of
practice offered and relevance to life situations.

TABLES

Table 1-1: The Percentage of Each Race Group Who Were Urban Dwellers in
South Africa in 1970 and 1980

	Urban Dwellers - %	
	1970	1980
White	86,8	88,9
Coloured	74,1	77,3
Asian	83,7	91,3
African	33,1	37,8

Source: Gordon, L. ed. Survey of Race Relations in South Africa 1980,
Johannesburg. The South African Institute of Race Relations, 1981, p.68.

Table 1-2: Black Poverty in South Africa: 1980[1]

a.	No. of Blacks	No. of Families (5.5 persons to a family
Urban	5,320,418	967,349
White farm areas	4,323,545	786,099
Homelands	11,338,308	2,061,511
	20,982,271	3,814,959

b.   Taking Poverty Datum Line at R200 p.m. per family: %

25% of urban families average shortfall R50 p.m.	= R 12.0m	6.5
50% of rural families average shortfall R80 p.m.	= R 31.4m	13.6
75% of homelands families average shortfall R120 p.m.	= R185.5m	80.1
	R228.9m	

or R2.747 billion per year

1.   The table was compiled by N Reynolds (1981:7) and the figures
were taken from C E W Simkins, The Distribution of Personal Income,
DSRG Working Paper No. 9 Pietermaritzburg: University of Natal, 1979.

Table 1-3: Growth of Urban Population[1]

	1960	1970	1980
Actual	46.7	47.8	47.3
Predicted[2]	49.6	55.3	56.7

1. Drawn from C E W Simkins, The Economic Implications of African Resettlement, SALDRU, Cape Town, 1981.

2. Based on a model by Chenery and Syrquin, Patterns of Development, 1950-1970.

Table 1-4: African Population Residing Legally in Cape Town

	Langa[1]	Nyanga[1]	Gugulethu[1]	Other[2]	Total
Men	24 977	10 275	16 082	12 510	63 844
Women	2 350	2 942	12 422	-	17 714
Children[3]	3 705	3 823	25 565	-	33 093
Total	31 032	17 040	54 069	12 510	114 651
Men in Single Quarters	23 622	8 019	4 691	12 510	48 842

Sources: Hansard, No. 5, 4 March, 1975, Questions Columns 352-3.
David Selvan (1976), pp. 9-10, Table 5.

(1) Statistics at 31.12.1974

(2) "Other" includes the S.A. Railways and Harbours compounds in the docks and bordering on Langa and other licenced premises such as the Hout Bay compound and building sites. The figures in this column are for 1976.

(3) Children are below 16 years of age.

Table 2—1: Family Data

	ANTA	BHURHU	CIRA	DYANI	FENI	GONYA	HLEKE	JWARA	KETSHE	LUSIZINI	MAQOMA	NTINDE*	PAYA	QASANA
FAMILY SURNAME:														
MOTHER:														
age	39	38	40	40	30	32	34	37	46	35	32	24	24	40
education (standard)	6	4	5	8	0	1	4	3	6	7	6	3	5	0
marital status	married	married	married	separated	widow	married	married	married	married	married	married	unmarried	married	separated; current union not formalized
children alive (dead)	5	4 [2]**	4 (1)	7	3 (1)	5 (1)	4 [4](1)	5 (1)	6 [9](2)	4	2 (1)	2	1 (1)	4 [6](4)
FATHER:														
age	45	58	50	52	?	33	48	42	52	43	41	32	30	48
education	6	0	3	3	0	5	0	6	6	0	5	5	2	5
number of wives	1	2nd (1st deserted him)	1	1 (separated)	1	1	2	1	2	1	1	0	1	as above
MOVE TO CAPE TOWN:														
mother	1970	1962	1963	1966	1979	1976	1966	1972	1959	1964	Born in CT	Born in CT	1975	1960
father	1957	1945	1950	1952	-	1963	1953	1957	1950	1961	1959	-	1968	1954
MOVE TO CROSSROADS:														
mother	1975	1976	1976	1975	1979	1976	1975	1976	1975	1975	1975	1978	1976	1975
father	1975	1976	1977	-	-	1976	1975	1976	1975	1975	1975	-	1975	1975
PASS STATUS:@														
mother	+	10(1)(b)	+	+	none	+	+	+	+	+	10(1)(a)	10(1)(a)	none	+
father	+	10(1)(b)	10(1)(b)	10(1)(b)	-	+	10(1)(b)	+	+	contract	+	contract	none	+
HOUSE:														
own	/			/	/	/								
relative's		/	/				/	/	/	/	/	/		
lodging													/	/

KEY:

* Ntinde is Gedja's mother's family name. Gedja's father is called Ndlambe.

**[ ] Children by either partner from another union.

@ + represents a Crossroads' Pass (see text p.89). Table continues p.65.

Table 2-1: Family Data (continued)

	ANTA	BHURHU	CIRA	DYANI	FENI	GONYA	HLEKE	JWARA	KETSHE	LUSIZINI	MAQWA	NTINDE*	PAYA	QASANA
FAMILY SURNAME:														
CHURCH MEMBERSHIP:														
mother	Wesleyan Methodist	Dutch Reformed	Anglican	Roman Catholic	None	Apostolic Faith Mission	Anglican	United Presbyterian	Roman Catholic	Baptist	Seventh Day Adventist	Zion	Roman Catholic	None
father	Wesleyan Methodist	Dutch Reformed	Anglican	Roman Catholic	-	Apostolic Faith Mission	Anglican	United Presbyterian	Roman Catholic	Baptist	Seventh Day Adventist		None	Methodist
SIZE OF FAMILY LIVING IN HOUSE:														
adults	2	3	3	3	3	7	6	3	3	5	5	5	2	2
children	5	4	2	5	7	14	7	3	9	4	4	4	2	7
total	7	7	5	8	10	21	13	6	12	9	9	9	4	9
IF OWNED, NUMBER OF LODGERS:														
adults	3													2
children	3													3
total	6													5
IF LODGING, NUMBER OF OTHER INHABITANTS:														
adults			3		2			2					11	
children			3		1			2					9	
total			6		3			4					20	
TOTAL NUMBER OF PEOPLE IN HOUSE:														
adults	5	3	6	3	5	7	6	5	3	5	5	5	13	4
children	8	4	5	5	8	14	7	5	9	4	4	4	11	10
total	13	7	11	8	13	21	13	10	12	9	9	9	24	14
FAMILY INCOME, PER WEEK:														
mother	-	R10.00	- (After May) R15.00	R20.00	R4.00	-	R25.00	R15.00	R25.00	R12.00	R12.00	R14.00	-	R25.00
father	R38.00	R35.00	R20.00	Deceased husband's	Deceased husband's	R35.00	R36.00	R30.00	R50.00	R32.00	R30.00	-	R25.00	R36.00

Table 4-1: Scores on the Felt Map Task

Child*	No. of items mapped	Accuracy out of 10
Tozama	77	7
Lungiswa	74	6
Peliswa	34	6
Togu	29	6
Mlawu	21	6
Cebo	41	5
Nomvula	14	2
Hintsa	17	2
Yameka	19	1
Nukwa	15	1
Gwali	12	1
Zuziwe	16	0
Saliswa	16	0

---

*Gedja was away when this task was done.

Table 4-2: Results of the Three Mountains Task

Photographs:		Number incorrectly chosen	Number correctly chosen
	a	1	1
	b	9	-
	c	9	2
	d	1	2
	e	4	-
	f	6	1
	g	7	2
	h	10	1
	i	6	-
	j	3	-

Table 5-1: Results on Piaget's Kinship Test

	Lun.	Toz.	Zuz.	Pel.	Tog.	Nuk.	Sal.	Hin.	Yam.	Ged.	Nom.	Gwa.	Ceb
Scores according to Piaget's definitions	12	10	11	10	8	7	4	7	5	5	3	2	2
Additional marks awarded for use of kin terms in accord with children's definitions	6	7	4	4	4	5	7	2	1	0	1	2	1
Total out of 18:	18	17	15	14	12	12	11	9	6	5	4	4	3

237

Table 5-2: Household Membership

	Yam+	Tog	Zuz+	Nom	Sal	Toz+	Ged	Hin	Lun	Pel	Ceb	Nuk+	Gwa
Child's March 1980 List	4	5	8	10	1	8	8	3	1	5	3	2	6
					(3)				(7)		(6)		
Child's Nov.* 1980 list	6	7	13	14	14	11	13	9	8	7	8	9	7
No. in household: my Nov. 1980 count	24	19	17	16.	14	12	12	9	8	7	7	6	6

+ Ego included in each count although 9 children did not include themselves - those without a +.

() Brackets represent the number listed after prompting.

* It should be noted how many more members per household were named by the children in November than in March. Given that many psychological tests are administered only once to each subject, the disparity is noteworthy. Had the children "learned" by November how to respond to my questions on the basis of their experience in March? Or had their familiarity with me and my interests rendered them less shy and thus more willing or able to provide full answers, or, indeed, to be more observant of their surroundings in relation to my interests. The methodological question is : how much impact do test experiences or familiarity with context have on children's performances? The question was discussed in Chapter 5.

Table 5-3: Use of Kin Terms in Address

Scores on Puppet Calls (Total Possible - 20):

Pel	Toz	Lun	Yam	Tog	Ceb	Nuk	Sal	Gwa	Ged	Zuz	Hin	Nom
20	18	15	12	12	8	7	7	7	7	7	6	3

Table 5-4: Puppet Play and the Use of Kin Terms

The number of children who called family members

correctly using kin terms when holding each

puppet in turn

Puppets Names:	Kin Identity:	Number of Possible Terms				
		4	3	2	1	0
Nopinki	Daughter	5	8			
Zolani	Son	4	8			1
Thandeka	Mother	5			2	6
Nosipho	Grandmother	2		1	2	8
Bhololo	Grandfather	2		1	3	7

Table 7-1 : Results of Piagetian Tests

Administered to the Sample

and Control Groups

		CONTROL (25)		SAMPLE (14)		SAMPLE (10)	
		C	N	C	N	C	N
TEST NUMBER:	I	15	10	7	7	5	5
	II	14	11	10	4	8	2
	III	9	16	7	7	5	5
	IVa	11	14	7	7	6	4
	IVb	15	10	9	5	7	3
	Va	2	23	4	10	3	7
	Vb	4	21	5	9	3	7
PRE-TEST:							
	II	–	–	2	12	2	8
	IVa	–	–	1	13	1	9
POST-TEST:							
	II	–	–	8	6	7	3
	IVa	–	–	9	5	8	2

C - conservers

N - non-conservers

Table 7—2: Results of a Variety of Counting Tasks

	A COUNTING:				B RECOGNISING NUMERALS:			C ADDING:			D WRITING:	E DICE/DOMINOES:		F CONSERVATION:		
	Feb.	June	Sept.	Nov.	Feb.	Nov.	Nov.	Feb.	Sept.	Nov.	Nov.	Feb.	Nov.	Feb.	June	Nov.
MLAWU	40/12	40/12	20/12	70/12	Yes	Yes	Yes	Yes	Yes	Yes	Yes	Yes	-	N	C	C
PELISWE	40/12	40/12	20/12	70/12	Yes	Yes	Yes	No	No	Yes	Yes	Yes	Yes	N	C	C
TOGU	40/12	40/12	20/12	70/12	Yes	Yes	Yes	Yes	Yes	Yes	Yes	Yes	Yes	N	C	C
LUNGISWA	44/12	40/12	20/12	71/12	Yes	Yes	Yes	Yes	Yes	Tes	Yes	Yes	Yes	N	C	C
NUKWA	11/-	12/12	15/12	57/12	No	Few	No	No	No	No	No	Yes	Not Well	N	N	C
NOMVULA	30/12	20/12	20/12	21/12	No	Yes	Few	No	No	Yes	Yes	Yes	Not Well	N	N	N
ZUZIWE	11/-	20/12	20/12	70/12	No	Yes	Few	No	Yes	Yes	No	Yes	Yes	C	C	C
CEBO	6/-	12/12	6/-	15/-	No	No	No	No	No	No	No	No	Not Well	N	N	N
TOZAMA	40/12	40/12	20/12	70/12	Yes	Yes	Yes	No	Yes	Yes	Yes	Yes	Yes	N	C	C
HINTSA	12/12	12/12	20/12	20/12	No	No	No	No	No	No	No	Yes	Yes	N	N	C
GWALI*	5/-	5/5	5/-	4/-	No	No	No	No	No	No	No	No	Yes	N	N	N
GEDJA*	40/12	40/12	20/12	20/12	No	Few	No	No	No	No	No	Yes	Not Well	N	N	N
YAMEKA*	0/-	12/12	20/12	30/12	No	No	No	No	No	No	No	No	Yes	N	C	C
SALISWA*	12/12	12/12	20/12	30/12	No	No	No	No	No	No	No	No	Not Well	N	N	N

KEY : N - non conservation

+Section A has four columns each with two figures, the bottom one shows whether or not each child could count to 12 and the top one shows how far each could count. Each column represents a different occasion in February, June, September and November. Section B has three columns : the first shows whether or not each child could recognize numerals up to 31 in February. In November, I noted which children could recognize numerals up to 10 (column 2) and over 10 (column 3). Section C is a note of each child's ability to make small additions in February, September and November. The September estimate is derived from the shopping exercise which involved the addition of small amounts of money up to two rand. In the other two tests no aids were used although the children's fingers and toes were available as counters and, indeed, were used as such. Section D records whether or not the child could write numerals up to 20. In Section E, a rough estimate of the children's success in playing a game of dice in February and dominoes in November is given. Section F gives the results of the number conservation test using beads administered thrice during the year.

Table 7-3: Results of Test on Perceptual Motor Co-ordination

	Mlawu	Peliswe	Togu	Lungiswa	Nukwa	Nomvula	Zuziwe	Cebo	Tozama	Hintsa	Gwali*	Saliswa*	Yameka*	Gedja*
Geometric Shapes: TOTAL : 4	2	2	2	2	1	0	3	0	4	1	0	1	4	1
Write Name: TOTAL : 4	4	4	4	3	0	3	2	0	4	0	0	0	0	0
Rhythmic Writing: TOTAL : 12	11	11	10	9	5	5	6	1	11	6	5	5	6	3
Draw with Chalk: TOTAL : 16	16	14	16	16	14	16	15	13	16	13	11	15	16	15
Physical exercises: TOTAL : 108	108	99	107	104	108	107	107	90	103	85	90	102	108	94
TOTAL ON 5 SECTIONS TO BASE OF 100	442	422	432	396	255	316	368	172	487	235	194	255	350	231
TOTAL : 500	(2	4	3	5	9	8	6	14	1	11	13	9	7	12)
TOTAL ON 4 SECTIONS - WRITING NAME	342	322	332	321	255	241	318	172	387	235	194	255	350	231
TOTAL : 400	(3	5	4	6	8	10	7	14	1	11	13	8	2	12)

N.B.

1. The table gives score totals and relative position on the five groups of tasks. I marked leniently, granting success if the task was achieved no matter in what fashion.

2. When Section 2 is removed (Write name), two of the Abas.* (Saliswa and Yameka) are seen to have scored well although they have had little experience with chalk or pen and paper.

3. Figures in brackets are positions among the 14 sample children.

Table 7-4: Height and Weight of the Sample Children

Name*	Sex	HEIGHT (in metres)	% of Standard on Boston Scale	WEIGHT (in kilos)	% of Standard on Boston Scale
Tozama	F	1.230	98	25	98
Yameka	F	1.185	95	25	98
Mlawu	M	1.100	87	25	98
Lungiswa	F	1.205	96	25	100
Saliswa	F	1.205	96	23	95
Hintsa	M	1.300	105	24	96
Gedja	F	1.160	96	24	103
Peliswe	F	1.180	98	18.5	80
Nukwa	M	1.080	89	16	67
Togu	M	1.170	96	22	94
Nomvula	F	1.160	96	25	110
Gwali	M	1.155	98	22	100
Zuziwe	F	1.150	98	19.5	90
Cebo	M	1.105	92	21	95

60-80% of the standard weight equals undernutrition.

60% of the standard weight equals marasmus.

*The children are listed in order of age, eldest first.
Exact age was used in comparing their height and weight
with the Boston scale. Thanks are due to Dr I Thom
of the Empiliswenii South African Leadership Assembly
Clinic in Crossroads for measuring and weighing the
children and to Dr T Waterston of the University of
Zimbabwe Medical School, for computing the percentages.

Table 7-5: Results of Three Seriation Tasks

	I Piaget's Stick Task:	II Animal Task:	III Figure Task:
SCHOOL CHILDREN:			
Peliswe	C	B	B
Togu	C	B	A
Lungiswa	B	B	A
Nukwa	C	B	B
Nomvula	C	B	C
Zuziwe	B	A	A
Cebo	C	C	C
Tozama	B	A	A
Hintsa	C	A	C
CHILDREN NOT AT SCHOOL:			
Gwali	C	C	C
Gedja	C	C	C
Yameka	B	B	B
Saliswa	C	C	C
TOTAL NUMBER OF CHILDREN WHO ACHIEVED – A:	0	3	4
B:	4	6	3
C:	9	4	6

KEY: A – operational level

B – intermediate level

C – pre-operational level

Table 7-6A: Scores on Developmental Items on HFDs Administered to the Sample Children on Three Occasions

	Column: A Scoring According to Koppitz			B Score Minus Item 10- Hair			C Score Minus Item 22- Legs in two Dimensions			D New Score* Minus Items 10 & 22			E EQUIVALENT I.Q.'s On Scoring According to Koppitz			F On New Scores*		
Test Number:	1	2	3	1	2	3	1	2	3	1	2	3	1	2	3	1	2	3
Sample Children:																		
Mlawu	4	3	3							4	3	3	110	90	90	110	90	90
Peliswe	3	4	3	3	5	4				3	5	4	90	110	90	90	120	110
Togu	5	5	5							5	5	5	120	120	120	120	120	120
Lungiswa	3	4	3	3	4	4	4	4	3	4	4	4	90	110	90	110	110	110
Nukwa	2	4	1							2	4	1	80	110	70	80	110	70
Nomvula	4	3	4	5	4	5				5	4	5	110	90	110	120	110	120
Zuziwe	4	4	4	5	5	5				5	5	5	110	110	110	120	120	120
Cebo	3	3	4							3	3	4	90	90	110	90	90	110
Tozama	4	3	4	4	4	4				4	4	4	110	90	110	110	110	110
Hintsa	2	2	1							2	2	1	80	80	70	80	80	70
Gwali	2	2	3							2	2	3	80	80	90	80	80	90
Gedja	2	2	4	3	2	4	2	3	4	3	3	4	80	80	110	90	90	110
Yameka	4	3	1	5	4	2	4	4	1	5	5	2	110	90	70	120	120	80
Saliswa	2	1	3	2	2	3	3	2	4	3	3	4	80	70	90	90	90	110

*Scores that have been altered have been underlined.

KEY: Interpretation of Individual HFD Scores**

HFD Score	Level of Mental Ability.
8 or 7	High Average ro Superior (I.Q. 110 upwards)
6	Average to Superior (I.Q. 90-135)
5	Average to High Average (I.Q. 85-120)
4	Low Average to Average (I.Q. 80-110)
3	Low Average (I.Q. 70-90)
2	Borderline (I.Q. 60-80)
1 or 0	Mentally retarded or functioning on a retarded level due to serious emotional problems (I.Q. less than 70)

N.B. In the above table, the higest I.Q. score in each range has been used.

** SOURCE: Koppitz (1968:331).

<u>Table 7-6B: Summary of 7-6A</u>

<u>The Number of Human Figure Drawings (Total 42) Scored for Developmental Items</u>
<u>on the Scale 5 to 0 on:-</u>

	A KOPPITZ'z Manual		B THE NEW SCORE:	
Score: 8 or 7	0		0	
6	0		0	
5	3	40.5%	11	57.1%
4	14		13	
3	13		10	
2	8		6	
1	4	59.5%	2	42.9%
0	0		0	

The above percentages group together the scores from low average
upwards (a score of 4 or more) and those of a low average downwards (a score
of 3 or less).

Table 7-7A: Scores on Emotional Indicators on HFDs Administered to the Same Children on Three Occasions*

Column:	A			B			C			D			E		
	Scoring According to Koppitz on the 30 E.I. Items			Score Minus Item 7— Tiny Figure			Score Minus Item 24— Omission of Nose			Score Minus Item 6— Slanting Figure			New Score Minus Items 7+ 24 and 6		
Test Number:	1	2	3	1	2	3	1	2	3	1	2	3	1	2	3
Sample Children:															
Malwu	3	1	3	2	1	3	3	1	2	2	1	2	_1_	_1_	_1_
Peliswe	5	2	0	4	2	0	4	2	0	4	1	0	_2_	_1_	0
Togu	3	3	2	2	2	1	3	3	2	2	2	2	_1_	_1_	_1_
Lungiswa	1	0	2	1	0	1	1	0	2	1	0	1	1	0	_0_
Nukwa	5	5	5	4	4	5	4	4	4	5	5	5	_3_	_3_	_4_
Nomvula	3	2	1	2	1	1	3	1	1	3	2	1	_2_	_0_	_1_
Zuziwe	1	0	0	0	0	0	1	0	0	1	0	0	_0_	0	0
Cebo	4	5	5	3	4	5	3	4	4	4	4	5	_2_	_2_	_4_
Tozama	2	1	2	1	1	2	2	1	2	2	1	2	_1_	1	2
Hintsa	4	4	5	4	3	4	3	3	4	4	4	4	_3_	_2_	_2_
Gwali	5	4	2	4	3	2	4	3	1	4	4	2	_2_	_2_	_1_
Gedja	5	5	2	4	4	2	4	4	1	4	4	2	_2_	_2_	_1_
Yameka	2	1	5	2	0	5	2	1	4	1	1	5	_1_	_0_	_4_
Saliswa	1	1	0	1	1	0	0	0	0	1	1	0	_0_	_0_	0

*It should be noted that whereas a high score on tests for developmental maturity (Table 7-6A) reflects relative success, a high score on tests for emotional problems (Table 7-7A) and school achievement (Table 7-8A) reflects failure.

+Scores that have altered have been underlined.

Table 7-7B: Summary of Table 7-7A

The Number of Human Figure Drawings (Total 42) Scored for Emotional Indicators on the Scale of 5 to 0 on:

		A KOPPITZ's MANUAL		B THE NEW SCORE:	
SCORE:	5	11 ⎫		0 ⎫	
	4	4 ⎬ 69.0%		3 ⎬ 40.5%	
	3	5 ⎪		3 ⎪	
	2	9 ⎭		11 ⎭	
	1	8 ⎫		14 ⎫	
	0	5 ⎬ 31.0%		11 ⎬ 59.5%	

The above percentage group together scores of two or more which, according to Koppitz, indicate the presence of emotional problems on HFDs, and of one or less which suggest the absence of emotional problems. The same applied for Table 7-7C.

Table 7-7C: Summary of Table 7-7A

Changes in Scores Across Time on Each Drawing Session:

		A KOPPITZ's MANUAL TEST NUMBER:				B THE NEW SCORES:			
		1	2	3		1	2	3
SCORE:	5	4	3	4	SCORE: 5	0	0	0
	4	2	2	0	4	0	0	3
	3	3 78.5%	1 57.1%	1 71.4%	3	2 50.0%	1 35.7%	0 35.7%
	2	2	2	5	2	5	4	2
	1	3	4	1	1	5	4	5
	0	0 21.4%	2 42.9%	3 28.6%	0	2 50.0%	5 64.3%	4 64.3%

Table 7-8A: Scores on School Achievement Indicators on HFDs
Administered to the Sample Children on Three Occasions

Column:

	A			B			C			D		
	Scoring According to Koppitz on the 7 School Achievement Items			Score Minus Item 6- Slanting Figure			Score Minus Item 21- 3 Figures or more			New Score Minus Items 6 and 21*		
Test Number:	1	2	3	1	2	3	1	2	3	1	2	3

Sample Children:

Mlawu	3	1	1	2	1	0	3	1	1	2	1	0
Peliswe	3	1	0	2	0	0	2	1	0	1	0	0
Togu	1	2	0	0	1	0	1	2	0	0	1	0
Lungiswa	0	0	1	0	0	0	0	0	1	0	0	0
Nukwa	2	2	1	2	2	1	2	2	1	2	2	1
Nomvula	1	0	0	1	0	0	0	0	0	0	0	0
Zuziwe	0	0	0	0	0	0	0	0	0	0	0	0
Cebo	2	3	1	2	2	1	2	3	1	2	2	1
Tozama	1	0	0	1	0	0	0	0	0	0	0	0
Hintsa	1	0	2	1	0	1	1	0	2	1	0	1
Gwali	4	2	0	3	2	0	3	2	0	3	2	0
Gedja	3	1	0	2	0	0	2	1	0	1	0	0
Yameka	2	0	1	1	0	1	1	0	1	0	0	1
Saliswa	0	0	0	0	0	0	0	0	0	0	0	0

*Scores that have been altered have been underlined.

Table 7-8B: Summary of Table 7-8A

The Number of Human Figure Drawings (Total 42) Scored for
School Achievement on the Scale of 4 to 0 on:

	A KOPPITZ'S MANUAL:	B THE NEW SCORE:
SCORE: 4	1 ⎫	0 ⎫
3	4 ⎬ 28.6%	0 ⎬ 16.7%
2	7 ⎭	7 ⎭
1	12 ⎫	9 ⎫
0	18 ⎭ 71.4%	26 ⎭ 83.3%

The above percentages group together scores of two or more
which, according to Koppitz, indicate the likelihood of low
school achievement, and of one or less which suggest the
absence of problems with school achievmenemt. The same
applies for Table 7-8C.

Table 7-8C: Summary of Table 7-8A

Changes in Scores Across Time on each Drawing Session On:

	A KOPPIT'S MANUAL TEST NUMBER:				B THE NEW SCORE:		
	1	2	3		1	2	3
SCORE: 4	1 ⎫	0 ⎫	0 ⎫	SCORE: 4	0 ⎫	0 ⎫	0 ⎫
3	3 ⎬ 50.0%	1 ⎬ 28.6%	0 ⎬ 7.1%	3	0 ⎬ 28.6%	0 ⎬ 21.4%	0 ⎬ 0.0%
2	3 ⎭	3 ⎭	1 ⎭	2	4 ⎭	3 ⎭	0 ⎭
1	4 ⎫	3 ⎫	5 ⎫	1	3 ⎫	2 ⎫	4 ⎫
0	3 ⎭ 50.0%	7 ⎭ 71.4%	8 ⎭ 92.9%	0	7 ⎭ 71.4%	9 ⎭ 78.6%	10 ⎭ 100%

Table 7-9: Rank of Sample Children on A Variety of Tasks Scored
During the Year

		Rank Order of the Fourteen Children	Rank Order of the Ten School Children
CHILD:	Tozama	1	1
	Mlawu	2	2
	Lungiswa	3	3
	Yameka	4	–
	Togu	5	4
	Zuziwe	6	4
	Peliswe	7	6
	Nukwa	8	7
	Gedja	9	–
	Nomvula	10	8
	Hintsa	11	9
	Saliswa	12	–
	Cebo	13	10
	Gwali	14	–

BIBLIOGRAPHY

ACOTT, M. (1980). 'Repudiate Smit, PM Urged.' The Cape Times, 5 June.

ATHLONE ADVICE OFFICE. (1981). Annual Report, October 1980-December 1981. Cape Town: Black Sash and SAIRR.

AUERBACH, F. (1979). Measuring Educational Development in South Africa. Johannesburg: SAIRR.

BELL, A., ed. (1980). The Diary of Virginia Woolf, vol. 3, 1925-1930. London: Hogarth Press.

BIESHEUVEL, S. (1943). African Intelligence. Johannesburg: SAIRR.

BLACKING, J. (1964). Black Background. The Childhood of a South African Girl. New York: Abelard-Schuman.

BLUESTEIN, N. and ACREDOLO, L. (1979). 'Developmental Changes in Map Reading Skills.' Child Development 50:691-97.

BOWER, E., ILGAZ-CARDEN, A. and NOORI, K. (1982). 'Measurement of Play Structures. Cross-cultural Considerations.' Journal of Cross-Cultural Psychology 13(3):315-29.

BRUNER, J., JOLLY, A. and SYLVA, K., eds. (1976). Play: Its Role in Development and Evolution. Harmondsworth:Penguin.

BUDOW, M. (1976). 'Urban Squatting in Greater Cape Town 1939-1948.' B.A. Honours Dissertation, University of Cape Town.

BUHRMANN, V. (1978). 'Tentative Views on Dream Therapy by Xhosa Diviners.' Journal of Analytical Psychology 23(2):105-21.

_____. (1981). The Inthlombe (ritual dance) as Applied to Dream Material.' Journal of Analytical Psychology 26(4).

_____. (1982). 'Indigenous Healers: Mental Health and Ill-Health.' In: Freed, ed., op. cit.

BUNDY, C. (1979). The Rise and Fall of the South African Peasantry. London: Heinemann.

BURGESS, A. (1981). Earthly Powers. Harmondsworth: Penguin.

BURMAN, S. and REYNOLDS, P. eds. (1986). Growing Up in a Divided Society: The Contexts of Childhood in South Africa. Johannesburg: Ravan Press.

CAPLAN, P. (1979). 'Erikson's Concept of Inner Space: A Data Based Reevaluation.' American Journal of Orthopsychiatry 49(1):100-08.

COLE, M. (1978). 'Ethnographic Psychology of Cognition - So Far.' In: Spindler, op. cit.

_____, and MEANS, B. (1981). Comparative Studies of How People Think: An Introduction. Cambridge, Mass.: Havard University Press.

CRAMER, P. and HOGAN, K. (1975). 'Sex Differences in Verbal Play Fantasy.' Developmental Psychology 2:145-54.

DANZINGER, K. (1957). 'The Child's Understanding of Kinship Terms: A Study of the Development of Relational Concepts.' Journal of Genetic Psychology 91:213-32.

DAVENPORT, J. and HUNT, K. (1974). The Right to the Land Cape Town: David Philip

DEREGOWSKI, J. (1980). 'Some Aspects of Perceptual Organization in the Light of Cross-Cultural Evidence.' In: Warren, ed. op cit.

DESMOND, C. (1978). Limehilll Rivisited: A Case Study of the Long Term Effects of African Resettlement. Natal: DSRG/MPN.

DONALDSON, M. (1979). Children's Minds. Glasgow: Fontana/Collins.

DONOHUE, J. (1982). 'Some Facts and Figures on Urbanization in the Developing World.' Assignment Children. A Journal Concerned with Children, Women and Youth in Development. Geneva: UNICEF 57/58.

DOUGLAS, M. (1978). Cultural Bias. London: Royal Anthropological Institute of Great Britain and Ireland, Occasional paper no. 35.

_____. (1980). Evans-Pritchard. Glasgow: Fontana.

ELLIS, G. et al. (1977). The Squatter Problem in the Western Cape. Some Causes and Remedies. Johannesburg: SAIRR.

ERIKSON, E. (1951). 'Sex Differences in the Play Configurations of Preadolescents.' American Journal of Orthopsychiatry 21:667-92.

_____. (1965). Childhood and Society. Harmondsworth: Penguin.

_____. (1968). Identity, Youth and Crisis. New York: W.W. Norton.

_____. (1974). 'Once More the Inner Space: Letter to a Former Student.' In: Strouse, ed., op. cit.

FICK, M. (1939). The Educability of the South African Native. Pretoria: South African Council for Educational and Sociological Research, Research Series no. 8.

FINLEY, G. and LAYNE, L. (1971). 'Play Behaviour in Young Children: A Cross-Cultural Study.' Journal of Genetic Psychology 119:203-10.

FOUCAULT, M. (1966). The Order of Things. An Archeology of the Human Sciences. New York: Vintage Books (1973).

_____. (1976). The History of Sexuality. Vol. 1: An Introduction. Tr. by R. Hurley. New York: Vintage Books (1980).

_____. (1980). Power/Knowledge. Selected Interviews and Other Writings 1972-77. Ed. by C. Gordon. New York: Pantheon Books.

FREED, E. ed. Aspects of Psychiatry among the Black Population of Southern Africa. Johannesburg: University of Witwatersrand Press.

FREUD, S. (1918). 'Infantile Neurosis.' In: Collected Papers, vol. 3. Tr. by A. and J. Strachey. London: Hogarth Press (1925).

GARVEY, C. (1977). Play. Glasgow: Fontana.

GEBER, B. and NEWMAN, S. (1980). Soweto's Children: The Development of Attitudes. London: Academic Press.

GEERTZ, C. (1973). The Interpretation of Cultures: Selected Essays. New York: Basic Books.

GINSBERG, H. and OPPER, S. (1979). Piaget's Theory of Intellectual Development. Englewood Cliffs, N.J.: Prentice-Hall.

GLUCKMAN, H.M. (1950). 'Kinship and Marriage among the Lozi of Northern Rhodesia and the Zulu of Natal.' In: Radcliffe-Brown and Forde, eds., op. cit.

GOODENOUGH, F. (1926). Measurement of Intelligence by Drawings. New York: Harcourt, Brace and World.

_____. (1928) 'Studies in the Psychology of Children's Drawings.' Psychological Bulletin 25:272-83.

_____. and HARRIS, D. (1950). 'Studies in the Psychology of Children's Drawings, II: 1928-1949.' Psychological Bulletin 47:369-433.

GOODY, J. (1972). Domestic Groups. New York: Addison Wesley.

GORDON, L., ed. (1981). Survey of Race Relations in South Africa, 1980. Johannesburg: SAIRR.

GRAAFF, J. and MAREE, J. (1977). Residential and Migrant African Workers in Cape Town. Cape Town: SALDRU, Working paper 12.

GREENBAUM, C., and KUGELMASS, S. (1980). 'Human Development and Socialization in Cross-Cultural Perspective: Issues Arising from Research in Israel.' In: Warren, N., ed., op. cit.

HABERMAS, J. (1968). Knowledge and Human Interests. Tr. by J. Shapiro. New York: Beacon.

HAMMOND-TOOKE, W. (1962). Bhaca Society: A People of the Transkeian Uplands, South Africa. Cape Town: Oxford University Press.

_____. (1969). 'The Present State of Cape Nguni Ethnographic Studies.' In: Ethnological and Linguistic Studies in Honour of N.J. van Warmelo, Ethnological Publications 52 Pretoria: Government Printer.

_____, ed. (1974). The Bantu-speaking People of Southern Africa, 2nd ed. London: Routledge and Kegan Paul.

HARRIS, D. (1963). <u>Children's Drawings as Measures of Intellectual Maturity</u>. New York: Harcourt, Brace and World.

HAVILAND, S., and CLARK, E. (1974). 'This Man's Father Is My Father's Son: A Study of the Acquisition of English Kin Terms.' <u>Journal of Child Language</u> 1:23-47.

HORRELL, M. (1978). <u>Laws Affecting Race Relations in South Africa, 1948-1976</u>. Johannesburg: SAIRR.

HUNKIN, V. (1950) 'Validation of the Goodenough Draw-a-Man Test for African Children.' <u>Journal of Social Research</u> 1:52-63.

HUNTER, M. (1963). <u>Reaction to Conquest. Effects of Contacts with Europeans on the Pondo of South Africa</u>. London: Oxford University Press.

IRVINE, S. and CARROL, N. (1980). 'Testing and Assessment across Cultures. Issues in Methodology and Theory.' In: Triandis, <u>op. cit.</u>, 'Methodology' vol. 2, ed. by Triandis and J. Berry.

JAHODA, G. (1979). 'The Construction of Economic Reality by Some Glaswegian Children.' <u>European Journal of Psychology</u> 9:115-27.

_____. (1981a). 'The Development of Thinking about Economic Institutions: The Bank.' <u>Cahiers de Psychologie Cognitive</u> 1:55-73.

_____. (1981b). 'Pictorial Perception and the Problem of Universals.' In: Lloyd and Gay, <u>op. cit.</u> 41.

JOHNSON-LAIRD, P. and WASON, P., eds. (1977). <u>Thinking. Readings in Cognitive Science</u>. Cambridge: University Press.

JOYCE, J. (1937). <u>Ulysses</u>. London: Bodley Head.

KIERNAN, J. (1980). 'The World about Us: The Cosmic Model in an Expanding Universe.' Anthropology Conference Paper, Rhodes University.

KOPPITZ, E. (1969). <u>Psychological Evaluation of Children's Human Figure Drawings</u>. New York: Grune and Stratton.

KRADER, L., ed. (1974). <u>The Ethnological Notebooks of Karl Marx</u>. Assen: Van Gorcum.

LABORATORY OF COMPARATIVE HUMAN COGNITION. (1979). 'Cross-Cultural Psychology's Challenges to our Ideas of Children and Development.' <u>American Psychologist</u> 34(10):827-33.

LAURENDEAU, M. and PINARD, A. (1970). <u>The Development of the Concept of Space in the Child</u>. New York: International Universities Press.

LEVINE, R., and PRICE-WILLIAMS, D. (1974). 'Children's Kinship Concepts: Cognitive Development and Early Experience among the Hausa.' <u>Ethnology</u> 13(1):25-44.

LLOYD, B. (1981). 'Cognitive Development, Education and Social Mobility.' In: Lloyd, and Gay, eds. op. cit.

_____, and GAY, J., eds. (1981). Universals of Human Thought: Some African Evidence. Cambridge: University Press.

LYNCH, K. (1960). The Image of the City. Boston: M.I.T. Press.

MACHOVER, K. (1949). Personality Projection in the Drawing of the Human Figure. Springfield, Iii.: Charles C. Thomas.

MACKWORTH, N. and BRUNER, J. (1971). 'How Adults and Children Search and Recognise Pictures.' Human Development 13:149-170.

MALHERBE, G. (1977). Education in South Africa, vol. 2 (1923-1975). Cape Town: Juta.

MALINOWSKI, B. (1931). 'Culture.' In: The Encyclopedia of the Social Sciences 4:623.

MAREE, J., and CORNELL, J. (1978). Sample Survey of Squatters in Crossroads, December 1977. Cape Town: SALDRU Working paper 17.

MEAD, M. (1928). Coming of Age in Samoa. New York: William Marrow.

_____. (1930). Growing Up in New Guinea. New York: William Morrow.

MILLAR, S. (1968). The Psychology of Play. Harmondsworth: Penguin.

MURRAY, C. (1976). 'Keeping House in Lesotho. A Study of the Impact of Oscillating Migrants.' A dissertation submitted for the degree of Doctor of Philosophy, University of Cambridge.

_____. (1979). 'The Work of Men, Women and the Ancestors: Social Reproduction in the Periphery of Southern Africa.' In: Social Anthropology of Work ASA 19. London: Academic Press.

NASH, M. (1978). Squatter Camp Demolition: The Human Cost. Cape Town. BSR.

_____. (1980). Black Uprooting from 'White' South Africa. The Fourth and Final Stage of Apartheid. Braamfontein: South African Council of Churches.

NTLOKO, L. (1980). 'The Sage of Crossroads.' Energos 2.

OPPER, S. (1977). 'Concept Development in Thai Urban and Rural Children,' in Dasen, P. ed. Piagetian Psychology: Cross-Cultural Contributions. New York: Gardner.

PAGE, J. (1973). 'Concepts of Length and Distance in a Study of Zulu Youths.' Journal of Social Psycholoogy 90:9-16.

PIAGET, J. (1921). The Child's Conception of the World. Tr. by J. and A. Tomlinson. Totowa, N.J.: Littlefield, Adams (1972).

_____. (1928). Judgement and Reasoning in the Child. London: Routledge and Kegan Paul.

_____. (1935). Science of Education and the Psychology of the Child. Tr. by D. Coltram. New York: Orion Press (1970).

_____. (1941). The Child's Conception of Number. New York: W.W. Norton (1965).

_____. (1947). The Psychology of Intelligence. Tr. by M. Piercy and D. Berlyne. London: Routledge and Kegan Paul (1950).

_____. (1948a). The Language and Thought of the Child. New York: W.W. Norton (1952).

_____. (1948b). The Moral Judgement of the Child. Tr. by M. Gabian. New York: Free Press (1965).

_____. (1951). Play, Dreams and Initiation in Childhood. Tr. by C. Gattegno and F. Hodson. New York: W.W. Norton (1962).

_____. (1966). The Psychology of the Child. Tr. by H. Weaver. New York: Basic Books (1969).

_____. (1970a). Genetic Epistemology. Tr. by E. Duckworth. New York: W.W. Norton (1971).

_____. (1970b). Main Trends in Inter-Disciplinary Research. London: George Allen and Unwin (1973).

_____. (1972a). The Child and Reality: Problems of Genetic Psychology. Tr. by A. Rosin. London: Frederick Muller (1974).

_____. (1972b). The Child's Conception of the World. Tr. by J. and A. Tomlinson. Totowa: Littlefield, Adams.

_____, and INHELDER, B. (1948). The Child's Conception of Space. Tr. by F. Langdon and J. Lunzer. New York: W.W. Norton (1967).

PINNOCK, D. (1980). Elsie's River. Cape Town: Institute of Criminology, University Press.

PLATZKY, L. (1978). Crossroads. What is Happening? Cape Town: Cape Western Region Black Sash, March (mimeo).

PRESTON-WHYTE, E. (1974). 'Kinship and Marriage.' In: Hammond-Tooke, ed., op. cit.

PRICE, R. and ROSBERG, C., eds. (1980). The Apartheid Regime. Political Power and Racial Domination. Berkeley: University of California Perss.

RADCLIFFE-BROWN, A. and FORDE, D., eds. (1950). African Systems of Kinship and Marriage. London: Oxford University Press.

READ, M. (1968). Children of their Fathers: Growing Up among the Ngoni of Malawi. New York: Holt, Rinehart and Winston.

REID, J. (1966). 'Learning to Think about Reading.' Educational Research 9.

REYNOLDS, N. (1981). The Design of Rural Development: Proposals for the Evolution of a Social Contract Suited to Conditions in Southern Africa. Cape Town: SALDRU working paper 40.

REYNOLDS, P. (1984). Men Without Children. Second Carnegie Inquiry into Poverty and Development in Southern Africa: Paper 5. Cape Town: University of Cape Town Press.

RICHARDS, A. (1956). Chisungu: a Girl's Initiation Ceremony among the Bemba of Northern Rhodesia. London: Faber and Faber.

ROACH, E. and KEPHART, N. (1966). The Purdue Perceptual Motor Survey. A Direct Action Approach to Nonachiever Problems. Columbus, Ohio: Charles E. Merrill.

ROBINSON, J. (1960). Collected Economic Papers, vol. 2. Oxford: Blackwell.

SAHLINS, M. (1977). 'Colors and Cultures.' In: Dolgin, J., Kemnitzer, D. and Scheneider, D. eds. Symbolic Anthropology. A Reading in the Study of Symbols and Meanings. New York: Columbia University Press.

SAIRR. (1954). Memorandum on African Housing in the Peninsula. Cape Town: SAIRR.

_____. Annual Reports, 1966-67, 1976-77, 1978-79, 1979-80, 1981-82. Johannesburg: SAIRR.

SCHWANTES, F. (1979). 'Cognitive Scanning Process in Children.' Child Development 50:1136-43.

SCRIBNER, S. (1977). 'Modes of Thinking and Ways of Speaking: Culture and Logic Reconsidered.' In: Johnson-Laird and Wason, op. cit.

SEAGRIM. G. and LENDON, R. (9180). Furnishing the Mind. A Comparative Study of Cognitive Development in Central Australian Aborigines. Sydney: Academic Press.

SELVAN, D. (1976). Housing Conditions for Migrant Workers in Cape Town 1976. Cape Town: SALDRU, Working paper 10.

SERPELL, R. (1976) Culture's Influence on Behaviour. London : Metheun.

_____. (1980). 'Intelligence, Education and Adaptation in a Rural Community.' Paper presented at PAZ Conference, Lusaka, May.

SIMKINS, C. (1981a). The Distribution of the African Population of South Africa by Age, Sex and Region-Type 1960, 1970 and 1980. Cape Town SALDRU working paper 32.

_____. (1981b). The Economic Implications of African Resettlement.
Cape Town: SALDRU working paper 43.

_____. (1982). A Note on Projecting African Population Distribution and
Migration to the Year 2000. A paper submitted to the Commission on
Urbanization. Johannesburg: SAIRR.

SINGER, J. (1973). The Child's World of Make-Believe. New York: Academic
Press.

SOUTH AFRICAN OUTLOOK. (1976). 'Crossroads' 110(1259).

_____. (1977). 'The Squatter Problem' 107 (1269).

_____. (1978). 'Crossroads' and 'Crossroads - the
Statistical Picture' 108(1280)

_____. (1980). 'Solidarity with the Poor' 110(1312).

_____. (1982). 'The Czech Connection' 112(1332).

SPIEGEL, A. (1980). 'Changing Patterns of Migrant Labour and Rural
Differentiation in Lesotho.' Social Dynamics. 6(2):1-13.

SPINDLER, G., ed. (1978). The Making of Psychological Anthropology.
Berkeley: University of California Press.

STARR, J. (1979). Continuing the Revolution: The Political Thought of Mao.
Princeton, N.J.: Princeton University Press.

STEYN, G. (1969). 'Main Features of Educational Development in the Republic
of South Africa, 1910-1967.' In: 1968 Statistical Yearbook.
Pretoria: Government Printer.

STROUSE, J., ed. (1974). Women and Analysis. New York: Dell.

THOMAS, T. (1974). The Children of Apartheid. A Study of the Effects of
Migratory Labour on Family Life in the Ciskei. London: African
Publishing Trust.

TRIANDIS, J., ed. (1980). Handbook of Cross-Cultural Psychology, 6 vols.
Boston: Allyn and Bacon.

TUKULU, A. (1979). 'White Counselor, Black Client - Problem or Possibility.'
.Psychology Honours Paper, University of Cape Town (unpublished).

TWALA, R. (1951) 'Beads as Regulating the Social Life of the Zulu and
Swazi.' African Studies 10:113-123.

UNESCO (1972). A statistical Study of Wastage at School. Paris Geneva:
UNESCO IBE.

VAN TROMP, J. (1948). Xhosa Law of Persons: A Treatise on the Legal
Principles of Family Relations among the AmaXhosa. Cape Town: Juta.

VAN WARMELO, N. (1931). 'Kinship Terminology of the South African Bantu.'
Ethnological Publications 2. Pretoria Government Printer.

_____. (1935). Preliminary Survey of the Bantu Tribes of South Africa.
Pretoria: Government Printer.

VERSVELD, B. (1978). 'Africans in Cape Town.' South African Outlook
108(1289).

WARREN, N., ed. (1980). Studies in Cross-Cultural Psychology, vol. 2.
London: Academic Press.

WEST, M. (1980). 'The "Apex of Subordination": The Urban African Population
of South Africa.' In: Price, R. and Rosberg, C., eds. op. cit.

_____. (1982a). 'From Pass Court to Deportation: Changing Patterns of
Influx Control in Cape Town.' African Affairs 81(325):463-77.

_____. (1982b). 'Total Onslaught in Cape Town.' South African Outlook.
112(1337):171-78

WILBERTS, J. and FLORQUIN, F. (1977). ['Fluctuations of Relative Importance
in Variables of Intelligence and Perceptual-Motor Structuring of
Space while Learning to Read in the First Primary Year']. Revue
Belge de Psychologies et de Pedagogie 39:75-84.

WILSON, F. (1971). 'Farming, 1866-1966.' In: Wilson, M. and Thompson, L.,
eds. op. cit., vol. 2.

_____, (1973). 'Focus on Family Life.' South African Outlook.

_____. (1975). 'The Political Implications for Blacks of Economic
Changes Now Taking Place in South Africa.' In: Thompson, L., and
Butler, J., eds., Change in Contemporary South Africa. Berkeley:
University of California Press.

WILSON, M. (1948). 'Some Possibilities and Limitations of Anthropological
Research.' Inaugural Lecture, Rhodes University College.

_____. (1977). For Men and Elders. Changes in the Relations of
Generations and of Men and Women among the Nyakyusa-Ngonde People
1875-1971. London: International African Institute.

_____, and MAFEJE, A. (1963). Langa: A Study of Social Groups in an
African Township. Cape Town: Oxford University Press.

_____, and THOMPSON, L., eds. (1971). The Oxford History of South
Africa, 2 vols. Oxford: Clarendon Press.